Julie — 6-21
You will be missed!
ENJOY THIS NEXT CHAPTER
IN YOUR LIFE... THANKS
FOR BEING YOU & ALWAYS
CONTINUE TO PRAY FOR
THE TRUTH!
Hugs,
Kim

Too Blessed to be Stressed... Inspiration for Every Day

DEVOTIONAL JOURNAL

Debora M. Coty

BARBOUR BOOKS
An Imprint of Barbour Publishing, Inc.

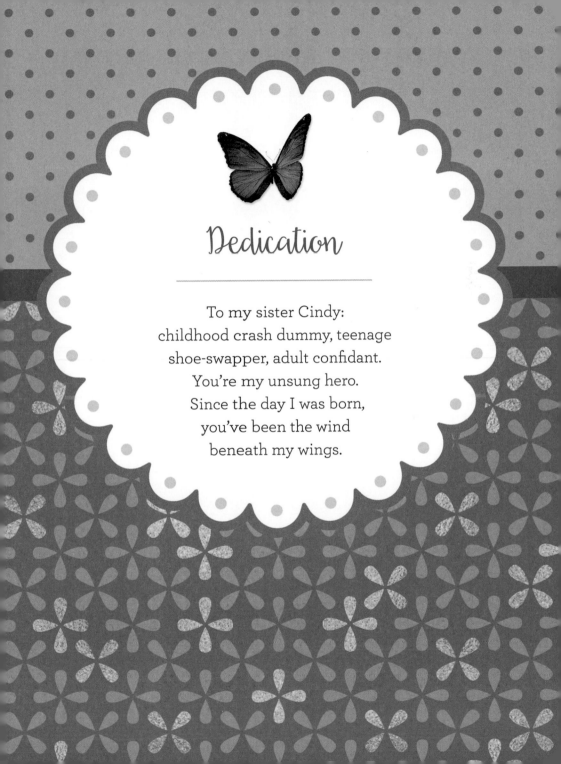

Dedication

To my sister Cindy:
childhood crash dummy, teenage
shoe-swapper, adult confidant.
You're my unsung hero.
Since the day I was born,
you've been the wind
beneath my wings.

Acknowledgments

- Buckets of gratitude to the awesome team at Barbour Publishing and my bodacious editor, Kelly McIntosh. You people rock my world!

- HUGE high five to my agent, Greg Johnson of WordServe Literary Agency.

- Heartfelt thanks to the fine folks who graciously allowed me to share their stories to help you (and me!) on our daily faith journeys: Rose McClellan, Linda Pugsley, Bethany Quinn, Kim Rate, Nancy Buckley, Rick Christensen, Andie Hardee, Cheryl Bodden, Bill George, Mariana Enlow, Ruth Ellinger, Jack Fernandez, Darlene Hobbs Brown, Gloria Foster, Caryl Music, Ginny Jones, Marianne Cali, Nancy Hernandez, Lynn Agnew, Diana Flagg, Julia Thomas, Sandi and Bob Dorey, Lali Stanley, Pat Glickman, Jan McRae, Eddie Aikens, Debbie Cali, and Suzanne Woods Fisher.

- A stress-relieving back rub to my long-suffering husband, Chuck, for all he does to haul me out of the potholes on the literary road; cuddles and kisses to my kids & grands for patiently waiting on me to emerge from my writing cave.

- A special belly tickle to Fenway, my loyal, loving, deaf-as-a-post doggy who, like his mistress, is graying (and fraying) a bit around the edges. Hey, do they make canine Clairol?

- Lotsa love to my parents, Adele and Frank Mitchell, both nearing ninety now, who still continually encourage and motivate me to keep writing, no matter what. I couldn't be prouder to be your daughter!

- And as always, mega praise and honor to my dearest Papa God, who never leaves my side.

Introduction

I never intended to become a potty writer. But, well. . .there 'tis.

My readers tell me the short, quick-read chapters in my books make them perfect bathroom fodder for read-and-run convenience. At least I gain a manly readership that way; I just love getting letters from menfolk who say their wives left me in the bathroom where they picked me up.

Oooo-kay. Nothing like a little potty humor to start things out, eh?

So here's another selection to add to your Debora Coty bathroom collection. Possibly the best yet. Because it's full of everyday kisses from Papa God. Yep, a warm, toasty reminder that your heavenly Father's there, He's aware, and He cares about you every single day of your life.

I hope you'll laugh with me, perhaps cry a little, and hopefully consider some exciting new aspects about your faith that haven't crossed your mind. Like how to combat killjoys that sabotage your peace, the surprise ministry Papa may be preparing you for, and why sphincter-pucker moments are actually a good thing.

Hmm. Maybe we shouldn't discuss potties and sphincters on the same page.

This would be a grand time to thank you for sharing my offbeat blend of humor and hope, wit and near-wisdom, through my books and speaking ministry. My BFFs (Blessed Friends Forever) mean the world to me; you're the reason I write.

So here we go again, this time a year-long quest to fully embrace the fact that we're loved, cherished, and *Too Blessed to be Stressed.* (Hey, somebody should write a book by that title!)

And please. . .don't squeeze the Charmin.

Fresh Hope

"Those who hope in me will not be disappointed."
ISAIAH 49:23 NIV

I awoke before dawn on New Year's Day in a fog of gloom. I was bummed by recent family problems, pressing decisions, and the sudden death of a close friend right before Christmas.

After wading through depressing headlines and unfunny comics in the Sunday paper, I dressed and headed to church alone. Spouse was under the weather. Wouldn't you know, the day I needed company most. . .zilch.

As I pulled out of my driveway and nosed the car around the first curve, I was immersed in light. Beautiful, sparkly, utterly amazing white light from a magnificent array of sunbeams. Maybe it was a unique combination of sheen and mist; perhaps the angle of the sun was different than usual, I don't know, but it was as brilliant as an elaborate Disney light show.

Okay, here you need to know that I'm a sunbeam connoisseur. Yep. Since I was a little girl, I've taken special joy in early-morning sunbeams—those translucent fingers of Papa God reaching down to earth to touch His creation with the first light of a brand-new day. Hope! That's what they make me feel. . .hope.

Such promise! Such possibilities! *Anything* could happen.

On the first day of a fresh beginning, those hope-filled sunbeams cut through my mental fog and clutter to reach right in and caress my careworn heart. I was surrounded with luminescent, soul-stirring reminders that I'm not alone—that Papa God is right here with me.

He's with you too, ya know, girlfriend. And He will continue to be throughout the upcoming year.

Hope Eternal,
Help me see You in the first
light of a brand-new year. Such
possibilities! Such promise!
Anything could happen.

Everybody Needs a Papa

*You received God's Spirit when he adopted you as his
own children. Now we call him, "Abba, Father."*

ROMANS 8:15 NLT

It started in 2004 when I began writing my novel, *The Distant Shore*. The plot is based on the true story of a young girl sent away—for mysterious reasons that are gradually revealed—to live on Florida's remote, untamed Merritt Island in 1904.

Emma-Lee finds island life with crusty spinster Aunt Augusta bewildering and lonely until she's befriended by kindly Captain Stone, an Irish freighter captain.

Captain Stone is a godly man and introduces Emma-Lee to his beloved heavenly Father, whom Emma-Lee wholeheartedly embraces as "Papa God," the heavenly papa who will never abandon or forsake her like her earthly papa.

Papa God fills a hollow hole in her heart.

Along with Emma-Lee, I began referring to Him as Papa God and have done so ever since. Acknowledging that the Almighty views us through the lens of a faithful, unconditionally loving parent fulfills a deep need for belonging in each of us.

Abba is the intimate Aramaic form of *Father* used in the Bible numerous times, most notably by Jesus, referring to God the Father. *Abba* is translated into current-day *Daddy* or *Papa*. I love the term *Papa God*—it's warm, protective, and delightfully cuddly. What name could more richly express our close relationship with our heavenly Daddy?

I invite you to join me. I think you'll be surprised how quickly—and almost magically—the secret, deep longing in your heart for nonjudgmental, all-accepting, all-forgiving love will be fulfilled.

After all, He's your Papa too.

> Papa God,
> Thank You for adopting me
> into Your family as Your adored,
> cherished daughter. You truly
> are my Papa.

Purse Politics

Prepare your minds for action.
1 PETER 1:13 NASB

Have you ever noticed that purse loyalties divide womandom like politics divide our nation? Such devotion toward swatches of leather and fabric!

Okay, you've got your two basic purse parties: bullmastiff (massive and intimidating) and Maltese (petite and adorable), with various trendy independent parties toting contraptions like moving vans with straps, Tic Tac–sized micro-clutches, and glorified horse feed bags.

My kids roll their eyes while claiming that my tendencies run toward the latter, but I never hear them complain when I happen to have the very item they need at the moment, be it dental floss, a blow dryer, or half a chocolate éclair. (You must be prepared; never know when you might become stranded on a deserted island.)

Of course, there are sporadic bipartisan crossover occasions like beach trips or formal dinners when party lines blur, but in general, each purse party feels absolutely certain that its platform is superior and will fight to the death to defend it.

According to my hilarious friend, author of *Purse-uit of Holiness*, Rhonda Rhea, "pursuing holiness is kind of like finding the perfect purse. You know it's out there—somewhere—if you could only find it."

If you could only find it.

It's my prayer that this little devotional will help you do just that. Pursue, discover, and embrace a deeper relationship with Papa God, the Master Designer. Trust me, regardless of your purse party, there's NO better designer label to wear proudly!

*Designer of Me,
I want more of You as much
as I want that Prada bag. No,
more. Help me be diligent
in my purse-uit.*

Killjoy

Be anxious for nothing. . .let your requests be made known to God. And the peace of God, which surpasses all comprehension, will guard your hearts and your minds in Christ Jesus.
PHILIPPIANS 4:6–7 NASB

I love this Bible chapter. Not only does it contain my favorite decom-stress verse (above); it teaches us how to deal with everyday stressors that steal our joy.

Grab your Bible as we look at four killjoys in the fourth chapter of Philippians:

- **Killjoy #1: Conflict** (verse 2)
  The apostle Paul sends a message to two women who can't get along. Know any of those? Women in Philippi were quite liberated and were allowed to take part in government and politics. But conflict divides and conquers; Paul cautioned them to make amends, not allow conflict to rob their joy.

- **Killjoy #2: Anxiety** (verse 6)
  We sometimes feel overwhelmed by daily fears and anxieties, but hey, we can be whelmed without being overwhelmed. Will we choose to serve our crazy, runaway feelings or the all-powerful One who helps us manage them?

- **Killjoy #3: Stinkin' thinkin'** (verses 8–9)
  Fear is like static blocking our inner faith voices. All we can pick up are those destructive, toxic voices that cast doubt on truth. Paul gives us a marvelous list here that enables us to change channels and focus on positives instead of negatives.

- **Killjoy #4: Fretting** (verse 10)
  Fretting is our feeble effort to maintain control.

  > F: False sense of
  > R: Responsibility for
  > E: Every little
  > T: Thing

But guess what? We've never actually been in control. Papa God is.

Emmanuel (God with Us), Make me more aware of the killjoys I allow to sabotage my abundant life in You.

Perfecting My Stinky Face

Encourage one another.
1 THESSALONIANS 5:11 NIV

My three-year-old grandbuddy, Blaine, watching me apply makeup: "What's that stuff do, Mimi?"

"Blush makes me look less dead. . .er, I mean it gives me more color."

"Oh. Why do ya wanna be pink?"

"I don't want to be pink. I just don't want to look like a walking marshmallow."

He contemplates this deep concept.

"What'cha doing now, Mimi?"

"Spraying perfume to make me smell pretty. See—[holding out wrist for olfactory inspection]—what do you think?"

[Making stinky face] "Ugghh. You smell like my Pull-Ups."

Swell.

I too have been perfecting my stinky face. Not intentionally. But sometimes when I pass a mirror, I'm floored at my gnarly expression. The thing is, I'm not angry. . .or sad. . .or even displeased. I'm just preoccupied. So preoccupied that I'm not aware of what my face is doing, and apparently when ignored, my facial muscles default to my mother's scowl.

I thought Mama was always mad at me. One time, I asked what I'd done, and she seemed surprised and said, "Why, nothing. I'm not upset; I'm focused on what I'm doing. Just ignore my face."

Well, of course that's impossible. The face is the window into the mind. Reading expressions is our feedback mechanism to know what's going on inside others.

So does my countenance bless or intimidate people? Does Jesus-joy shine through my eyes and encourage through my smile?

Hmm. Maybe I should tell my stinky face the good news in my heart more often. And ditch the Eau de Pull-Ups.

Sweet Lord,
Make me more aware of the
You I portray. I offer my coun-
tenance to You today as an
instrument of praise.

Crash Dummies

*"I have had a great struggle with
my sister, and I have won."*
GENESIS 30:8 NIV

Siblings are the reluctant instructors in our life classrooms. They're our crash dummies, our failed experiments, the unfortunate people we practice on to learn how *not* to treat others.

They unwittingly teach us civility by suffering the consequences of our mistakes as we forge the virtues of kindness, fairness, and helping one another. They're our first and last teammates, the ones we're forced to depend on. The ones who bring us secret joy when they actually come through.

Of course, we're their crash dummies too.

Yet despite trampled feelings, bruises, and occasional concussions, what would we do without them? They're as much a part of our DNA as our crooked noses. We love them, admire them, and are irritated senseless by them all at the same time.

We share memories no one else in the world fathoms; they understand where we're coming from even better than our spouses. Siblings are passengers in our lifeboat, and it would be suicidal to try to blow them out of the water.

So we might as well accept them as heaven-sent companions for this voyage of life and try to paddle in sync.

In the movie *In Her Shoes,* Rose Feller (played by Toni Collette) voiced every sister's sentiments when she was trying to explain the unexplainable bond she shared with her incorrigible sister, Maggie (Cameron Diaz): "Without her. . .I don't make sense."

No, without our siblings, we just don't make sense.

And strangely enough—despite the lumps, bumps, and hard knocks—we don't want to go it alone.

> *Prince of Peace,
> Motivate me to tell my
> crash dummies (siblings)
> that I love them before
> it's too late.*

Aging Gratefully

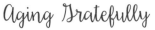

*I will still be the same when you are old
and gray, and I will take care of you.*
ISAIAH 46:4 CEV

As we cross that invisible half-century line, things begin to change.

Varicose veins pop and sizzle like tiny zags of electricity.

Harry Potter's got nothing on me—he may have a lightning bolt on his forehead but I have fifty on my left leg alone.

After decades of decorating ourselves with heavy earrings, those previously plump, robust earlobes droop to our Birkenstocks. Ever notice how in young folks, the piercing hole is a tiny dot? As we age, that dot elongates into a long wobbly slash.

I tell people Captain Jack Sparrow ran his sword through my piercing hole in a fit of passion. Right.

And our earlobes aren't the only things wobbling.

Cleavage suddenly quits cleaving and you find the best reason to wear low-cut blouses is to funnel crumbs down to collect in your belly button for a late-night snack.

My PAH theory—Physiological Aging Hypothesis—states that as a woman's age creeps northward, her body parts travel south, and hips expand to new horizons east to west. We hot mamas are all over the map!

But shouldn't maturity be the most productive season of life? After many years of trial and error, we finally get a grip on our unique sets of gifts and abilities and we can gratefully determine how best to use them for Papa God's glory.

Eyesight might be on the fritz, but insight is keener than ever. We've learned to take our eyes off the mirror and focus on things more important.

*Lord of My Later Years,
I refuse to die before my actual
death. I'm grateful to be here.
Use me to Your glory.*

The Revealing

*"He reveals deep and hidden things;
he knows what lies in darkness."*
DANIEL 2:22 NIV

Betty enjoyed being surprised when she gave birth back in the seventies. . .first she had one boy. Then another. Then a third. All unexpected marvels.

But she did *not* enjoy the surprise four decades later when her husband, Arthur, gave birth. . . sort of. . .to a turn signal lever from a 1963 Thunderbird.

The seven-inch metal lever had apparently impaled Arthur's arm in a horrific car accident. His life-threatening injuries took precedence over a little arm discomfort, so the imbedded metal wasn't discovered. Over time, a protective pocket grew around the lever, and Arthur went about his normal life, unaware of his strange bedfellow.

Then one day Arthur's courthouse visit mysteriously set off the metal detector. X-rays revealed a slender object, a little longer than a pencil, stuck in his arm. (Hey, if it'd been inflamed, do you think they'd have called it Arthur-itis? Tee-hee!)

There are times when we're all surprised at things stuck inside of us. Maybe not rusty T-Bird pieces, but other things. Ugly things like envy (*I wish my job paid as well as hers*), jealousy (*my sister's skinny little behunkus is SO not fair!*), or resentment (*I will never forget what my husband said to me ten years ago*).

We can just go on day after day, unaware of the ugliness festering deep inside, infecting our hearts. Or we can ask Papa God to x-ray our souls and reveal the foreign objects that need removing. The choice is ours.

*Great Physician,
Search me and reveal buried ugliness that needs to be excised. I'm sick of being sick. I'm itching to be healthy.*

Dis Equality

Keep your mouth shut, and you will stay out of trouble.
PROVERBS 21:23 NLT

The masculine sex has finally found their answer to the female's cover-all-sins catchphrase "Bless her heart."

It's always amused me how women—especially Southern gals—can say anything about someone, no matter how catty, scathing, or gossipy, as long as they end it with "Bless his/her heart." That little disclaimer supposedly makes everything palatable.

The vocabulary equivalent of ketchup.

Males have now gained *dis* equality. They've taken up a slang phrase that enables them to disagree, disparage, and disrespect without apology. And it's not only socially acceptable; it's considered hip. Ultra-cool. Tooled. Just sayin'...

In case, like me, you're not completely hip, ultra-cool, or tooled, I'm not just saying nothing here; that's the phrase: "Just sayin'..."

Oh, women use it too, but I've noticed the hairy gender has really latched on. Now they can shred, tear, and rip apart other people with a smile on their faces just like us girls.

"That's the stupidest thing I've ever heard. Just sayin'..."

"You can't believe anything he says. Just sayin'..."

"You're not really going out with *her*? Just sayin'..."

It might behoove us all to remember a well-known scripture about now: "If you can't say anything nice, don't say anything at all." No, wait. That's the gospel according to my mother.

Actually it's today's verse, Proverbs 21:23. Now there's sage advice. Plain. Wise. Always hip. Just sayin'...

God Who Cannot Be Deceived, Let me not deceive myself with weasel words. Please forgive my critical spirit and make me cognizant of what I'm really sayin' about other people today.

Journey to Dawn

My hope is in you all day long.
PSALM 25:5 NIV

My internal rooster woke me as usual at five for my predawn prayer walk. Blinking in sleepy confusion at my surroundings, I remembered that I had bivouacked at a writer's retreat for a little physical and spiritual renewal.

After my first lap around the large campground, the sky began gathering momentum in preparation for sunrise. It was still dark, but hints of light appeared. One lone mockingbird braved a medley in the crisp air.

On my second lap, more light appeared over the lake, accompanied by streaks of pink and tinges of silver. A cooing pigeon joined the mockingbird.

By my third lap, layers of multihued crimson emblazoned the horizon. More color, more promise. Tag-playing squirrels scurried up a tree. The world was awakening to a new day.

Finally, nearly an hour after the journey to dawn began, the sun burst through low-slung clouds in a blaze of glory, casting shimmering jewels on the lake. A symphony of birds and bush-beasties celebrated daybreak.

What a difference the presence of the sun makes, transforming the world from stagnant darkness into teeming life!

You know, faith's journey is much like the journey to dawn. At first we fumble in darkness. But as trust grows and we mature as believers, our momentum builds until Papa God's appointed time when our debut arrives. Each phase of preparation is important and necessary to the end result. At last we burst through the clouds of obscurity to make an eternal difference in someone's life.

*Creator of New Dawns,
Fuel my faith, so that one fine
morning Your Son will rise in me
and erupt in dazzling Sonshine
that'll change someone's world.*

Crazy-in-Love

Children are a gift of the LORD.
PSALM 127:3 NASB

True, children are a gift. A blessing. Aack. Sometimes a mixed blessing.

Like the time my darling three-year-old Matthew appeared in the middle of our dinner party in nothing but his Spiderman underpants and dozens of my Kotex stuck to every square inch of his little body.

Or when he disappeared from his stroller in one of the most exclusive fashion boutiques in the mall and reappeared in the store's display window sitting on the lap of a mannequin, trying to squish a cookie between her painted lips.

How about the time adolescent Matthew accidentally drove the neighbor's riding lawnmower right through his screen pool enclosure?

Or when a horrified yowl resounded from teenage Matthew in the bathroom at seven o'clock one morning? He'd groggily begun brushing his teeth when he realized that the foul-tasting toothpaste he'd liberally applied to his toothbrush was his sister's yeast infection cream.

There are times you just want to hook a voltmeter up to their little punkin brains to see if anything is getting through.

Ulcer is *kids* spelled backward. Well, it should be anyway. The parent handbook should inform us of the risks before we swim upstream and spawn. Having a kid is like getting your tongue pierced; you're all in. Fully committed. No turning back. Life as you once knew it is over.

Yet we would do it all over again.

Are we crazy or what?

*Heavenly Father,
Thank You for making me
crazy-in-love with my children.
And thank You for being
crazy-in-love with me,
Your crazy daughter.*

Ride 'Em, Cowgirl!

*Martha was distracted by all the
preparations that had to be made.*
LUKE 10:40 NIV

I've always sympathized with Martha of the Mary/Martha sister duo. Martha was zipping around cleaning, cooking, running errands. . .doing all that needed to be done to host a passel of dinner guests.

I totally get that. How will things get done if someone doesn't DO them? How will the bronco get broken if someone doesn't take the bull by the horns and ride him?

Is that cowgirl usually you?

So while the chickens were strutting around fully feathered and a mountain of unpeeled potatoes avalanched on Martha's head, Mary was sitting at the feet of Jesus, contentedly listening.

Martha probably would have *loved* to lounge around listening to the Messiah too, but she was too distracted. "Lord, don't you care that my sister has left me to do the work by myself? Tell her to help me!" (Luke 10:40 NIV).

Many of us identify with Martha. We yearn to focus our attention on Jesus, but we're distracted by our perpetual to-do lists too. So much to do, so little time. Don't fib now—haven't you ever jotted down your grocery list in church?

Jesus' response to distracted Martha shakes me to my cowgirl core: "You are worried and upset about many things, but few things are needed—or indeed only one. Mary has chosen what is better" (Luke 10:41–42 NIV).

What? Didn't Jesus realize His dinner would never materialize if *every*one sat at His feet? How did He expect the grapes would get squeezed, the bread dough kneaded, the chickens fricasseed?

Hmm. Maybe, just maybe—He was trying to tell us that hearts are more important than stomachs.

*My Beloved Savior,
Help me buck all distractions
today and focus solely on You.*

He Got It

A little child shall lead them.
ISAIAH 11:6 KJV

It was a gorgeous Sunday morning at our remote Smoky Mountain cabin. Three-year-old grand-buddy Blaine had enough of a cough and runny nose to keep us away from traditional church, so we decided to worship at the Church of the Prayer Rock.

It really *was* a prayer rock—two boulders shoved together in the woods to form a crude bench facing a wooden cross nailed to a towering elm. The perfect setting to drink in the beautiful and majestic workmanship of the Creator.

Brother Blaine led us in singing "Jesus Loves Me" and "Amazing Grace." Pastor Pop-Pop (my husband, Chuck) shared a made-up-on-the-cuff, toddler-friendly sermon about three little boys learning to be good in order to please Jesus, not just their parents, mimis, or pop-pops.

Then when Blaine pointed to the cross on the tree and asked why Jesus died there, Mimi (moi) had the privilege of explaining that because we all do naughty things, someone had to be punished (THAT concept he understands all too well).

I told him that Jesus loves us so much, He chose to die on the cross as punishment in our place so that we could live with Him and Papa God forever and ever. Blaine's little forehead wrinkled in deep thought. He slowly nodded. He got it. Let me tell you, there wasn't a dry eye in the Church of the Prayer Rock that day.

Does your heart still melt when someone meets Jesus? Are you tenderized to the God-shaped holes in the lives of people you know?

Master Creator,
Thank You for saving my
soul through the willing
sacrifice of Your Son, Jesus.
Help me stay tenderized to
others' need to know Him too.

Returning Your Call

When I called, you answered me.
PSALM 138:3 NIV

Nancy spent decades praying for just the right time to share Jesus with her hostile father. But he always cut her off at every mention of her faith or the Bible. Wanting nothing to do with "foolish God talk," he grew hardened and bitter, isolating himself from everyone.

Then one night, as she drove home from an unsettling visit with her ill, elderly dad in the hospital, Nancy felt an unshakable urge to go back. She resisted but finally turned the car around.

As she re-entered the hospital room, Nancy found him crying. Shocked by the image of her strong, fiercely self-sufficient father breaking down, she could only stand and gape.

"What's wrong, Dad? Are you in pain?"

"Not physical pain. No."

"What kind of pain then?"

"I'm. . .well, I'm lonely. Nobody comes to see me except you. And you never stay long." He flicked a tear off his wrinkled cheek. "I hate this. . .being alone."

Nancy sensed that the time was finally right. Jehovah was returning her call.

"Well, Dad," she said gently, "if Jesus were in your heart, you'd never be alone. Will you let me tell you about Him?"

Twenty minutes later, Nancy was overjoyed to lead her father in a prayer to accept Christ as his Savior and constant companion for all eternity.

According to our human timetables, God is sometimes slow, but He's never late. In the eleventh hour, He often shows up with the key that unlocks a bolted door. Or a map to a path we never knew existed.

We may be on "hold" for a while, but Papa always returns our calls.

Ever-Loving Lord,
I'm so glad that in Prayer World
dropped calls don't exist.

Fear Monsters

*"Do not be afraid or discouraged, for the LORD will
personally go ahead of you. He will be with you;
he will neither fail you nor abandon you."*
DEUTERONOMY 31:8 NLT

In my travels as an event speaker, I've encountered countless women like me who've spent years running from their own personal fear monsters.

Some fears have names and specific countenances; others are faceless, frightening creatures lurking in the shadows just out of sight. But we know they're there. We *feel* them. And we yearn to boldly step up to those fear monsters and yank off their masks.

In preparation for writing my book *Fear, Faith, and a Fistful of Chocolate,* I wanted to pinpoint real fears women struggle with on a daily basis. So I conducted a survey of five hundred random women between ages eighteen and eighty. The results surprised me.

In ascending order, here's the bottom half of the top ten fear list:

#10: Being judged unfairly
#9: Specific critters (snakes, roaches, rats, etc.)
#8: Rejection
#7: Dependency on others
#6: Loneliness

Do you experience some of these same fears? Which ones and how often?

What fears do you struggle with even more than these?

Sometime today, stop and jot down your worst fears. Then tomorrow, you'll find what the survey said were the top fears that women face. Try to figure out the top fear (now don't cheat and look ahead!).

I'll give you a hint: the #1 fear was w-a-y out in front of the others. In fact, across all age categories, twice the percentage of women named it their greatest fear. What do you think it is?

....

....

....

*Slayer of Fear Monsters,
Help me identify my greatest
fears; I know that's the first
step toward defeating them.*

Rising Above It

For God has not given us a spirit of fear and timidity,
but of power, love, and self-discipline.
2 TIMOTHY 1:7 NLT

Yesterday I shared with you women's #6 through 10 greatest everyday fears. I asked you to identify your own worst fears and decide what you think is the #1 greatest fear of women across all age ranges.

Are you ready? Here, in ascending order, according to my survey, are women's five biggest fears:

#5: The unknown/death
#4: Old age
#3: Failure
#2: Debilitating illness/terminal disease
#1: Loss of a loved one (spouse/child/parents)—includes separation as in divorce, prodigal child leaving, and separation from parents

You know, our fears spotlight what matters to us most. . .those hidden corners of our life in which we trust Papa God the least. These are where we need to focus.

Fear first worms its way into our thinking and then it affects our actions. If we allow fear to continue to wreak havoc unimpeded, it can eventually erode our self-esteem, relationships, and even our faith.

The good news is that we don't have to continue being controlled by fear, hiding in timidity and cowering in anxiety. We can rise above it.

But remember, we can't embrace change until we let go of fear. And change is a direct product of today's verse. Say it aloud, considering each word. What three weapons does Papa God give us against fear?

We need change, don't we? Change from imprisoning phobias, destructive anxiety, and unproductive fretting. Change from worries that keep us stretched tighter than size 8 jeans over a size 12 tushie.

Instigator of Progress,
Motivate me to seek
change. Because a fearful
life is no life at all.

Soul Force

The ransom for a life is costly, no payment is ever enough.
PSALM 49:8 NIV

"We must forever conduct our struggle on the high plane of dignity and discipline. We must not allow our creative protest to degenerate into physical violence. Again and again we must rise to the majestic heights of meeting physical force with soul force."

Soul force. Indeed.

My heart is stirred every time I hear these words from Dr. Martin Luther King Jr. during his "I Have a Dream" speech, given on August 28, 1963, in Washington, DC. Dr. King, a Baptist minister, made an indelible mark on the world through nonviolent civil disobedience based on his Christian beliefs.

Although Dr. King was addressing African Americans striving for civil rights equality, his words are applicable to each and every Christ follower battling seen and unseen foes today.

Soul force. What do you think Dr. King meant by that?

I believe he was referring to spiritual warfare and the power of the Holy Spirit versus the power of:

- **The Evil One** (Matthew 13:19)
- **The Accuser** (Revelation 12:10)
- **The Enemy** (Matthew 13:39)
- **Your Adversary** (1 Peter 5:8)
- **Spiritual Forces of Wickedness** (Ephesians 6:12)
- **Father of Lies** (John 8:44)
- **The Tempter** (Matthew 4:3)

Yes, all these vile titles belong to the same despicable being: Satan. The one who delights in physical violence. The one who thrives on disunity, prejudice, and hatred.

The opponent of all Christians.

During this week as we honor Dr. King, let's seek to connect with the soul force he talked about. Because if that force is with us, we'll need no other.

*Holy Spirit,
Today I pray for peace
among mankind. Papa
God's powerful peace.*

Guts

Thank you for making me so wonderfully complex!
Your workmanship is marvelous.
PSALM 139:14 NLT

Piece o' cake, they said. No problemo. We'll knock you out and you'll wonder if you ever even had a colonoscopy.

Wrong.

I lay fully awake on my side watching a red-tinted version of Journey to the Center of my Girth on a monitor. My bare tush protruded from the hospital gown as the male and female MDs took turns guiding the little inner-spaceship through the twisting tunnel that was my colon. My blood pressure tanked after the first injection of woozy juice, so they couldn't give me more sedative until my BP elevated.

It never did.

Suddenly I felt a jerk on the camera tether followed by a strange *thwomp* behind me. "What was that?" I asked the nurse. She peered over my backside, her eyes wide as dinner plates.

"Um, I think we'll have a slight delay," she said, forgetting to close her mouth.

Turns out the female MD fainted. Yep. Passed out. Right on the floor. A team of people in scrubs rushed in with smelling salts and had a tea party within inches of my naked derriere. Quite humbling to realize everyone in this zip code has now been up close and personal with my hind quarter cellulite.

Eventually the male MD resumed. With a vengeance. Maybe he was trying to make up for lost time, or his breakfast burrito had too many chili peppers, but *whoa*, he jammed that joystick, baby.

When it was finally over, I had a moment of silent gratitude for my guts. . .something we rarely consider until they cease working properly. Say, have you thanked the Creator of your splendid innards lately?

Master Designer,
I'm grateful today for
ALL my working parts.

Repairing Walls

"You see the bad situation we are in."
NEHEMIAH 2:17 NASB

Grab your Bible and join me in studying the book of Nehemiah. We can learn a lot from that prophet of old in dealing with discouragement today.

- **Tears are okay.** "I sat down and wept. . .for days" (1:4). I can relate, can't you? Weeping and mourning are natural, healthy reactions to bad news. But we mustn't languish there.
- **Fatigue weakens our resolve** (4:21–23). When we're exhausted, it's easy to quit. Take regular rest breaks and fun frolics. Refresh yourself physically, mentally, and spiritually so your resolve stays strong.
- **Frustration rises as rubbish accumulates** (4:10). Clutter in our lives needs to be addressed and removed, not walked around.
- **Confusion halts momentum** (4:8). We must create a plan and diligently work it, revising whenever necessary.
- **Feelings of failure diminish hope** (4:1–3). If we lose hope, we also lose joy, peace, and our heart connection with Jesus. To counteract, we must change the way we see, think, and speak. Yesterday's failure doesn't dictate tomorrow's. Step away and pray to gain new *her*spective: How do my circumstances look from Papa's eternal viewpoint? What would Jesus do? (Cliché, I know, but sooo helpful!)
- **Fear spreads quickly and robs our faith** (4:14, 17). A surefire way to fight fear is to remember what the Lord has done for you. Rally with other believers. There's strength in numbers.

Nehemiah *knew* discouragement. He was tasked with repairing a decrepit city wall with no materials, time, or help. Despite horrendous obstacles, he prayed, developed a plan, and conquered his wall.

How's your wall going, sister?

....

....

....

*Yahweh Tsuri
(The Lord, My Rock),
My wall is falling apart piece by
discouraging piece. I trust You
to provide all I need to repair it.*

Fifty Shades of Play

Marriage is to be held in honor among all.
HEBREWS 13:4 NASB

Wanna play?

Adults don't get that question nearly enough. Especially from their spouses.

This revelation God-smacked me the other day when Chuck entered my writing cave and performed his customary early-morning greeting. He pressed his balled fist to his forehead and genuflected.

No kidding. He bowed.

Lest you think we have some sort of kinky bondage thing going, I'll 'splain.

Ever since evacuating estrogen morphed my fifty-something hair into hay, I've had to install a large pink roller each morning to make my bangs look less like a baby porcupine having a frizzy quill day.

At first Chuck stared with alarm at this hideous pink appendage assaulting his awakening senses. But then, as he has for the thirty-eight-plus years of our marriage, he started looking for the playful side of an unpleasant situation. He developed this ridiculous salute simulating his own forehead roller in homage to his queen and genuflects with the proper gestation due her royal hiney.

Or maybe that's gesticulation and highness. *Whatever*. It makes us both smile.

It's become our secret handshake of sorts. Like we're the only two members of an exclusive club. Anyone observing would roll their eyes and shake their head. Nobody gets us but us. Isn't that the way it should be with two people who choose to grow old and weird together?

Seriousness is taken far too seriously. Especially in marriage. There's enough gravity and solemnity in every other aspect of our life. Why not throw a little silliness glue into the relationship we plan on outlasting them all?

....

....

....

....

....

....

....

Forger of Forever Couples,
Help me apply more silliness
glue to the frayed edges
of my marriage today.

Just Do It

My response is to get down on my knees before the Father.
EPHESIANS 3:14 MSG

When Papa God asks us to serve Him, He doesn't mean as an advisor.

As much as we hate to admit it, Yahweh doesn't need or want us to tell Him what He *should* do. He wants to hear from us, absolutely, but what brings a smile to His big, beautiful face is when we open our spiritual ears to hear what His plans already are (Jeremiah 29:11).

And that means prayer. Communication. A dialogue, not monologue. Speaking AND listening.

We can pray anytime, anywhere. Like the apostle Paul (see today's verse), I tend to hit my knees when my soul is deeply troubled. Funny, isn't it, how dropping to our knees raises our spirits closer to heaven?

In biblical days, kneeling for prayer wasn't all that common. The average, garden-variety prayer position was standing with arms clasped as a symbol of helplessness and earnestness. Some, of course, raised their hands in worship like King David (Psalm 134:2; 141:2); others fell prostrate on their faces like the prophets of old (Joshua 5:14; Ezekiel 1:28; Daniel 10:9).

None of these positions is right or wrong. Papa God is happy to have you turning your undivided attention to Him in *any* position. As long as you just do it. Flat on your back in bed, sitting on the frozen bleachers at Junior's soccer match, or sprawling on your belly like a beached whale at exercise class.

Prayer knows no rules. No thees, thous, or witherfores. Just. . .pray. Pure, unplugged, heart-tuned-in communion with your eternal best Friend.

*Lord, Large and In Charge,
So grateful that when entering
into prayer, I may enter in
pieces, but I leave in peace.*

Aw Shucks

The more you get, the less you are.
PROVERBS 1:19 MSG

A strange rustling noise beneath my bed awoke me at 3:00 a.m. *What in the world?*

I dragged myself out and flipped on the light. Dropping to all fours, I peered under the bed. My heart lurched.

Dusty, my excited pup, cradled between his front paws the cash stash I'd been squirreling away as an emergency fund. It was hidden in an envelope buried beneath the boxes under my bed.

Apparently my treasure had been unearthed.

There sat Dusty, preparing to rip into my wad of bills. He'd peeled the envelope like a banana, and $200 in twenties dripped canine drool. My entire life savings was about to be devoured in a single slobbery gulp.

You know, there's something mystical about money. It lures us, intrigues us, controls us, and absorbs us if we're not careful. It does pry us out of bed in the morning to work, but the downside is attaining money sucks out our creative energies, often leaving only dregs for our family. . .like limp tea leaves in the bottom of a teacup.

Wealth tends to consume your soul, leaving you empty as a cornless shuck.

Well, you'll be relieved to hear that I did manage to rescue my stash, but Dusty taught me something important that night. To a dog, money has no more value than the pages of the novel he ripped apart yesterday.

Maybe we should start looking at it that way too.

Bountiful Giver,
Never, ever do I want to gain
the world but lose my soul.
Keep my cob in its shuck,
Lord, until harvesttime.

Cat Tale

Pride lands you flat on your face.
PROVERBS 29:23 MSG

One spring morning as I was sweeping my front steps, my cat Sammy-Q (as a kitten he was Suzy-Q until the vet assured me his plumbing begged to differ) belly-crawled up in fierce jungle-cat mode. He attacked the straw broom head with fangs bared and claws a-blazing.

Intent on completing my task, I impatiently pushed him aside and continued the chore. Undaunted, Sammy-Q launched an air-raid attack, knocking the broom handle from my grip.

With growing annoyance, I not-so-gently removed him from the premises and resumed my cleaning. He was not to be dissuaded, however, and returned to attack the evil stick-monster again and again, regardless of how often I thwarted his efforts.

Then an odd thing happened. My irritation suddenly parted like the Red Sea, and in the dry riverbed of revelation, I saw myself mirrored in Sammy-Q's hardheaded behavior.

I too had been trying to accomplish tasks that I stubbornly refused to yield to Papa God, even when my own best efforts repeatedly fell short. Seeing only the goals that I wanted to accomplish, I missed the Lord's bigger picture.

Just as I couldn't explain to Sammy-Q what I was doing or why, he—in his limited feline capacity—was unable to grasp my human reasoning for not allowing his misdirected efforts to succeed. We were simply on different levels.

Likewise, I cannot, in my limited human capacity, ever completely comprehend God's divine blueprint for my life. Like Sammy-Q, I must learn to accept that my Master has reasons for allowing me to fail. . .whether I understand them or not.

Worthy Lord,
Help me trust that
even my failures are
part of Your divine plan.

Bamboozled

*Leah's eyes were weak, but Rachel
was beautiful of form and face.*
GENESIS 29:17 NASB

Have you ever felt like the punch line of a bad joke?

No doubt Leah did. Hunky Jacob labored seven long years to marry Leah's gorgeous sister, Rachel. Leah must've silently watched, year after year, embarrassed that she, the eldest, wouldn't wed first—the custom of the day—and envious that a man desired a woman that much.

But not her. Never her.

Then, at the last minute, the girls' squirrelly father secretly switched his daughters at the altar.

Jacob shouted, "What is this you have done to me?" (Genesis 29:25 NASB). Leah must have felt like the booby prize. A worthless catfish when Jacob was fishing for salmon.

Like Leah, we often feel that we don't measure up. That we're not good enough. That Jehovah made a mistake in our blueprints and chucked the model after viewing the prototype.

But Psalm 139:13 assures us that our unique qualities are no accident: "You made all the delicate, inner parts of my body and knit me together in my mother's womb" (NLT).

We don't have to be "beautiful of form and face" to be used mightily of God. Like Leah, we might need Coke-bottle glasses or sweat out reciting marriage vows only if the groom is bamboozled by a slick trick.

But hey, Leah gave birth to six of the twelve tribes of Israel, the cornerstone of Judeo-Christendom.

And Papa God has a mighty plan for all of us other Leahs too.

*Elohim (Mighty Creator),
Some days I wish I was
"beautiful of form and face."
But then I remember Leah,
and I'm encouraged that You
bless the "beautiful of heart
and gut" just as much.*

Horse Sense

"Ask the animals, and they will teach you."
JOB 12:7 NIV

Pedaling my bicycle past a rural pasture one afternoon, I spotted something remarkable. Two horses stood side by side, facing opposite directions, simultaneously scraping their teeth along the lower back of the other.

I half expected to hear a satisfied Mr. Ed-ish "Ahhh" at any second.

How very clever! So did humans come up with "Scratch my back and I'll scratch yours," or did we borrow that from innovative equines?

I shouldn't be so astonished at the ingenuity of these marvelous creatures. My niece Bethany, a longtime horsewoman, says training horses requires two hundred repetitions of the desired behavior. And smart horses take longer.

Longer? Really? Wouldn't the *dumber* ones take longer?

Nope. If you let them get away with doing the task incorrectly after 198 correct times (and the smart ones *will* test you), you'll have to start over. From scratch.

We're not so different from our horsey friends, are we? In trying to replace a bad habit with a better one, we may do it perfectly 198 times. . . We'll stick to 1,400 daily calories, floss faithfully, read the Bible, or run a mile every morning, and think we've got it nailed.

But on the 199th day, we'll sneak a Krispy Kreme, toss the floss, read *Fifty Shades of Grey* instead of Genesis, or only run two blocks "so I won't get my hair sweaty."

Then it's much easier to forego the new behavior next time. Before we know it, that habit's not a habit at all.

So when we're honing a new habit, it's wise *not* to fall off the wagon. Even once. Especially a horse-drawn wagon.

*Almighty Father,
Give me the stamina to stick
it out when establishing
new, better behaviors.*

Be Still & Know

"Be still, and know that I am God."
PSALM 46:10 NIV

A few years ago, I stumbled across a special spot in the woods near my mountain cabin. The minute I saw the fallen logs that formed a cozy woodland seat and back support amid the beautiful forest greenery, I knew.

This was the spot Papa God had earmarked just for me. For the time we would spend together. For the precious hours I would sit, be still, and just *know* (see today's verse).

Why do I need such a place? Why do *you*?

With our hectic schedules and crazy-busy lifestyles, sometimes it's hard to get a bead on that still, small voice of God. And that's exactly what it takes—being still—to truly *know* what He's whispering to our hearts.

In order to internalize the incredible goodness and *Godness* of our heavenly Papa, we must mute the cacophony of the world and find stillness of our bodies, minds, and emotions. Only then can our hearts ingest this truth. Only then can we really *know* He is God.

My special spot is off the beaten path, so it's secluded. No unexpected visitors, loud noises, or interruptions (I always turn my phone off during my Be Still & Know time). It's near the humongous tree I call the Wall of Wood that reminds me of Papa's vastness and incredible power.

A few yards away, there's a reflection pool filled with chilled mountain springwater that reflects Papa's majestic mountains and towering treetops. My soul just can't drink in enough.

Have you considered rooting out a Be Still & Know place for yourself?

Creator of the Universe,
Convict me of my need to get
quiet before You. I need to hear
You, to feel You, to know You.

Golden Eggs

"Come with me by yourselves to a quiet place."
MARK 6:31 NIV

Eureka! I found it!

A little soggy maybe, and sometimes mosquito infested, but still, I love it. It's the special "Be Still & Know" place Papa God picked out especially for me near my home in Florida.

Yesterday we talked about our need for a Be Still & Know place. So let's take it a step further. How do we find this elusive stillness?

As wonderful as my mountaintop cathedral is, I'm not up there much of the year. I'm down here. . .in flat, hot, humid Florida. So I petitioned the Lord for a Be Still & Know spot here too. And He provided one.

So what that it borders a marsh? I'm experienced in gator evasion.

That it's halfway submerged after a hard rain? I can borrow my grandbuddy's rubber Spiderman boots.

Who cares about a few (dozen) mosquito bites? *Off!* is cheaper by the case.

The good news is that it's secluded (who else in their right mind would go there?); the resident sandhill cranes have welcomed me with open wings; and best of all, Papa meets me there every single time I show up.

Not as majestic as the mountains maybe, but hey, this is Florida. The only mountains we have are speed humps.

So whether you live in the desert, swamp, hills, plains, seaside, or badlands, Papa God has a special meeting place ready and waiting. You just have to find it. Like searching for the golden Easter egg, it's a bit of effort, but more than worth it.

Lord of My Secrets,
I cherish my time with You.
Just me, just You.

Wassup, Dude?

*"God has brought me laughter, and everyone
who hears about this will laugh with me."*
GENESIS 21:6 NIV

I knew the moment I uprooted Carrot Dude from my garden that he was someone special, with his long knobby carrot legs and chubby root arm encircling his conjoined twin.

He was so. . .Carrot Grant. Suave and elegant, with a witty flair to his orangeness.

After I brought him in and scrubbed the dirt from his little face (or maybe that was his bum—hard to tell!), he completely captured my imagination. I started carrying him around the house with me, propping him up on counters to keep me company. And then it happened.

We bonded. I was smitten with a vegetable.

So why not share Carrot Dude with the world? Off we went—to work, shopping, gardening, the playground. . .and I documented our exciting adventures (visit DeboraCoty.com for the hilarious video). I couldn't believe the scores of followers Carrot Dude collected; I had to stay up late at night to keep up with all the comments:

- "I'm really enjoying Carrot Dude! Please don't stop!"
- "Digging new friends from the garden? Deb, I'm a little worried. Remember, it IS a carrot."
- "Kind of like Flat Stanley, only orangier."
- "Carrot Dude gets out more than I do!"
- "A funky little heavenly reminder that we're all different."

And my favorite: "Where's his head?" My answer: "Carrot Dude was born headless. The good news is that it's not fatal—many people are born with this handicap and aren't hindered in the least. They become politicians."

....

....

....

....

....

....

....

> *Lord of the Harvest,
> Thanks for laughter,
> the best stress reliever
> there is. Send me more today!*

Believing in Fences

Our God gives you everything you need.
2 Thessalonians 1:2 MSG

Dang. Another hole. Fenway's been digging again.

It's the tenth escape since we fenced our backyard two weeks ago. The conclusion is obvious: my dog simply doesn't believe in fences.

Should've known that from the beginning; after all, that's how the scruffy little guy became part of our family nine years ago. I found the one-year-old pup, barely out of Huggies, trotting down the center line of a packed rush-hour highway. The vet said judging by the filthy dreadlocks matted to his bony body and his calloused paws, he'd been on the road for months.

A travelin' man.

As years passed, he overcame most of his born-to-run tendencies.

Then comes this dastardly fence. Grrr. Fenway stares down the slatted foe taunting him with definitive boundaries.

He's clearly risen to this new challenge, presenting me daily with big innocent chocolate eyes and a dirt-encrusted snout. Neighbors testify that he pops over to visit then pops back under before his homies catch on.

Although we've tried to thwart his escapes by digging chicken wire beneath the fence, Fenway perseveres, constantly testing the perimeter for weaknesses like a *Jurassic Park* raptor.

You know, I recall many times I've dug my way under boundaries Papa God has erected in my life. My forays into the wild have turned out badly. . .penalties to pay, backtracking to do, holes to cover (but some just won't stay hidden).

So I've learned to respect those boundaries and recognize that my Master doesn't want me to get hurt. Or lost. Or neglected. Because He's my Papa and He loves me dearly.

Even when my snout is clogged with dirt.

Master Protector,
Thank You for loving
me with fences.

Someone Special

Let your love, G<small>OD</small>, shape my life.
P<small>SALM</small> 119:41 MSG

I'm not Catholic, but for the past two decades, I've had my own priest. Actually, he wasn't exclusively mine, but I admired, loved, and respected Father Fitzgerald as if he were. But then everyone felt that way about him.

I first met Father Fitz the day I angrily presented him with a petition demanding that his new church install a speed hump at the entrance bordering my property. His speeding parishioners MUST stop putting my children and pets at risk.

Father Fitz defused my ticking bomb by graciously accepting the petition, enveloping my hand warmly in both of his, and inviting my family to dinner.

That speed hump was already installed before our dinner the following week. Despite jokes about proselytizing each other, we became fast friends. The clincher was when this wonderful Catholic priest kept a (mostly) straight face after asking my four-year-old daughter if he could see her dolly (which she was holding tightly to her chest) and she replied, "Not now. I'm milking her."

I even modeled one of the main characters in my first novel after Father Fitz. He was just the wise, kind, godly Irishman with a keen sense of humor that I needed. When *The Distant Shore* was released, I hand delivered a copy to him and explained that he was the inspiration for Captain Stone. When his eyes misted, I knew he understood how special he was to my family.

Is there someone in your life—an unlikely friend, perhaps—whom you consider special but have never told them so? Perhaps today could be the day.

*Creator of All Humanity,
Help me reach out in love
today to tell that special
person I appreciate them.*

Scratches

He gives a greater grace.
JAMES 4:6 NASB

My pastor, Mark Saunders, got a new office desk. But before he could use it, he had to clean out the old desk. . .which led to an afternoon of purging his entire office.

As he furiously grubbed and stacked and sorted through piles of clutter that accumulated then decumulated (Mark's creative nonword) on his desk, the unthinkable happened. A scratch. Right in the center of the beautiful new desktop.

No, not just a scratch—in Mark's eyes, it was a gouge. Maybe even a gorge. The Grand Canyon now graced Mark's brand-new desk. In his effort to achieve perfection, he'd induced the very opposite—imperfection.

Isn't this how it often is with you and me as we strive—in our own strength—to purge our personal lives apart from Papa God's grace? We make a little progress; we may even imagine that we're nearing perfection. But suddenly it's all stripped away in moments of weakness or disregard or neglect. . .*poof.*

We undo all the good we've done.

Scratches happen in our marriage—we have a good day together; we're really connecting for a nice change; and then. . .*poof.* One thoughtless comment sparks an inferno.

Scratches mar our self-discipline too. We lose three pounds and start eyeing the skinny clothes in our closet (the ones draped in cobwebs) then. . .*poof.* We relax our resolve and succumb to the temptation of a breakfast brownie. Sigh.

Mark's desk now displays a strategically placed Bible. It covers the scratch and reminds him that his life goal is to simply surrender and let Jesus do the purging.

Him Whom My Soul Loves,
I am thankful today that Jesus
covers the scratches of my life.

Wag More

"I will watch my ways and keep my tongue from sin;
I will put a muzzle on my mouth."
PSALM 39:1 NIV

The other day while driving home, I stopped for gas. The bushy-bearded driver in front of me suddenly stopped his multidented pickup *ten feet* from the curb, got out, and walked away. The fifty-something heavyset man casually strolled through the busy gas pump traffic and disappeared into the convenience store. He'd left his car door wide open, blocking the traffic lane so everyone was forced to stop. And wait.

The drivers of four cars (including me) had no alternative but to sit there staring at each other until he finally reappeared, toting a package of chewing tobacco. Oblivious to the rest of the world, he moseyed back over to his truck, climbed in, nonchalantly fiddled with the radio, and eventually drove away.

Many people march to the beat of their own drummer playing the ever-popular song: "It's All About Me." We can't help but encounter them in the course of our every day. Some may be self-centered, careless, or ignorant. But I suspect most are like you and me—busy, worried, and distracted.

Not intentionally thoughtless, just preoccupied with the burdens of life.

So how should we respond to these toe stompers? Sit on our horns? Spew blistering words? Set that idiot straight?

The Bible says to put a muzzle on it. Yep. To keep our tongues from sin. No matter how much the offender might appear to deserve it. Guilty or not. Grateful or not. Grace is the name of the game if we truly want to emulate Christ.

Giver of Grace,
Loan me Your holy muzzle
today. Instead of attacking
like a mad dog, help me
wag more and growl less.

Destiny

My life is God's prayer.
PSALM 42:8 MSG

I was thrilled to receive a Facebook message from a long-lost childhood friend. Ginny was my neighbor and summer bum-around pal when we were kids. Together we scarfed down many a bowl of freshly popped Jiffy Pop swimming in a whole stick of melted butter.

Mmm. The good old days: no diets, no cares, no cholesterol counts.

Ginny said she'd happened across a book called *Too Blessed to be Stressed* and laughed her head off. She just had to look me up to see if that Debora Mitchell Coty and I could possibly be one and the same. Surely not, right?

"Maybe you were funny when we were young, but I don't remember it."

True, I was a serious (and chubby) child. But Papa God began preparing me for my future ministry as a humorist by surrounding me with funny people. Mama loved to make other people laugh (still does at eighty-seven) and Daddy, a true southern gentleman (now eighty-nine), had a wonderfully wry wit, but nobody knew it because he was drowned out by Mama.

My sister, two years my elder (she HATES it when I say that), would rather laugh than eat. When we weren't wrestling or fighting over shoes, we were giggling.

Then I married Chuck, one funny, twisted soul, let me tell you. That man keeps me chuckling after nearly forty years.

So I turned out to be an inspirational humorist. It was divinely planned all along.

Take a moment, think back, and ponder. . . What ministry has Papa been preparing you for your whole life? ("Sleeping" is not an acceptable answer!)

Fulfiller of Destinies,
Thanks for routing out mine.
Now please send me the map.
And a stick of butter.

Wrinkled Ben

"God is opposed to the proud,
but gives grace to the humble."
JAMES 4:6 NASB

Cricket frantically searched her pockets yet again. It was no use. The $100 bill was gone.

My grown daughter and I had been perusing garage sales for Christmas bargains; she'd brought along the cash her husband had been paid at work the night before. But no one had change for the hunky bill, so she'd folded and stored it in the place she thought would be safest—her jeans pocket.

Now we were both wallowing in deep muck.

"If it fell out of your pocket, somebody would have snatched it up immediately," I said, feeling terrible for her. "Maybe they really needed it."

"They couldn't have needed it worse than me." Cricket's eyes welled up and her hands started shaking. "That was all we had to spend for the baby's Christmas."

So with nothing left to be done, we prayed. Geesh. Wouldn't you think we'd have done that *first*?

As we poured our grief out to Papa and begged for His grace in somehow finding or replacing the money, Cricket, in desperation, thrust her hand back into that same empty pocket she'd already tried five times. Only this time it wasn't empty. Her hand came out clutching a wrinkled green portrait of Ben Franklin.

"Look! God put it back in my pocket!" Cricket cried, as we burst into screaming celebration.

Ben was lost but now is found. Just like you. Just like me. That's grace.

> *Giver of Endless Grace,*
> *Help me notice—and be grateful*
> *for—the marvelous grace*
> *You give me in so many different*
> *ways every single day.*

Second Banana

*I can do all things through
Him who strengthens me.*
PHILIPPIANS 4:13 NASB

In high school, I was always *second* best. Red ribbon in the science fair, runner-up in the talent show, backup singer in the choir, one-tenth of a point behind my best friend's GPA.

And I'll never forget the All Sport's Banquet in twelfth grade. It was my turn to receive the Most Valuable Player award for tennis. It always went to a senior. I was the only senior on the team. No-brainer, right?

So I spent hours getting dolled up (there were football players to impress) and rehearsing my acceptance speech (humbly gracious, of course). The athletic director finally mounted the stage holding the MVP trophy. My palms sweated. My heart pounded.

But for the first time ever, the tennis MVP went to a junior. The gal who'd sneered at me the entire season because I couldn't beat her.

Sigh. Second banana again.

Then a funny thing happened that summer after high school. The passive little girl who'd always accepted her lot in life as second banana got, well, fired up.

Today's verse lit a spark in my soul. Was it true? It didn't say *some* things. . .it said *all* things. In my blossoming faith, I finally had a creed, a powerful truth to embrace, the confidence I needed to go for the gold in pursuing my life goals. Silver was no longer good enough if I was going to live my very best for God's glory.

*Victorious Lord,
The day I transcend this life,
I'm gonna run up the steps to
the stage of eternity, hold my
arms Rocky-high, and thank
the One who gave His life so
I might win first prize.*

Life-Altering Moments

Please don't give up on me!
PSALM 119:8 NLT

Linda, an Air Force nurse, was in charge of a medical team training mission; her team was to board a large aircraft, the interior of which was basically an empty warehouse, rig it to suspend medical plinths and carry other medical equipment and patients safely, and then disembark in London for a little R&R.

Configuring the aircraft was no small task, requiring tedious hours of hard labor, but finally it was completed. Linda and her team took their seats. The aircraft taxied for takeoff.

Suddenly, the plane decelerated and Linda heard the pilot's voice through her headphones, "Medical Team Leader, sorry to inform you: you've been bumped for cargo."

Grumbling broke out as Linda and her coworkers began the arduous task of de-configuring the aircraft, transferring all the equipment to another plane, and starting the entire procedure all over again, this time to a much less exciting destination.

Visions of Harrods shopping evaporated; Linda and her coworkers were disappointed and angry.

When they finally arrived, exhausted, at their rerouted destination at 3:00 a.m., Linda learned that as the plane they'd been booted from had approached England, freak wind shear currents ripped off a wing and the aircraft plummeted to earth.

There were no survivors.

Linda was stunned. She could have been on that plane. It was a life-altering moment that would lead her to eventually give her life to Christ and become a military chaplain.

Life-altering moments sneak up on us when we least expect them. How will Papa God get your attention when a change is needed?

Living Lord,
Teach me to pay attention
when You're trying to
tell me something.

Flab Is Drab

We will not compare ourselves with each other....
Each of us is an original.
GALATIANS 5:26 MSG

Ever feel defined by your behind?

I do. Too much junk in my trunk.

I totally get author Jeannette Barber's drastic method of weight control: "When I buy cookies, I eat just four and throw the rest away. But first, I spray them with Raid so I won't dig them out of the garbage later. Gotta be careful, though, because Raid really doesn't taste that bad."

When I turned fifty, I turned hungry. And discovered OOPS: my Obstinate Orca Propagation Site. You too might battle OOPS—those humpback whales beached on your outer hips. One morning you wake up and OOPS, there they are. Obstinate orcas, refusing to return to the open sea.

Like me, many women gain a pound or two every year. Not enough to worry about, right? Wrong. This "Boo Baggage" sneaks up on you until one day ten years down the road, twenty rotten, stinkin' pounds jump out and yell, "Boo!"

Nearly every woman I know is somewhere on the "concerned" to "obsessed" continuum about her weight. Not surprisingly, weight gain ranks in the top fifteen fears of women. In one study, 15 percent of women surveyed said they'd rather be blind than overweight. Forty-nine percent said they would trade five years of their life not to be obese.

How tragic that almost half of us would rather be dead than fat.

Sure, appearance seems important, but inner beauty is more important—the evidence of the Holy Spirit's presence in our lives. Inner beauty translates into outer beauty, regardless of what's in our trunk.

Lord of Lean AND Large,
I want to honor You with my
body as well as my spirit.

Garden Party

"Where, O death, is your victory?
Where, O death, is your sting?"
1 CORINTHIANS 15:55 NIV

I was one of a dozen friends gathered for a springtime garden party, the beautiful backyard vibrant with colorful blossoms of renewed life.

In macabre contrast, we were there to honor a dying friend. Melva had been diagnosed with an aggressive malignant brain tumor and was given little time to live.

Melva had us draw numbers from a hat that had recently adorned her chemo-induced bald head. We were to choose, as Melva's parting gift to us, one of the purses she brought forth and displayed on a table.

Now these weren't new purses; they were well-loved, well-worn bags that bore the finger-prints of Melva's life. Some were dressy, some casual, others quirky, but all represented facets of Melva's essence and spirit. She wanted to give this little part of herself to her special friends as a token of love and legacy of remembrance.

"Please. . .I want *you* to have them," was Melva's heartfelt bequest.

The navy clutch I brought home reminds me daily of the fragility of life. That one day we will all leave a legacy of remembrance with our family and friends. But what will that legacy be? Will it be the power of prayer, of unconditional love, of faith that floats even when we're floundering in despair's septic tank? Will it be memories of a life well lived, moments savored, laughter shared?

I sincerely hope so.

A blue clutch sitting on my dresser implores me to make it happen.

El Olam (The Everlasting God),
Thank You for life. . .now and
hereafter. Help me make the
most of my days on earth and
leave behind a legacy of hope.

Pond Scum

*"Let your light shine before others, that they may see
your good deeds and praise your Father in heaven."*
MATTHEW 5:16 NIV

Trudging across the parking lot to speak at a church luncheon, I felt weighted down by heavy personal problems, my spirit lower than pond scum.

A salt-and-pepper-haired man with his back toward me was gazing at a poster bearing my photo. He turned and a smile lit his face.

"Why, it IS you, Debbie!" he cried, spreading his arms wide. "Remember me?"

I 'bout dropped my teeth. It was a mature version of wild and crazy Jack, the strapping twenty-year-old I'd worked alongside thirty years before. Amid joyful hugs, I learned that Jack is now a strong Christian leader in that very church.

That was the biggest thrill of all, for Jack had been heavily into ninja and the "dark arts" back in the day.

I floated on air as Jack introduced me to his lovely wife and son. "You know, Debbie, I wouldn't be here if it weren't for you," Jack said. "You were the first person I ever saw act out Christianity. Your faith was real. You lived what you believed and I took notice. I may not have said anything, but I was watching."

My eyes sprung a leak.

"I was real mixed up spiritually for a long time, but God finally got my attention and I turned my life over to Him. Thank you for impacting my life."

Now isn't that just like Papa God? To light up a pond scum day with brilliant Sonshine?

*Son of Man,
It's such a privilege to live my
faith as a beacon to You. Shine,
Jesus, shine, even when my
embers ebb. Rekindle my flame
with Your grace and mercy.*

Love Story

"You'd better think fast,
for there is going to be trouble."
1 SAMUEL 25:17 TLB

Abby was frantic; some might even call her a desperate housewife. She'd just received a call that would forever change her life. But then maybe that wasn't so bad. Her life story sure wouldn't make the Hallmark channel.

It had all seemed so promising in the beginning—ten years before when she'd met Nabe, an ambitious college sophomore intent on making a splash in the business world. Abby had fallen in love with his boundless energy and his lust for the good things of life. She had willingly dropped out of school to work three jobs to finance his education in pursuit of his goals. . .*their* goals.

But when he'd finally clawed his way to the top of the financial ladder and was head of his own Fortune 500 company, she wasn't so sure this was the life she'd bargained for.

Nabe had changed. Abby rarely saw him; when he was home, he was always parked in front of that confounded computer or conferring with some lawyer or CEO on the phone.

Worse, he'd gained a reputation as a financial black hole, gobbling everything in his path to satisfy his own greed. But it was never enough. He needed more, always more. Newscasters called him "The Butcher of Wall Street," and he'd insisted that everyone call him Butch, including his wife.

Abby's life felt empty, void of meaning. At twenty-nine, she was still beautiful, but already she could see hollowness in the pale blue eyes staring back from the mirror. Could this be all there was to life. . .and love?

Continued tomorrow. . .

God of Hope,
Please give me more
for my marriage.

The Plot Thickens

"Who does this son of Jesse think he is?"
1 Samuel 25:10 nlt

(Continued)

Then out of the blue came the call from Carol, Butch's executive assistant, confiding that the world was about to end.

"He really did it this time, Abby. The damage is irreversible," Carol whispered, her voice tinged with fear.

"What do you mean? What did he do?" Abby asked, her stomach clenching.

"You've heard of Dave Jesseson, the CEO of Kingdom Enterprises?"

"Well sure, who hasn't? Isn't KE the fastest growing conglomerate in the world?"

"That's right. It's downright miraculous how that company has exploded onto the scene. Some say God Himself must be at the helm. Anyway, it turns out that Mr. Jesseson's people have been quietly protecting some of Butch's interests from opposing companies—the wolves waiting in the wings to scarf up anything they can. Butch has no idea what a mess he'd be in if the KE guys hadn't interceded on his behalf."

Carol took a deep breath and continued.

"So this morning, Mr. Jesseson called Butch and asked—very politely—if he'd be interested in forming a partnership with KE to develop and market a revolutionary invention to transform the livestock industry."

"What did Butch say?" Abby braced herself. She knew Butch's volatile temperament all too well.

"Oh, he was rude and insulting, told Mr. Jesseson he'd made his fortune on his own and would never consider sharing any of it with the likes of him. Then Butch hung up on him."

"Oh no!" Abby blanched and reached for the roll of Tums she chewed like candy.

Continued tomorrow. . .

*Adonai Eloheinu
(The Lord Is Our God),
Help me always remember
that I accomplish nothing
on my own; every blessing
comes from Your hand.*

Time for Action

Abigail wasted no time.
1 SAMUEL 25:18 NLT

(Continued)

"That's not all." Carol's voice squeaked. "My friend Louise, a KE employee, just texted me that Dave Jesseson and his army of lawyers are headed over here, *as we speak,* to initiate a hostile takeover and destroy Butch. But Butch is in a meeting and gave me strict orders not to disturb him under any circumstances. You're his wife; what should I do?"

Abby woefully shook her head as the phone slid from her hand. What could anyone do? Butch was probably three sheets to the wind, drinking it up with his corporate buddies behind closed doors as usual on Friday afternoons.

She knew the reputation of Dave Jesseson—strong, but fair. Surely he'd listen to reason if she was quick enough. Abby flew into action, opening her home safe and filling a briefcase with her twenty-thousand-dollar coin collection. She grabbed Butch's half-million-dollar 1909 Honus Wagner baseball card and the 1952 Mickey Mantle worth thirty-five thousand dollars.

Racing against time, Abby drove to Butch's building, dashed through the double glass doors and across the marbled lobby where a dozen suited men stood before the bank of elevators. To Abby, they looked like a firing squad. Recognizing Dave Jesseson from *Newsweek* covers, Abby threw herself between him and the opening elevator door.

"Wait, please, Mr. Jesseson! I'm Butch's wife, Abby, and I beg you to hear me out."

Dave stepped back, surprise registering on his hardened, determined face.

Continued tomorrow. . .

Master Creator,
You gave me a good mind,
able to sort things out, even in
emergencies. Please move me
to action when the time is right
and not waste precious time
waiting for someone else
to solve my problems.

Happy Ending

David wasted no time in sending messengers
to Abigail to ask her to become his wife.
1 SAMUEL 25:39 TLB

(Continued)

"I know my husband has returned evil for your good," Abby said to Dave Jesseson, "but I implore you to overlook this foolish thing he's done."

She opened the briefcase and held out her valuables to him. "Please accept these gifts and restrain from shedding corporate blood to avenge yourself. The Lord is with you; I know you'll never forgive yourself if you act rashly in revenge. Please forgive Butch, but most of all, forgive me for not being more aware of my husband's vile ways so I could intervene sooner."

Dave stared at her, his face softening.

"You're right," he said. "I *am* acting rashly and would most assuredly regret this act of revenge when my blood quit boiling tomorrow. Thank you for stopping me. You're quite a woman. Because of you, I won't destroy Butch. God bless you and keep you, Abby."

Later, when the security guard informed Butch what had *almost* happened, he suffered a stroke and became as stone. Ten days later, he died.

Soon after the funeral, Abby was busy sorting out Butch's mess when the doorbell rang. A messenger bore three-dozen pink roses and a card reading

> *"Dearest Abby,*
> *You're as smart as you are gorgeous. I can't stop thinking about you. You've*
> *won my eternal admiration. Will you marry me?*
> *Your smitten suitor, Dave."*

So, girlfriend, I'm sitting here grinning; are you?

Recognize the updated story (with a smidge of literary license) of David and Abigail from 1 Samuel 25? You've just gotta read the original love story; Papa God, the author of romance, tells it best.

Ahh, Lord,
Thanks for creating
sweet romance; some
days it keeps me going.

Wedding Bells

Someday your children will come home....
Then all you have done for them will be greatly rewarded.
JEREMIAH 31:16 CEV

Wedding bells chimed as my only son, Matthew, hitched his star to the lovely Rebecca, the new Mrs. Coty.

It was both easier and harder than I expected.

Easier in that sweet Rebecca thoughtfully took care of all the details to make it as simple as possible for me during the crazy-busy demands of a new book release.

But it was harder than I thought it would be to watch my little buddy present his heart to another woman. I thought I'd worked through all that. After all, he's twenty-eight and has been living away from home a decade. He's had girlfriends. . .girls I learned to share his heart with. For a time.

But this one's for all time.

As I watched him kneeling, tuxedoed and handsome, at the unity candle altar, I flashed back to Captain Buttertub, our nickname for three-year-old Matthew running around the backyard in his Spiderman underpants, an old buttertub from the sandbox jammed upon his little blond head as he fought valiantly with his stick-sword to protect his mama from invisible villains.

And now he's vowing to protect someone else from the world's villains.

I realize our motherly job is to raise our sons to this end, that they will fulfill the biblical mandate to leave and cleave to their wife in adulthood as they did their mother in childhood.

I know. I know. But still it aches somewhere in a hollow place deep inside. . .a secret ache mamas share.

Heavenly Father,
It's so hard to let go as our
children fulfill their destinies.
But You—Father of Jesus—
already know that, don't You?

Matchmaker

*Love is always supportive,
loyal, hopeful, and trusting.*
1 CORINTHIANS 13:7 CEV

The Almighty deserved a high five when He matched me with my Chuck. But we're not one of those palsy-walsy couples who do everything together; we understand and respect our differences.

Chuck's into quality. I'm into quantity. He'll painstakingly fix a broken fifty-cent item if it takes all week. I'll toss it and buy another.

We do home projects together. Just not at the same time.

For example, I slap on wallpaper willy-nilly (YES, wallpaper!) and then exit. Chuck enters and spends many hours methodically doing all the precision trimming (while I start three more projects). We inspect our work together and congratulate each other on a job well done.

When Chuck makes dinner, he carefully slices a fresh pineapple into perfect one-inch cubes, never allowing them to touch another food so their unique flavor may be savored.

I randomly chop apples, strawberries, tomatoes—whatever I can find that's remotely fruit-like (hey, aren't onions fruit?) into a hodgepodge salad, some pieces peeled, some not so much.

Could these different styles of ours annoy each other? You betcha.

Yet love is a many-splintered thing. Providence often brings odd couples together; the only way we can make the relationship work is to follow the guidelines in 1 Corinthians chapter 13 (please take time to read the entire chapter).

I draw comfort in Papa's promise that true love never fails because my heart-shaped hamburgers on Valentine's Day sure did. After shrinkage and burnage (new grill!), Chuck thought I was serving him two-headed moles.

But he ate them anyway. Now dat's amore!

*Divine Matchmaker,
Today, Valentine's Day, I'm
thankful for evolving love, the
frosting on our relationship
cupcake. Today was good, but
tomorrow will be even better!*

Zing

When you lie down,
your sleep will be sweet.
PROVERBS 3:24 NIV

I overheard a revealing conversation between two young mothers in a grocery store checkout line. One was draped over her cart, trying to comfort a whimpering baby while her toddler tossed a package of gnawed cheese at the cashier's head.

The disheveled mother turned to the woman behind her, who was balancing a baby on one hip and a jumbo package of diapers on the other. Pointing to a tabloid headline heralding "Man Awakens From 30-Year Sleep," she asked wistfully, "Doesn't that sound heavenly?"

"Ooooohhhhhh yeah," came the heartfelt reply.

Sleep. Do we ever get enough?

Papa God never meant for us to keep going nine hundred miles per hour all day. He built triggers into our bodies to cue us when it's time to escape consciousness. Wise people listen to those cues, such as notable nappers Albert Einstein, Thomas Edison, and Ronald Reagan.

Happy naps are an effective cause-pause in the nonstop stress of our day. They're little slices of heaven that revive our energy, clarity, and motivation. Our *zing*. They're womankind's front line of defense against the assault of acute nastiness resulting from fatigue.

When I miss my nappy, ain't nobody happy.

I average five hours of sleep at night, so I try to take an afternoon nap whenever possible. *Try* is the operative word here, for many times I lie in bed thinking about all the things I should be doing instead. But occasionally I'm blessed with an hour of blissful, degrumpifying unconsciousness, for which the occupants of my little world are extremely grateful.

So, girlfriend, how do you revive when you're sagging?

Restorer of Zing,
I'm immensely grateful
for a good night's sleep.
May I please put in a
request for one tonight?

Darth Wader

*Your enemy, the devil, is. . .sneaking
around to find someone to attack.*
1 PETER 5:8 CEV

The moon hid behind clouds as I walked down the street to my daughter's house after dinner. Suddenly, something rushed out at me from the dark, snapping at my bare calves.

Ouch! The horrible thing bit me. And then kept lunging at my heels as I high-stepped down the street, shrieking.

"Met the Phantom Attack Duck, did ya?" the neighbor hollered.

"Duck? I thought it was an alligator," I huffed, trying to catch my breath.

"Might as well be. Jaws strong as a gator. She's got a nest in those bushes."

That was my first encounter with the devil in feathers that terrorizes my neighborhood. I call her Darth Wader. This evil warlord is cleverly disguised as long-necked poultry, black as coal from beak to webbed feet.

You know, that's how Satan operates too—hiding in the peripheral darkness of our lives. When we're naively wandering through our days on autopilot, unaware of his presence and completely off guard, he attacks.

And like Darth Wader, he won't stop dogging us once he's had his first nip, his first taste of victory.

"I got away with that little fib; one more won't hurt."

"I have another prayer request about Jill. You won't *believe* what she did this time!"

Remember "Resist the devil and he will flee from you"? (James 4:7 NASB). Don't be a wimp! Be a warrior! Why settle for Olive Oyl when you could be Xena the warrior princess?

*Mighty Father,
I know caving to the dark side
isn't my destiny. For You are my
Force above all other forces, the
one true, all-powerful, living God.*

Exquisite Mysteries

*"Call on me and come and pray to me,
and I will listen to you."*
JEREMIAH 29:12 NIV

I've just finished doing something that made me feel bad. *Really* bad. I immersed myself in a vat of scalding pain. Someone else's pain.

- The shell-shocked parents who lost their beautiful twenty-four-year-old daughter to suicide with no warning. No symptoms. No goodbyes.
- The mom who went in to wake up her twenty-one-year-old son for work and found him not breathing.
- The writer friend my age who, out of the blue, suffered a debilitating stroke that will alter her entire life.

Yes, I immersed myself in their pain and I did it intentionally. Yesterday, today, and I'll do it tomorrow too.

Why? Because I wholeheartedly believe in the power of prayer. And I'll bet you do too.

Prayer is one of those exquisite mysteries of faith. It's hard to believe that the Creator of All Things would actually *want* our input and for us to tell Him (even though He already knows) our desires and petitions. It blows my everlovin' mind.

Yet He asks us to pray. And promises He'll listen.

So we'll go on intentionally allowing our hearts to break alongside someone else's. Someone who is aching with more pain than they ever imagined was possible. Because we know the One who can help them. And He knows us too.

....

....

....

....

....

....

....

....

*Healer of Hearts,
I willingly enter into the pain
of others through prayer. I have
faith that during my darkest hour,
someone will do this for me. Hear
my earnest requests, O Lord, and
touch these broken lives with Your
healing mercies. . . [Go ahead
and finish, sister. . .you're on.]*

More Than You Paid For

"Your Father already knows your needs."
LUKE 12:30 NLT

The jittery, middle-aged woman arrived at London's Chessington Zoo carrying a box. Well, *carrying* might be a strong word—it dangled by her fingertips as far from her body as humanly possible.

She told the zookeeper that she'd bought something online and when the package arrived, she spotted something she *didn't* order in the bottom of the box.

"Here," she said, thrusting the carton into his hands before fleeing toward the parking lot, "I don't want to keep it."

Ya think? Skittering angrily around the box was a gigantic, hairy tarantula.

"We don't know what the product was, or where she ordered it from," said the zookeeper, "but the spider is very fast, very aggressive, and *very* big."

Ooookay. Cancel my mail-order surprises.

Sometimes we get more than we pay for, don't we? A spouse with an abusive past, a coworker with a hidden agenda; an online friend with a shameful true identity, a new girlfriend who—we find out too late—gossips about our deepest secrets.

We might even carry a few scary secrets ourselves, skittering around the darkest recesses of our soul. Things we don't want to keep, but we don't know where or how to unload them.

Know what? Papa God already knows. And He's got His big, loving arms extended, ready to take those nasty things from us. If we'll just hand them over.

Resolver of Secrets,
Here are mine. Take them. I don't
want to keep the gigantic, hairy
creatures another second. Clean
out my dark corners. Fumigate
my soul. Thank You, Lord.

Don't Miss the Music

Embrace peace—don't let it get away!
PSALM 34:14 MSG

It began with a hurried, worried, late-night drive to the ER with Spouse in severe abdominal pain. During countless tests, surgery, a gigantic railroad-track scar, and weeks of recovery, I was forced to set aside busy life as I know it and sit. Just sit.

And I could hear the music again.

It was the same music I'd heard on a trail just a few weeks earlier at our Smoky Mountain cabin. I was walking along the secluded woodsy path when I felt the need to rest a bit. So I parked my behunkus on a boulder to catch my breath.

That's when I heard the music.

It was gentle and humble and unpretentious—pretty hard to tune in to at first. But the longer I sat there, the melody grew and filled my insides with its glory. The buzz of bees, the trickle of a hidden waterfall, the rumble of distant thunder, tree branches rustling in the breeze. . .the epitome of sweetness in life all combined to create music for my soul.

It was truly beautiful and oh so satisfying. Peace. It sounded like peace.

Then it occurred to me: if you walk by too fast, you'll miss the music.

So I vowed not to walk so fast all the time. To slow down and listen. But as soon as we returned home, I hit the road running. It took an emergency room run to put on the breaks.

To stop. And hear Papa's beautiful music playing in my soul.

Most Abundant Provider,
Help me remember to take
a few moments today to stop,
sit down, and catch my breath.
I'm listening for Your gentle
melody in my heart.

Bringing Home the Bacon

*Whatever your hand finds to do,
do it with all your might.*
ECCLESIASTES 9:10 NASB

After the Sochi Olympics, Swiss cross-country double gold medalist Daris Cologna's proud country presented him with a pig.

While Russian and American athletes received hundreds of thousands of dollars cash and merchandise from their governments, Daris received a little pink porker for his lifetime of hard work.

At the ceremony, Daris smiled broadly, thanked everyone graciously, and named his prize Sochi. Then he hit the slopes to begin practicing for the next Olympics.

So why would Daris continue such grueling training when the reward is so meager?

Why do you continue that activity—the one that eats (like a pig) your valuable time, attention, and energy—although the payout is miniscule?

We all have them. . .projects/jobs/dreams that we pursue because we just can't let go. The return for our investment may not be in dollars; it may be in sense—the sense that you've helped someone, improved yourself, or that you've accomplished a task the Lord customized for your unique gifts and abilities.

Whatever the motivation, it's there, it's strong, and it keeps us going. Because there's satisfaction in harvesting the fruit of our passion and following Papa God's calling. Whether it brings home the bacon or not.

Maybe I'll call my next book Porker as a reminder that some things in life are worth doing . . .just because.

*Seer of Deeds Great and Small,
Help me remember that my
future reward for today's
thankless task is worth more
than gold. Or pigs.*

Mud

We will be confident when we stand before God. Even if we feel
guilty, God is greater than our feelings, and he knows everything.
1 JOHN 3:19–20 NLT

It was my first day of sixth grade at a newly built school. So new, in fact, that mounds of dirt and deep holes dotted the schoolyard. Overnight rain had filled the holes with black, muddy water.

Gwenda and I were part of a group of girls admiring each other's back-to-school clothes. Gwenda stood with her back to a mudhole, laughing merrily; I reached over to finger the butterfly appliqué on her pretty pink sweater.

What happened next is recorded in excruciating slow-mo in my memory. As my hand extended toward her, Gwenda inadvertently stepped backward. Down, down, down she went, her whole body immersed in that gooey, disgusting mud.

Words cannot express the horror that seized my soul.

I stood helplessly by as teachers fished Gwenda out of the slime pit, every sixth grader witnessing her utter humiliation. I blinked back tears as they ushered her into the office to call her mother.

"Sorry" wasn't big enough to cover the magnitude of my transgression.

Although no blame was officially cast my way, I secretly wallowed in guilt mud for years. I could barely look Gwenda in the face, although she remained as sweet and friendly as if it had never happened.

With today's scripture, at last, my heart found peace. I was graciously forgiven by Gwenda, mercifully forgiven by Papa God, and begrudgingly forgiven by myself, my toughest critic.

Dear girl, is there something you need to forgive yourself for today?

Loving Father,
You know my heart. You know
my mudholes. Please help
me deal with any unresolved
guilt in my life today.

Debts

*"If you forgive other people when they sin against you,
your heavenly Father will also forgive you."*
MATTHEW 6:14 NIV

In her book *Amazing Love,* Holocaust survivor Corrie ten Boom recounts staying with a Kansas farm family. Incorrigible seventy-something Corrie loved learning to ride horses, drive tractors, and furrow fields with a horse-drawn plow.

But she noticed a subtle sadness pervaded the home. Corrie learned that a huge blowout several months before between the father and eldest son had severed their relationship. He was forbidden to ever enter the house again.

Corrie was deeply troubled, for she had grown very fond of this American family. So she prayed for God to present an intervention opportunity.

Several days later, Corrie was horseback riding (more plodding than riding, she admits) when the farmer rode up alongside her. It was the answer to her prayer.

"Have you ever prayed, 'forgive us our debts as we forgive our debtors'?" Corrie asked. The farmer nodded. "If you believe in Jesus Christ and belong to Him, your sins were cast into the depths of the sea. But then He expects that you will also forgive the sins of your boy and cast them into the depths of the sea. Just imagine how you would feel if your son had to go into service and was killed in action. Don't you think you should forgive him?"

After a long silence, the farmer said, "I'm going to see my son tonight."

Corrie silently rejoiced when the man laid his hand on his son's shoulder, saying, "My boy, will you forgive me?" His son replied, "But Father, I should ask you for forgiveness."

*Abba Father,
I mean every word of the Lord's
Prayer as I personalize it now:
Forgive me of _____, as I
forgive _____.*

Cooing, Not Pecking

*"Just as the heavens are higher than the earth,
so my ways are higher than your ways and
my thoughts higher than your thoughts."*
ISAIAH 55:9 NLT

My friend Pati is a Christ follower. Her husband, Cliff, although an upright and moral man, is not.

Pati, whose intimate relationship with Jesus began shortly after her marriage to Cliff, yearns for her husband to become part of the family of God through saving faith in Christ and spend eternity with Pati and their son in heaven.

Who among us doesn't want that, right?

So for the past decade Pati has argued, cajoled, pleaded, and bombarded Cliff with evangelical materials to the point of, well. . .nagging.

One evening when Pati was revving up her Jesus sales pitch to Cliff, their five-year-old son Brandon beckoned her to the hallway, out of his father's hearing.

"Mom," Brandon said, looking earnestly up into her eyes. "Do you know what the symbol for the Holy Spirit is?"

Flustered at her inability to reach Cliff, coupled with her son's seemingly off-the-wall question, Pati answered with hand on hip, head-rocking, snarky flair, "No, Brandon, what is it?"

"A dove," Brandon said quietly. "It's a dove, Mom. Not a woodpecker."

Yo. Out of the mouth of babes (although I personally think that child was born thirty and should have been named Solomon. You would not *believe* the profound spiritual truths that come out of his mouth!).

So nowadays, whenever Pati, in her impatience, pushes Cliff too hard, Brandon makes a discreet wood-pecking gesture with his hand—and Pati is reminded that the Lord's perfect timing isn't always ours.

....

....

....

....

....

....

....

....

....

*Most Complete God,
Sometimes I want something so
badly, I push too hard.
Strengthen my anemic trust
that You've got everything—
everything—under control.*

Getting Engaged

My heart bursts its banks.
PSALM 45:1 MSG

Awareness slapped me a wet towel.

For the past decade I've been rising at 5:00 a.m., fixing breakfast, doing my job, tending my chores, walking the dog, waving to Spouse as we go in opposite directions, making sure everyone's fed and clothed.

Executing my duty well.

But I'm floating through my days aloof and disengaged, going through the motions, rarely *feeling*. And you know what? I'm not satisfied with that anymore.

Perhaps it has something to do with cuddling a new grandbaby in my arms. A fresh body and spirit just embarking on the fantastic journey that is life. . .so pure and eager. So into every picture I've passed a thousand times unnoticed. So mesmerized by a tree blowing in the wind. Or the magic of a balloon.

Not yet schooled that the best way to avoid feeling pain is to turn off the spigot.

I pray he doesn't get to age sixty and stare in the mirror one day thinking, *Where did the time go? What did I do with all those lost years*?

You know, the prune is still plum-y beneath the wrinkles. It's when the wrinkles permeate the core that the soul begins to shrivel.

I want to stay a plum. But how?

Got it. . .engage. Yes!

My new goal: to be fully present in mind, spirit, and senses for the rest of this day. Like a baby, I will see, touch, smell, hear, feel, and *enjoy* each activity I undertake. Experiencing old things for the very first time.

Won't you join me?

Nourisher of My Soul,
Fill me with the freshness and
vitality of life. What a gift this
day can be! Help me unwrap it
and enjoy every moment.

Gettin' Jiggly Wid It

"He will renew your life and sustain you in your old age."
RUTH 4:15 NIV

It was a dark day when I arrived at my first senior tennis match. Yes, *senior*. As in over fifty-five.

The two gals my partner and I were playing sure didn't look like seniors. They looked like hard-bodied, uber-energetic thirty-year-olds who'd forgotten their moisturizers that morning. Until you got up close enough to see a few crow's-feet, you'd never know these trim, ponytailed, cellulite-free gals were past the potty-training years.

I became acutely aware of the gray sprigs springing wildly from beneath my headband, my under-eye totes, and the thigh-u-lite that kept jiggling after I stopped running.

Hey, why can't women shed old excess skin like snakes do? Take my reptilian pal, Servius Snake, who drapes himself along the top of our fence. I found a perfectly intact four-foot snake-skin caught in the vines, but Servius wasn't in there. He was three yards down the fence basking in the sunshine. He looked so jubilant; I thought he might burst into song at any moment, "I feel pretty, oh so pretty. . ."

How utterly wonderful for him. Every spring he gets a full body makeover. So why couldn't we women shed our saggy, baggy, crinkly wrapper each spring and start over fresh with unmarred, supple, beautiful new skin, soft as a baby's bottom?

Alas, for some reason, Papa God didn't think this system would bode well for humans. Pity.

So instead we have to figure out ways to contain the jiggles with spandex, squeegee out the facial wrinkles, and invest in vats of skin lard.

Rock of All Ages,
Help me be content in my skin.
No matter how jiggly it is.

Bear Necessities

God made all sorts of wild animals....
And God saw that it was good.
GENESIS 1:25 NLT

What a shocker! I glanced through the front window of our mountain cabin; a large black, furry face peered back at me.

Yikes!

A fully grown black bear was perched on the deck railing, gleaning sunflower seeds from our birdfeeder with his long, protruding, pink tongue. He was so startled when our eyes met, he nearly fell overboard.

He gathered himself, leapt from the railing to a nearby tree, his sharp claws extended and strong muscles rippling beneath his fur coat as he shinnied down to the ground while we humans ran around like crazies snapping photos.

My twenty-eight-year-old daughter heard the commotion from the shower and dashed bare-foot and dripping into the 45-degree twilight, chasing the fleeing bear with her camera, wearing only a towel.

That's when we discovered the birdseed was merely dessert. Dinner had been three full garbage bags awaiting transportation to the dump.

But Joe Black Bear, as we named him, wasn't finished.

The next day Spouse went to make himself a smoothie. The jumbo plastic jar of protein powder he'd left in the carport was missing. A scouting expedition turned up the jar smashed on a log in the woods like a gigantic egg, protein powder scooped up by the pawfuls.

How Joe heisted it remains a mystery. The gallon jar was too big to fit in his mouth, so he must've carried it with his front paws, walking on his hind legs. That surely would've been a sight to behold!

Now we just have to keep our eyes peeled for Joe toting a blender into the blackberry patch.

Creator of Creatures
Great and Small,
You were right. It IS good.

Who's Da Man?

*Therefore humble yourselves under the mighty hand of God,
that He may exalt you at the proper time.*
1 PETER 5:6 NASB

At one point during my thirty-six-year career as a health care professional, I was heavily recruited by a company competing with my then-employer.

"Well, I've certainly made a name for myself," I reveled with a smug smile. "They must have heard about my wonderful personality and superior work skills to keep pursuing me like this."

My ego swelled to zeppelin size.

Then I overheard a conversation that made me realize it was not *me* they were after, but the account I controlled. It actually had nothing to do with my personal qualifications or accomplishments; it had everything to do with gaining access to business of which I happened to be gatekeeper.

My zeppelin turned to lead and sank into the deep blue sea.

Sometimes we all get a little carried away by our accomplishments when we excel at something. And there's certainly nothing wrong with performing a skill so well that it draws praise and accolades. Papa God loves it when we take Ecclesiastes 9:10 seriously: "Whatever your hand finds to do, do it with all your might" (NASB).

The problem arises when we lose sight of *who* provided our gifts and abilities, who is ultimately responsible for the circumstances that produced our acclaim, who should get all the glory.

Take a moment today and think of three things you excel in. . .three accomplishments you're most proud of. Now lift your palms and give glory to the One who made them happen.

> *Breath of Life,*
> *I gratefully acknowledge*
> *that You made me and all*
> *that I am. I happily give*
> *You all praise and honor.*

Another One Bites the Dust

*My imprisonment in the cause of Christ has become
well known throughout the whole praetorian guard.*
PHILIPPIANS 1:13 NASB

Today's verse can be quite puzzling. It's in a letter written by the apostle Paul in AD 61 during his imprisonment in Rome for preaching about Christ. Who, I wondered, was the praetorian guard Paul mentions, and why was it significant that they'd heard Paul's story? (Ironically, *praetorian* is pronounced "pray-torian.")

A little research revealed the praetorian guard was an elite legion of soldiers (separate from the regular Roman army or police) selected to serve the Roman emperor. These were super serious imperial soldiers—no messing around.

Paul must've been considered an important political prisoner, for he was chained to a praetorian guard 24-7. This awkward arrangement left Paul no room for privacy, but at the same time provided a captive audience to continuously hear Paul share the good news that the Savior of the world had come in the personage of Jesus.

When—inevitably—the guard chained to Paul was converted to Christianity, he was transferred to a different position throughout the Roman world (where he shared his newfound faith) and was replaced by a new guard—from Paul's perspective, a believer waiting to happen.

Paul was spreading the Gospel to the world via the captive audience in his prison cell!

Just imagine the praetorian captain signing *more* transfer papers, shaking his head, muttering, "Another one bites the dust."

Got me thinking. . .who is my praetorian guard—the captive audience Papa God has placed in my little world? Are these coworkers, neighbors, and family members who are stuck in my presence continuously hearing the good news about Jesus?

*Worthy Lord,
Help me take sharing
the good news seriously—
one praetorian guard at a time.*

Dry Bones

" 'This is what the sovereign Lord says to these bones:
I will make breath enter you, and you will come to life. . . .
Then you will know that I am the Lord.' "
Ezekiel 37:5–6 niv

Today's Bible story reads like a sci-fi novel. God Almighty plunks the prophet Ezekiel down into a desert valley full of dry bones. "Wha-da-ya think, Zeke?" (my paraphrase). "Can the dead come to life?"

"Beats me." Ezekiel shrugs.

"Just do it!" Yahweh commands like a Nike commercial. "Tell 'em to rise!"

So Ezekiel obeyed God's seemingly absurd instructions and sure enough, amid a mighty clamor, our guy was surrounded by an army of rattling skeletons. They formed the framework of real men but were missing something vital. Like the skeleton pirates Captain Jack Sparrow (Johnny Depp) battled in *Pirates of the Caribbean*—pathetic bones strung together by gristle and shredded pirate garb.

The dead masquerading as the living.

Ezekiel realized these spiritless skeletons before him were worthless. Without the breath of God to infuse them with life, they were powerless, ineffectual. . .completely incapable of accomplishing anything of eternal value.

But God wasn't finished yet. "Come from the four winds, O breath, and breathe on these. . . that they might live" (Ezekiel 37:9 nkjv). And what d'ya know. . .they did!

I sometimes feel like one of those lifeless bags of bones, don't you? The dead masquerading as the living. A pathetic counterfeit of the real thing.

And then I realize what's missing.

Without the breath of God, my own bones will remain dead. Lifeless. Incapable of accomplishing anything of eternal value.

Living God,
On days like today when my
bones feel dead and dry,
breathe into me Your breath of
life. Bring me back to life.

Kindred Spirits

*I have no one else of kindred spirit
who will genuinely be concerned.*
PHILIPPIANS 2:20 NASB

When Marilla and Anne went home, Diana went with them as far as the log bridge. The two little girls walked with their arms around each other. At the brook they parted with many promises to spend the next afternoon together.

"Well, did you find Diana a kindred spirit?" asked Marilla as they went up through the garden of Green Gables.

"Oh, yes," sighed Anne.

When I was young, L. M. Montgomery's *Anne of Green Gables* set the bar high for my expectation of the kindred spirit that I too dreamed of having one day. Then in the sixth grade, Papa God sent Jan, my bosom buddy ever since we got bosoms.

We now live three hours apart but remain very close. There's still something comforting and precious about Jan's familiar face—a steadiness, a dependable feeling of security that's been forged through decades of sharing secrets, goals, successes, and failures. No one knows me, heart-and-soul, like Jan. And the miracle is, she loves me anyway!

Jan was the inspiration for the "best friend" in my novel *The Distant Shore*. Her Punkin taught the main character, Emma-Lee, how to be brave and stand up for her beliefs, just like Jan did for me in real life. And Punkin is an absolute hoot, like Jan. I attribute much of my humorous *her*spective of life to Jan, who always saw things a bit offbeat and was never shy about straying from the beaten path.

So do you have a Diana or Jan in your life? Who is your kindred spirit?

....

....

....

....

> *Light of the World,
> I promise to tell my kindred
> spirit today how much I
> love and appreciate her.*

Besties

And they kissed each other and wept together.
1 SAMUEL 20:41 NASB

Yesterday we began talking about kindred spirits. . .bosom buddies. . .besties. Nowhere in the Bible is this special friendship exemplified better than 1 Samuel chapters 19–23. I encourage you to read this fascinating story.

I picture David and Jonathan doing all kinds of male bonding activities together: rooting for their favorite gladiator at chariot races (ancient version of NASCAR), tossing a wadded-up sheepskin back and forth (the precursor to football), sharpening swords (honing weapons is said to be a timeless testosterone release), and of course hunting and fishing (no doubt a friendly competition to bag the baldest eagle or snookiest snook).

After David was booted by the paranoid and emotionally combustible King Saul (Jonathan's dad), Jon not only became a spy to save his friend's life but dodged his own father's spear hurled with the intent of taking him down because of his loyalty to Dave (20:32–33).

Jon was willing to give his all for his bosom friend, and Dave reciprocated. They weren't ashamed to show emotion to and for each other (see today's verse). Faith was the glue that bonded the two young men: "'The LORD will be between me and you, and between my descendants and your descendants forever'" (20:42).

At their last earthly encounter, when conditions were bleakest, "Jonathan. . .went to David. . .and encouraged him in God" (23:16).

And that's what it's all about with besties, isn't it? Encouraging each other with God, through God, and toward God. No matter what.

Heavenly Father,
I know that if I want to have a
bestie, I need to BE a bestie.
Show me the kindred spirit I can
"encourage in God" today.

Celebrating Wannabes

Prepare your minds for action and exercise self-control.
1 PETER 1:13 NLT

After watching a dolphin arc above blue Daytona Beach waters, my attention was captured by the simple elegance of nine pelicans flying in V formation. They adjusted their ranks to maintain that perfect letter from one end of the skyline to the other.

Enter the wannabe platoon.

Just behind that gloriously regimented squadron flew five additional pelicans trying their durndest to stay in line. Four did pretty well, tipping a wing here, snagging an up-current there to tweak their position and maintain a reasonably tight line.

But then there was Herbie (he reminded me of Rudolph the Red-Nosed Reindeer's misfit elf friend who never quite fit in).

Try as he might, avian Herbie couldn't fit in either. He dipped and weaved when he should have glided, nearly body-slamming the bird beside him. When the others finally gave up on him and boxed him out, Herbie tagged himself onto the end of the line, flapping like a spastic dot at the bottom of an exclamation mark.

I can identify with Herbie, can't you? We all feel like misfits at some point in our lives. Like we're the wobbling dot beneath the exclamation mark of successful people with whom we're trying to fit in.

But you know, being a Herbie isn't all bad.

Wannabe status keeps us striving to improve ourselves, to never stay complacent. To keep practicing our dipping and weaving so we can fly in formation when we want to, and not be ashamed to be the maverick when we don't.

So here's to the Herbies of our world! Are you one of us?

*Lover of Herbies,
Teach me, Lord, that
with due diligence
I'm not just a wannabe. . .
I'm a gonnabe.*

The Dark Side

Seize life! Eat. . .with gusto. . . . Oh yes—
God takes pleasure in your pleasure!
ECCLESIASTES 9:7 MSG

Okay, I'll admit it. I've been seduced by the Dark Side. Dark chocolate, that is. I'm the step beyond chocoholic; I'm a choco-athlete. I exercise just so I can consume more chocolate.

Yes, I suffer from CDD: Chocolate Deficit Disorder. And I'm not the only one. Our Master Designer created many women with a craving for the creamy, luscious stuff. It's the silk thread that connects us at a deeper level. A visceral level.

The way to a girl's heart is through her Ghirardelli, right?

But the Dark Side has a dark side: addiction. We can't stop scarfing. Then we must stoop to subterfuge. I mean really, which of us hasn't stashed Tootsie Rolls among the potted plants? Or hidden M&M's in her ibuprofen bottle? Or buried telltale Snickers wrappers inside balled-up paper towels in the trash can?

Sometimes we get desperate. Like the woman who was arrested for chasing her roommate with scissors and whacking her over the head with a board for stealing her Thin Mints. C'mon, now. Jail over Thin Mints? Nah.

Samoas, maybe. . .

I saw a wonderful definition of feminine might on a plaque: "True strength is breaking a chocolate bar into four pieces barehanded. . .and then eating only one."

Hey, there's an upside to chocolate: What better way to get rid of wrinkles than to fill them out? I call this my Fabulous Anti-Aging Theory (FAAT). Creases disappear and skin appears smooth as a baby's bottom. Plus, the oils in chocolate act as a terrific moisturizer—like the baby's bottom got lubed with butt paste.

Creator of Cacao Beans,
Thank You for taking
pleasure in my pleasure,
small, large, and dark.

Punk Dog

The Lord watches over all who love him.
PSALM 145:20 NIV

My dog had gone punk. Seriously. He looked like he'd taken up electric guitar and joined KISS.

It all started when he wouldn't stop chewing a hole in his back just north of his tail. I tried to find a nontoxic healing medication that would taste so terrible he'd leave the crater alone. Hydrogen peroxide, of course.

I never even considered the other properties of peroxide until my daughter's teenage boyfriend commented, "Sweet! A tie-dyed dog!"

Sure enough, his ebony hair was electrified with orange, red, and blond streaks like a miniature Joan Jett groupie.

It occurred to me, as I continued to lavish love on my pooch just as I did before his hairdo malfunction, that Papa God takes care of us in much the same way. He loves us unconditionally, no matter how our souls are packaged.

One look around my community reveals an immense diversity of earth suits. Few of us resemble the adorable little bundles of joy our Creator sent our parents upon our births. We've managed to pierce, tattoo, spike, enhance, tint, or inflate these bodies that have been entrusted to us.

I guess we're all punk dogs in a way.

Yet Yahweh looks past our crusty exteriors to our soft, sensitive underbellies, where we were created in His image. And He adores us, just the same.

Most Loving Lord,
I find it miraculous and wonder-
ful that You look past my flawed
exterior and embrace my heart.
Even a punk dog like me. I am
humbled. I am awed.

Foul!

"Lord, doesn't it seem unfair to you...?"
LUKE 10:40 NLT

Martha wasn't one for hiding her feelings. Not even to the Son of Almighty God. Nope, she let 'er rip when she thought her sister was stiff-arming the chores (today's verse). She was not only miffed at Mary; she was annoyed with Jesus for not stepping in and fixing it.

She probably had the same snarky attitude when she bluntly pointed out that her dead brother would be mowing grass instead of pushing up daisies if Jesus had actually come when she'd summoned Him (John 11:21).

Then in the next breath, she implored Jesus to fix it: "Yet even now I know that God will do anything you ask" (John 11:22 CEV). In other words, DO SOMETHING! Some nerve, eh?

"Yeesh," we lament, shaking our heads. "What a whiner!"

Well, yes she was. When she perceived that something was unfair, Martha complained, grumbled, and cried foul. Just like you. Just like me.

But she also loved Jesus with all her heart. Just like you. Just like me.

And He appreciated her honesty. Jesus didn't want her to hock up some fake smile. He never expected her to swallow her opinions and mask her feelings. He wanted her to be real. To talk to Him honestly, friend to friend. To withhold or hide nothing from Him, good, bad, or ridiculously childish.

Jesus didn't take offense at Martha's outbursts. Instead, He responded with grace, compassion, and understanding. Then He heaped more love on her than her scrawny arms could hold.

Just like He'll do with you. And with me.

Joy of My World,
Please forgive me when I whine,
cry foul, and demand that You
fix it. I really do love You.

Divine Providence

God is our refuge and strength,
a very present help in trouble.
PSALM 46:1 NKJV

On September 23, 2014, a Boca Raton, Florida, woman named Ruby gave birth to a healthy baby girl. But then something went drastically wrong.

Amniotic fluid entered Ruby's bloodstream and created a vacuum in her heart, stopping circulation. Forty-year-old Ruby was without a pulse for forty-five minutes while medical personnel worked frantically to resuscitate her. But to no avail.

Ruby's vital signs flatlined. Her distraught family was called in to say tearful good-byes to the unconscious new mother. Doctors were preparing to make the death pronouncement when suddenly the heartbeat monitor blipped. And then blipped again.

Ruby's was truly a double miracle, for not only did she survive without a heartbeat for nearly an hour, she suffered no brain damage. She was able to return home, completely healthy, to care for her infant daughter.

A hospital spokesman said that doctors had no explanation for her survival. Ruby did: "Divine providence."

I love that phrase, don't you? Divine providence. In other words, a *miracle*.

As Ruby's story attests, Papa God still performs miracles. They're not just within the pages of your Bible—miracles are within hearts and lives today. I've experienced numerous mini-miracles in my own life (although I'm not sure you can call any miracle "mini"; it's kind of like being only a little pregnant) and a few blockbuster miracles as well.

No doubt you have too. Or you will. Because Papa loves you dearly and He's in the miracle business.

Divine Miracle Maker,
Bring to my attention today all
the miracles that demonstrate
Your love to me. And help me
have enough faith to recognize
them when I see them.

Stuck

Trust the LORD and live right! The land will be yours.
PSALM 37:3 CEV

I pumped my bicycle pedals furiously that stifling summer day in 1992, trying to rid myself of pent-up frustration from eighteen months of trying to sell the tiny starter home we'd lived in for twelve years. It was a buyer's market and nobody was interested in our little house. My growing family was stuck; we couldn't move until it sold.

On impulse, I took an unexplored road and rolled into a secluded cul-de-sac. My vision was drawn to a large, deserted house with an overgrown yard; it seemed to actually glow in the shimmering heat. I couldn't tear my eyes away.

Then a still, small voice whispered, "Your wait is over. This is your new home."

I raced home and gushed the story to Chuck. We learned that the house had been up for sale for eighteen months. (The irony that it'd been listed the same time as our house didn't escape us!) The owners were anxious to sell. We set up a showing and loved, loved, loved everything about the house. . .except the price.

It exceeded our budget by thirty thousand dollars. Please. Nooooo. . .

Tears flooded my eyes as we rose to leave. This dream could never come true.

Chuck saw my intense disappointment and turned to the owner. In desperation, he explained that we'd asked God for a house and He'd led us to this one. We wished we had more money to offer, but this was all we could afford to pay. Would they please reconsider?

Continued tomorrow. . .

He Who Knows the Future,
Thank You for planning
all the details of my life.
Help me learn to leave them
in Your capable hands.

Delighted

*Delight yourself in the LORD; and He will give you
the desires of your heart. Commit your way to the LORD,
trust also in Him, and He will do it.*
PSALM 37:4–5 NASB

(Continued)

I held my breath and prayed like mad as the owner of our dream home considered Chuck's words. We had no idea if this woman even believed in a deity who led anyone anywhere, but there it was. Take us as crazies or not.

"Well," she finally said, "I guess if God wants you to have this house, I won't stand in the way."

Stepping out in faith, we put a contract on the house with a contingency that ours sold within twelve weeks. Otherwise the deal would fall through. But no buyers appeared, even after we'd reduced the price twice. By the eleventh week, it looked hopeless.

Then I came across today's verse: a personal message just for me. I felt peace wash over me and was able to relax for the first time in months. We'd committed ourselves into Papa's hands, no matter what.

The next day, the doorbell rang. There stood a couple who'd looked at our house a year before then decided to build instead. But one thing after another went wrong and here they were, back to reconsider.

My entire family (parents, kids, dogs, cats, hamsters, and all) huddled nervously in the corner while they toured the house. We knew *everything* hinged on their decision.

At last they reappeared and—WHOA!—made an offer. We signed the contract that day and closed on my birthday.

And what a delightful birthday gift from Papa it was!

*Completely Good Father,
I DO delight in You. Thank You
for surprise presents.*

Just Gotta BARF

*"GOD will fight the battle for you.
And you? You keep your mouths shut!"*
EXODUS 14:14 MSG

I got up early and drove nearly an hour to a league doubles tennis match that was scheduled for 9:00 a.m. The location was posted repeatedly, even as recently as eight that morning when our captain texted us to say we were still on, rain threat or not.

At starting time, my opponents and I were there, but no sign of my partner (a gal I was teamed with just for that day). The three of us started warming up, expecting her to appear at any minute.

At 9:25, she drove up. I was livid. League rules state that you forfeit the match after twenty minutes if both players aren't there.

She laughed and said flippantly, "Oh, sorry. I went to the wrong court and took a nap in my car. By the time I realized my mistake, it was too late. Oh well. At least I have time to eat breakfast now."

My blood boiled. Okay, Deb. Deep breath. Time to BARF.

B: Back off. Withdraw to gain new perspective. I hit the water fountain.
A: Admit. Bullet prayers to tell Papa how irate I am at this gal's selfishness.
R: Redirect. Turn my anger toward Satan, my real enemy in losing my temper.
F: Forgive. The hardest part. Forgive my offender AND myself.

My blood pressure finally returned to normal. My earrings didn't melt. Through BARFing, I was able to see my offender through Papa God's eyes and realize that she, just like me, screws up sometimes. But we're both still loved. (More about BARFing in *Fear, Faith, and a Fistful of Chocolate.*)

*Calmer of Storms,
Teach me that when
I'm angry enough to BARF,
I should just do it.*

Read the Signs

*Seek his will in all you do, and he
will show you which path to take.*
PROVERBS 3:6 NLT

My stove jammed yesterday. I took it as a sign from God.

Actually, an overturned pot in the metal drawer beneath the oven blocked it from opening and provided my moment of enlightenment: Aha! Papa God *wants* us to eat out tonight!

Aren't we always looking for signs of one kind or another from the Lord? Don't we beg for guidance with hairy decisions on a daily basis? Wouldn't we LOVE to have a giant hand jot personal instructions for us in the sky?

But would we recognize Papa God's handwriting if He did?

Like that scene in *Bruce Almighty* when Jim Carey's character was driving down the highway asking God to send him a sign. There, right smack-dab in front of him, lumbered a truck loaded down with street signs practically screaming messages in his face, CAUTION, TURN AROUND, WRONG WAY.

But he wasn't familiar with the Almighty's handwriting; he ignored the signs. BLAM!

There are many messages screaming in our face in this world, but they're not all divine penmanship. We must develop wisdom in discerning which signs are truly from the Holy Spirit as He supernaturally guides us.

And guide us He does when we actively seek His will—that means praying, sifting messages through the colander of God's Word, and consulting godly counsel. Then we can recognize legitimate signs directing us to His chosen path for us.

So I'm hoping my oven stays jammed just a few more restaurant dinners' worth. I prefer to think it's a sign from God.

*Gracious Father,
Teach me to read the signs by
seeing Your handwriting so
often I recognize it immediately.*

Never Underestimate Prayer

*But each day the LORD pours his unfailing love
upon me, and through each night I sing
his songs, praying to God who gives me life.*
PSALM 42:8 NLT

I passed my author friend Krystal in the hotel lobby the morning after the writer's conference. She was on her hands and knees dissecting her luggage.

"What's up, Krystal?" I asked, pausing en route to catch my waiting taxi. "Is something wrong?"

"I'm going batty trying to find my Kindle," Krystal admitted. "It's got to be here somewhere. I just can't live without that thing."

Unable to loiter and commiserate any longer, I told her I'd be sure to lift her situation up in prayer and proceeded to do so as my driver sped me away to the airport.

The following day, I emailed Krystal and asked if her Kindle quest had been successful.

"I searched both suitcases four different times before the shuttle arrived," she replied. "Couldn't find it. En route to the airport, I explained my dilemma to the two other ladies sharing the shuttle. I didn't even know them. Without a moment's hesitation, they launched a heartfelt prayer for the Lord to bring the prodigal Kindle back home. The driver thought we were nuts, having a prayer meeting in the backseat.

"While I was in line at the ticket counter, I unzipped the same compartment in my carry-on bag I'd already searched over and over. I'll be dipped if the Kindle didn't pop right up like a jack-in-the-box."

Her conclusion? "Never underestimate the power of prayer."

To that I say *Amen* and I'll be dipped.

*God Who Hears Me,
Help me make prayer a lifestyle,
not an isolated event.*

Genuinity

If you humble yourself, you will be honored.
MATTHEW 23:12 CEV

I'd become smitten with her delightful little novel decades ago. I'd never read anything quite like it. . . . My heart was moved. Uplifted. Inspired.

As I traversed my own writer's journey, I tried to contact her but met only dead ends. At last I uncovered an active e-dress and she responded. I was starstruck. I couldn't believe it was actually her!

As we corresponded and I learned more about her life and teachings, it dawned on me. Gradually. Painfully. She wasn't who I'd thought. I was so disappointed. My hero wasn't at all the person I'd imagined.

Sometimes people aren't what we'd hoped for. Or worse, not the person we thought we knew. I guess that's why genuinity (not a real word but should be) is so important to me. Above all, I want to be real—to demonstrate how a sincere follower of Christ can fall flat on her face but get up again and know she is just as beloved by her Papa despite her drastic mistakes in judgment.

No pretenses. No arrogance. No faux perfection.

I think Papa God looks *through* instead of *at* our mistakes with little round Benjamin Franklin lenses made entirely of love. The same kind I wear when my preschool grandbuddy does something intentionally defiant but I love him to pieces anyway.

It makes my day when someone says, "Deb, you write like you live." Transparency is good. Authenticity is good. Especially in fallible people, like Christians. Because realness is relatable and restores hope.

And for cryin' out loud, don't we all need more of that?

Lord without Beginning or End,
No one is more real than You.
Help me reflect Your genuinity
in a world of falsity today.

Closed Doors

In all your ways acknowledge Him,
and He will make your paths straight.
PROVERBS 3:6 NASB

When our granddog Rocky was a pup, he was a soul in need of guidance. He indiscriminatingly ingested trash, bugs, and flowers, regardless of toxicity level. Chewing, maiming, and destroying made him happy.

So in order to guide Rocky's behavior along the path of righteousness, doors had to close. The door to the bathroom, where he loved to redecorate the fluffy bathmat; the bedroom, where he routinely dismantled shoes; the living room door leading to the Berber carpet he enjoyed unraveling to the nub.

The only opened doors invited him to destinations previously prepared for his well-being. His course was set by a higher authority who knew what was best for him.

During the forty years I've been a believer, I've constantly prayed for Papa God's guidance. Looking back, I can see His divine hand setting parameters and closing doors. Many of those "no" answers were received with gnashed teeth, as if something unintentional slipped by while God took a potty break.

But Rocky has shown me that closed doors are an integral part of the guidance for which I've prayed.

Just as closed doors and physical restraints guide Rocky, allowing him freedom within borders established for his good, blocked pathways in my life keep me centered on the road Jehovah chose for me. Closed doors aren't a bad thing. They're a *good* thing.

Not accidents or oversights. They're part of the plan. Even when I whine and scratch and howl because I really wanted what was on the other side of that slab of wood.

Maker of Doors,
Keep right on guiding me,
even by closed doors.
I trust that when You close a
door, You'll open a window.

Frenzy

Be wise in the way you act toward outsiders. . . .
Let your conversation be always full of grace.
COLOSSIANS 4:5–6 NIV

We've all seen them. Some of us have been them: overzealous parents who scream, spit, and spew, caught up in the delirious frenzy of our children's sports competitions.

As believers, our greatest desire is to see our kids include their faith in every area of their lives. So how can we exemplify honoring Christ during sporting events?

- **Extend grace.** Show gracious appreciation to volunteers who clean fields, sell hot dogs, collect tickets, and sacrifice hours coaching.
- **Golden Rule it.** Coaches are human and will sometimes make mistakes. We should handle these mistakes with the same courtesy with which we wish to be treated when we blow it. Express your concerns privately to the coach as calmly and objectively as possible. If compromise or corrective action can't be reached, then consider approaching a coach's supervisor, being careful not to air grievances to children or other parents.
- **Think and speak positively**. Negative words develop into negative attitudes. If we approach games positively and avoid criticizing or making negative comments from the sidelines, our children (and we) will enjoy the game more.
- **Cage Godzilla.** When passion is involved, self-control can be a monster. It helps to make a plan *before* tensions rise and tempers flare in the heat of competition. Agree with your spouse or companion ahead of time on cues to keep you in check during a game. Take strategic trips to the concession stand or bathroom to decom-stress; strike up a pleasant chat; hum "This Little Light of Mine". . .whatever helps you muzzle the beast.

Light of the World,
Remind me that everywhere
I go I'm representing You.
Everywhere.

Roots

"Blessed are those who trust in the Lord.... They are like trees planted along a riverbank, with roots that reach deep."
JEREMIAH 17:7–8 NLT

For years it had been my chill-out chapel. My sanity sanctuary. And now it was gone.

I stared in dismay at the gaping hole in my backyard where the pre-hurricane stalwart oak had once stood, supporting one end of the hammock where I had literally hung out with Papa God when I needed a break from the world's stress.

"Hey, I'll fix it," Chuck volunteered. "I'll have that hammock back up in no time!" And he was off to purchase a fence post to replace the oak.

Three days later, the hammock appeared to be its old sturdy self. But on the trial run, as Chuck slowly lowered himself into the cotton webbing, dirt around the newly cemented post gave way, and it tilted bit by bit until Chuck was sitting on the ground.

One word sprang to mind: *roots*. That's what's missing here. Deep, far-reaching roots that create a stable foundation, a solid anchor. Dead posts don't have 'em.

The spiritual analogy slammed me. Am I a tree with roots that anchor and continuously strengthen me? Or am I a wooden post—a lifeless stick that appears stable but yields with the first application of pressure?

The cement of service—a smoke screen of busy activity in heaven's name—provides a false sense of security. Everything appears okay, but without roots, my faith eventually caves and I find myself sitting on the premises instead of standing on the promises.

Not where I want to be.

....

....

....

....

....

....

....

....

> *Root-Producing God,*
> *I don't want to be a lifeless post.*
> *Make me a living, thriving tree,*
> *watered, fertilized, and yes,*
> *pruned by Your loving hands.*

Bridges

*God. . .reconciled us to himself through Christ
and gave us the ministry of reconciliation.*
2 CORINTHIANS 5:18 NIV

I glared at the back of her head across the room. Karen had been my coworker for ten years. Then I was deeply wounded by something Karen did and felt justified cutting off all communication with her when I left for a new job.

And here we were at the same conference. *Awkward.* We sat on opposite sides of the room and averted our eyes when passing in the hallway.

I knew something had to give.

That night in my hotel bed, I argued with the Almighty about the injustice of the situation. I was the one who'd been wronged! Why did I have to chew my pride like tough gristle and be the one to gather hammer and nails to build a bridge?

"Because you're becoming more like Me. . .a carpenter," Jesus softly spoke to my heart.

The next day I looked for a chance to speak privately to Karen. Nada. "I tried," I told Papa. "If You want this to happen, You're gonna have to intervene."

I snuck out early to beat the checkout rush. As I left the building, guess who was standing just outside the door—all alone—checking her phone messages?

Reconciliation: resolve differences and restore harmony. It's not just a request. Or a suggestion. Or simply a nice thing to do. According to today's verse, it's our ministry as believers . . .our spiritual job.

And the Carpenter will equip us with the tools we need to complete any job He assigns us. Like building bridges.

*Master Builder,
Thanks for providing me with
a designer spiritual toolbox.
Now point me to the bridge I
need to start building today.*

Frozen

"As I have loved you,
so you must love one another."
JOHN 13:34 NIV

I scanned the faces of my audience, a denomination rumored to be the "frozen chosen." Yup. *Frozen.*

Being a humorist, I try to draw a smile from my audience. Maybe even a chuckle. Occasionally a profound belly laugh.

But nothing was happening here. A profusion of nothing. One lady in the back almost showed her teeth. Once. Or maybe that was a hot flash.

I had to remind myself that I couldn't *really* know what they were feeling, although their collective body language screamed "catatonic." They did seem to be warming up as I kept hacking away at their granite faces, and by the end, I believe I saw two partial plates and a gold filling.

To my amazement, as the solemn folks filed out, nearly all of them bought books and said something like, "Wonderful! I haven't laughed that hard in a long time."

Go figure.

Life's like that, isn't it? We never *really* know the effect we're having on other people. . .how much of us is rubbing off. They don't necessarily show it, but they're internalizing bits and pieces of us all the time. Just like we are of them. Little pieces that fit together like a puzzle to make us who we end up being.

And maybe one day, we'll take the opportunity to tell them how much a part of us they really are. How much they've meant to us. Because they surely won't know it from our frozen faces.

And then we can slap each other on the back and say, "Wonderful! I haven't loved that hard in a long time."

Lord of Love,
Defrost me. Move me to
tell those I love how much
they mean to me today.

Girls Will Be Girls

*"In this world you will have trouble.
But take heart! I have overcome the world."*
JOHN 16:33 NIV

Spouse and I were exhausted as we stood in the long security queue at the Venice, Italy, airport. A snaking line of luggage rested at the feet of weary travelers as far as the eye could see.

Along came a beagle-bloodhound mix, dragging a uniformed security guard. She sniffed her way along the procession, inspecting each bag for illegal substances.

My suitcase quickly passed scrutiny, but she suddenly halted before my mega-mama purse. Sniffing the exterior, Miss B (for beagle-bloodhound) became visibly excited. I was mortified. Everyone in the vicinity eyed me with alarm.

Miss B's snout completely disappeared into the depths of my purse. Her handler moved his hand toward his large handgun and commanded me in broken English to empty the contents of my purse onto the ground.

Gulp. I started sweating. Do they still have firing squads in Italy?

The silent crowd parted like the Red Sea.

I wrestled my purse away from Miss B and dumped out the embarrassing contents for all to enjoy. . .a baggie of chocolate wafers, half a ham sandwich, eighteen M&M's, two brownies, a half-eaten Snickers.

People tittered. Miss B quivered. The security guard nailed me with a glare that could melt steel. Then he rolled his eyes.

Humph. One minute I'm an international crime suspect and the next I'm insulted with an eye roll? Please!

He soundly rebuked poor Miss B, but hey, who could NOT get tail-wagging excited about chocolate? A girl's a girl in any species.

*Calmer of Nerves,
Give me Your supernatural
peace in times of trouble.*

Bad Habits

Don't worry about anything;
instead, pray about everything.
PHILIPPIANS 4:6 NLT

Have you ever been secretly scared that if you stop worrying, the very thing you're afraid might happen actually will?

That somehow the energy generated from your fretting is the force field keeping the dreaded outcome at bay, and if you lower the force field for even one minute. . .*BLAM.* The end of the world as you know it.

Yep, worry makes the average woman's world go round. We've watched our mothers, grandmothers, aunts, and sisters worry themselves into a tizzy, and we've learned to do the same thing.

Did you catch that? *Learned.* Worrying is a learned habit. And if it's been learned, it can be unlearned (more about that tomorrow).

Fretting and stewing and fussing seem perfectly normal because we're so used to it. We've fooled ourselves into thinking we're doing the responsible thing by agonizing over our dilemmas.

Worry is a type of fear that loves to masquerade as responsibility. By dwelling on our troubles, we think we'll somehow become enlightened with magical answers that will change inevitable outcomes.

Is there any other way to intimately care about family and friends besides obsessing over their problems? Actually, there is. It's found in today's verse.

Liberator of Worry,
Today, help me worry less and
pray more. Show me the differ-
ence in my stress level when I
turn my worries over to You.

Dissolving Worrywarts

Tell God what you need,
and thank him for all he has done.
PHILIPPIANS 4:6 NLT

Yesterday we talked about learning a bad habit: worry. Today I'd like to share some suggestions for unlearning this bad habit:

- **Morph worry into prayer**. Fretting is not productive. Prayer is. Prayer is the nerve that innervates the hand of God. Turn each problem into a prayer request and give it to the One who can actually do something about it.
- **Become a busybody**. When you begin to worry, redirect your thoughts by giving your body something to do. Action defuses anxiety. Get your hands busy; your mind will follow.
- **Go to your happy place.** Another gem for redirection, especially late at night when your whirling mind won't relax. Imagine you're in that special place that brings you calmness and happiness. . .maybe the warm surf of a fave beach or a beloved mountain trail. Ahh, feel the anxiety melt away.
- **Rest in the Word.** Another great worry buster for restless nights when you're more uptight than a twisted thong. Reflecting on a favorite scripture brings peace to your soul. Say it aloud and then let it roll through your mind over and over until you can think of nothing else.

You know, worry is the result of putting our faith in the wrong place—in ourselves instead of Papa God. We try to figure it all out, maintain control, and provide our own protection.

But that's not our job. Our loving Lord really will take care of us if we just let go of our worries and trust Him.

Faithful Father,
Help me remember that things
may not always turn out the
way I want, but they'll always
turn out the way You want.

Gates

Happiness makes you smile.
PROVERBS 15:13 CEV

Driving through an unfamiliar subdivision, I noticed an odd thing: a gate. Not a fence and a gate. Not a barn gate or a corral gate. Just a gate. It didn't lead to a path of any sort, nor was it the entrance to anything observable. It just stood solitarily in the middle of someone's yard. Calling my name.

As I slowed to take a better look, I could hardly contain myself. I just *had* to walk through that gate.

Of course the idea was silly. Why would I trespass in a stranger's yard to walk through a gate to nowhere? The sensible adult in me took over and I hurried away to my next appointment.

But I thought about that gate all day. Why on earth had I yearned to jump out of my car, race across the lawn, swing open and step through that gate? My heartbeat quickened just picturing it.

Suddenly I knew: it was the mystery, the fun, the adventure the gate represented.

Gateways to other worlds like Narnia, Oz, and Wonderland were thresholds for our childhood imaginations. Portals to visit magical places that refreshed our spirits and renewed our zeal for living.

Places we seldom have time to visit with the responsibilities of adult life.

I think we grown-ups need gates too. Our spirits yearn to be set free in glorious freedom and imaginative frolic just like children. But we're shackled by reality.

So maybe I'll rig up my own gate. . .in my mind. It'll look just like the gate Dorothy stepped through into the Emerald City. I'm already clicking my heels just thinking about it.

Creator of Imaginations,
Send me a gate to a
whimsical world today. And
remind me to come back.

Nekked

Make sure that your character is
free from the love of money.
HEBREWS 13:5 NASB

Ready for an eye-opener? Turn to Luke 19:1–10 and let's discuss Zacchaeus, whose life lesson from Jesus could be my own. And maybe yours too.

- Zacchaeus is a greedy tax collector for the Romans (who forcibly occupy Israel); he likely overcollects money from his own Jewish people and pockets the extra.
- He's therefore despised and friendless. Right. Just how you and I sometimes feel.
- Zach's a shorty (I can identify!), and since nobody will allow him through the crowd to see Jesus passing by (elbows up the ole snoz), he swallows his pride and climbs a tree (verse 4).
- To everyone's shock, the rock star chooses the despicable money-grubber as His lunch companion (verse 5). Zach nearly wets himself but shinnies down to accept the honor. He has no clue Jesus wants to be Lord of his life. . .and his *stuff*.
- It doesn't take long in the presence of Jesus for Zacchaeus to become convicted of his wrongdoings. Standing nekked before pure holiness tends to make us ashamed of our self-inflicted ugliness. (Nekked is quite different than naked; the Almighty created us naked with dignity and beauty; our own disrespect makes us nekked.)
- Zacchaeus not only repents but voluntarily offers to repay all he's stolen and more (verse 8). Jesus makes little people BIG.
- Zach isn't saved because of his changed actions but because of his changed heart (verse 10). A life change that affects the pocketbook is *real*.

I reread this story every time I begin to feel that my stuff owns me. Doesn't it give you a fresh *her*spective too?

Lord of My Nekked Wallet,
My stuff's all Yours. Take it.
Use it to Your glory.

Dents in My Fender

Don't hit back; discover beauty in everyone.
ROMANS 12:17 MSG

Harry is one of those difficult people you try to avoid but inevitably end up colliding with. I call them dents in my fender.

Harry invited Spouse and me to his milestone sixtieth birthday dinner. Despite reservations, we accepted, secretly fearing we might be the only ones there. You see, Harry's a bona fide genius who's socially nonfunctional. He's brilliant but clueless. People avoid him.

Blunt and *tactless* don't begin to describe Harry. He has offended us repeatedly with his dogmatic leftist opinions and droning insistence of the worthless banality of Christianity. Yet he considers us friends. Go figure.

So the DAY BEFORE his party, Harry emailed, "Deb, would you make my birthday cake?"

Seriously? Like I've nothing else to do? [Cue prayers for supernatural grace.]

"Okay, Harry. Which flavor—vanilla, chocolate, or strawberry?"

"Can't you make a hummingbird cake?"

"No, Harry," I typed. "I've never made a hummingbird cake. I have no recipe for a hummingbird cake. Besides, my shotgun isn't working and I'd have to use my bow and arrow. Those critters are so tiny it'll take ten to fill a measuring cup. See the choices above: pick one."

His reply was a link to a hummingbird cake recipe.

"Give me patience, Lord," I prayed. I knew that hasty words spoken in anger would make the best retort I would ever regret.

Once we embrace the magnitude of Papa God's divine grace, we can extend grace to others …despite the dings, dangs, and dongs they imbed in our fenders.

....

....

....

....

....

....

....

....

God of Graciousness,
Keep reminding me that in light
of eternity, people feeling
loved is much more important
than my bumpy fender.

Mountaintop Cathedral

Let everything that has breath praise the Lord.
PSALM 150:6 NASB

I was hanging out in our mountain cabin one spring morning, long before anyone else had risen. The sun had just slivered through the misty tree boughs and I'd cranked open the windows to breathe in the crisp morning air.

I love to play mountain music up there. You know the type of music I mean...dulcimer, banjo, mandolin, string bass—fast paced and free. Good ole foot stompin' stuff.

So I plugged in a CD, *Hymns of the Smokies*. I was puttin' my worship on, honey, singing and getting my bad self down on the dance floor, er, I mean living room rug.

And then the choir arrived.

As soon as the first notes of "Shall We Gather at the River" rang out, birds of all kinds started gathering at the window by the CD player. They perched on branches, even on the windowsill itself, singing along with that worship music at the top of their little birdie lungs.

They sang. I sang. We praised Papa God together. It was *awesome*.

I have no idea why they were attracted to that particular song, but when it ended, they took off for whatever it is mountain birds do in the mornings (besides church).

It tingles the toes of my soul to imagine that Papa's creatures might actually do just that ...church. In their own way, in their own language, in their own venues, far away from human eyes and ears.

And for my praise to have momentarily intersected with theirs is one of the greatest thrills of my life.

I just hope bear church is on another mountain.

Most Exalted One,
Today I join with all of
creation in praising You.

Heart and Soul

*The wife must see to it that
she respects her husband.*
EPHESIANS 5:33 NASB

Today's verse is excellent advice for women desiring to honor the biblical union of marriage. Studies show that the number one need of men is respect. What a marvelous difference it made in my marriage when I asked myself this key question: What does it look like to *respect* my man?

- **Pay attention to him.** That means listening with your eyes; stop what you're doing and look at him when he's talking. Ask questions. Look interested.
- **Esteem him.** Oughta be easy since you're always steamed about something he does, right? Actually, esteemed means "highly regarded." What makes him feel esteemed by you? Do it more often.
- **Brag him up to others.** Public praise lets him know you notice and are proud of his positive qualities. As a bonus, he'll likely do a repeat performance!
- **Pray together.** Chuck and I join hands and pray together every night in bed before we fall asleep. Trust me, this is an UNBEATABLE heart and soul melder.
- **Touch him.** And I don't mean in a sexual way (although you never know where it might lead). Show playfulness, intimacy, and affection by spontaneously touching him—brush hair from his forehead; pat his shoulder; give him a noogie. Okay, no noogie, but make some kind of physical contact. And do it often.
- **Go the extra mile.** Let him know you're thinking of him when you're not together. Notes are nice. Chuck and I hide plastic hearts in each other's belongings as a fun little surprise. Nothing says "I love you" like a crunch in your loafer.

*Creator of My Man,
Show me how to make him
feel my love and respect.*

Invasion

The Spirit who lives in you is greater
than the spirit who lives in the world.
1 JOHN 4:4 NLT

Oh. My. Stars. What a revelation!

I'd just posted a Facebook story about my adorable new hat when a comment from a child-hood chum suddenly transported me back to a memory I'd apparently blocked.

I was a dorky, sixth-grade, tousle-headed tomboy who never looked in a mirror except to brush my teeth. This particular day, I was slipping into my mother's classroom (she taught health at my school) to put something on her desk. The students' backs were toward me; I was tiptoeing and holding my breath, trying not to divert attention while Mama was up front teaching.

Suddenly, Mama stopped her hygiene lecture and proclaimed, "Class, if you want to see an example of poor grooming habits, turn around."

Thirty heads pivoted toward me in unison. I was mortified. Deer in headlights. Ducking my unkempt head, I dashed out the door just as the first wave of giggles rolled across the room.

Forty years later, I still flushed when reliving that horrible moment.

But then, I got it. My epiphany: *That's* why, all these years later, I wear so many hats; my past has invaded my present and I never realized it.

How about you? Maybe the secret fear lurking in the shadows of your mind isn't humiliation, but I'll bet some aspect of your current behavior—even something benign like wearing hats—is due to past events. Think about it.

The good news is that Papa God is bigger than all our fears. Even secret ones.

....

....

....

....

....

Mysterious Yahweh,
I know that my future includes
my past; I choose to hold
Your hand in the present.

....

....

....

....

Double Dipping

He awakens Me morning by morning,
He awakens My ear to listen as a disciple.
ISAIAH 50:4 NASB

I awoke from a nightmare at 4:00 a.m., my heart racing. An ominous cloud of fear enveloped my spirit. I needed a change of scenery.

So I slugged out of bed, hooked the leash to the dog as he leaned against the wall in a sleepy stupor, and pulled him outside for a walk.

My neighborhood was deafeningly quiet. Even the birds weren't up. Some might think the stillness eerie but I found it sublimely serene. The kind of profound serenity you can't find the rest of the day.

As I dragged the catatonic dog through the soundless, motionless peace, I happened to look up. There, in the sky's inky blackness, was the Big Dipper tilted on its side pouring out its contents. My eyes followed the invisible flow downward.

To my house.

Amazing! From that angle, you could draw a straight line directly to my roof.

Hmm. I think Papa God is trying to tell me something. But what?

An old hymn began flowing through my head: "Count your many blessings, name them one by one; and it will surprise you what the Lord has done."

Suddenly I knew.

Whether I'm aware or not, Papa God is constantly pouring blessings on my home. Lots of them: Spouse and I are well; we have work. We have shelter, love, enough to eat, three beautiful grandbuddies next door.

And just like that, my cloud of fear lifted. I sang that song worm all day, but it's really a caterpillar that eventually morphed into a butterfly of joy.

I am indeed blessed. So are you. Double dippered blessed.

Most Worthy of Praise,
I promise to count my
blessings today.

Dancing with My Star

*Wives, submit yourselves to your own
husbands as you do to the Lord.*
EPHESIANS 5:22 NIV

I've always had a problem with that *s* word in today's verse. I lean heavily toward Ruth Bell Graham's way of thinking: "There's a time to submit, and there's a time to outwit."

With nearly forty years of marital blitz (I mean bliss) under my belt, I'm still learning what submission really means.

The biblical progression of marital submission is that the woman submits to the man, and the man submits to God. Only in that context (the husband is a believer, choosing to submit to God) will the process be fruitful.

Men don't get off the hook. Everyone is called to yield to another authority, to answer to someone. The process of yielding involves willingly following, intentionally allowing another to take the lead.

It's like ballroom dancing. Marriage consists of two roles: the leader and the follower. The two move in unison to achieve their mutual goal: a beautiful harmony of expression. Otherwise, they are out of sync, stepping on each other, inflicting wounds and creating resentment.

Submitting doesn't mean that we're weak or any less capable than our husbands. It simply means we choose to let him lead the dance. It actually works to our advantage—we can relax and enjoy the moment, not worrying about the next step.

Of course Spouse will blow it at times. And we'll get ballistically frustrated. But Papa God set up the family structure for a reason.

Women may be smarter in some ways and quicker about fixing problems, but submitting to our partner, in love, is the best way to keep on dancing.

*Lord of the Dance,
Help me remember that You
are infinitely bigger than
my husband. Make Your will
happen through the channels of
authority You've designed.*

Call Me Pete

"You are Peter, and on this
rock I will build my church."
MATTHEW 16:18 NIV

I sometimes think my name should have been Peter.

Within Jesus' inner circle, Peter was the impulsive one. The leap-before-you-look dude. The first to jump into action. . .stepping out of a boat in the middle of a storm-tossed sea and *walking* across the water to reach his master's side; snatching a sword to cut off the ear of a soldier in the garden of Gethsemane; promising *never* to forsake Jesus, only to vehemently swear hours later that he never knew Him.

I so get Peter. I understand his zeal-driven rashness and recklessness, his willingness to plunge into foolhardiness if that's what it takes. I relate to his impatience, his inner drive to do something NOW. The way he jumped to conclusions and acted presumptuously, setting his twitching muscles in gear before his brain—just like me!

But on the flipside, I also understand Peter's deep regret, the darkness in his soul when he realized he'd once again done something incredibly stupid. I empathize with his earnest desire to please Jesus, whom he loved with all his heart and yearned to show it by his actions but just couldn't seem to get it right.

Yet, despite all his faults, Jesus loved and believed in Peter so much that He proclaimed Peter as the rock foundation of His worldwide church. Jesus used Peter for great and mighty purposes—impatience, foolishness, failures, and all.

Does that sound like anyone you know?

Rock of Ages,
You changed the world with
a brash, reckless, impulsive
person; won't You please, please
use another? My hand's up.

Togetherness

*Listen to your father. . .and do not
despise your mother when she is old.*
PROVERBS 23:22 NIV

My parents, avid RV enthusiasts, recently decided that we needed to enjoy a "family" vacation. This meant they—both in their eighties—and my sister and I—fifty-something—would cram together in a small camper out in the wilderness of north Florida for four days.

Fun, right?

We'd no sooner arrived at our rustic campsite a stone's throw from the Atlantic than a cold front blew in with temperatures nipping the midthirties. Hey, this was Florida, people. I had packed only shorts and flip-flops, anticipating our usual mild Easter weather. But this was the year of the freak Easter nor'easter.

Frigid winds blasted our tiny tin box, and I layered every scrap of clothing in my suitcase as my uniform for the entire trip. I looked like a plump s'more.

Who knew three people could snore loudly enough to rock a camper? Their hangy-balls had to be vibrating at seven on the Richter scale. My earplugs made no dent whatsoever. Hour after sleepless hour, I stared at the bleak lid of our sardine can.

The RV was snug for two, but four pushed the limits to whatever is beyond smooshed. With the couch-bed pulled out for my sister and me, there was no room to turn around, much less sit, so Daddy and I—both early risers—braved the blizzard winds on the beach until we could bear it no longer. Then we returned to defrost and try not to awaken the grouchy bears hibernating in the tin den.

Hang tight, the best is yet to come. . . . I'll finish tomorrow.

*Papa God,
Thanks for families who laugh
together. Without them, life
could really be a drudge.*

The Wood Ain't My 'Hood

Love wisdom like a sister.
PROVERBS 7:4 NLT

(Continued)

My sister, Cindy, had somehow avoided the camping experience her entire life, so she was nervous the evening of our first campfire. She found the dense woods surrounding the circle of firelight frightening.

"Wh–what's out there?" Cindy asked, wide-eyed.

"Don't worry," I replied. "The beasties are more afraid of you than you are of them." She scalded me with a sister look that silently accused, "Why should I believe the girl who washed my hair with mayonnaise and then laughed hysterically when I smelled like salad dressing for the prom?"

At that moment, the pounding of paws announced the arrival of a large raccoon plowing full speed into our campsite. Must have been mating season; she was closely followed by a jumbo specimen with a telltale gleam in his eye. Naturally the mini-stampede headed straight for Cindy.

My sedentary sister was suddenly atop the picnic table screeching like a banshee, performing some sort of ritualistic high-stepping dance.

The coons were as shocked as the rest of us and stood upright, their little hand-paws dangling in midair as they gaped at the furless pink creature's strange performance.

Daddy was the first to gather his wits and attempt to shoo the guests away. They seemed reluctant to leave, turning around several times to make sure the show was really over.

When assured that it was—due to the imminent mental breakdown of the diva—they returned to the wild, where life, no doubt, was comparatively peaceful.

Maybe before our next camping trip, I'll spot Sis a tutu and tap-dancing lessons.

*Abba Father,
I'm grateful for the sisters
You've blessed me with,
both blood sisters and
heart sisters.*

Sweet Message

Jesus said, "Let the children come to me. . . .
For the Kingdom of Heaven belongs to
those who are like these children."
MATTHEW 19:14 NLT

How about some chocolaty inspiration this Easter season?

Helen Cadbury was born in 1877 into a wealthy Christian family. Her grandfather had founded Cadbury Chocolates in Birmingham, England, and Helen's family of nine resided in Moseley Hall, an ancient estate with secret rooms and underground passages, lakes, and wooded acres.

Picture a slightly smaller version of Downton Abbey, with a lot less drama.

The entire household met before breakfast for daily Bible reading and prayer.

At twelve, Helen attended a ghetto street revival with her father. There, Helen went forward at the altar call, a well-dressed rich girl among the poor, to accept Christ as her Savior.

Helen had a new purpose in life: to share the joy and light of Jesus with her friends.

She took her huge Victorian Bible to school, but it was too cumbersome. Her father gave her a small New Testament she could carry in her pocket. Helen read from it to her friends every day and led many of them to faith in Christ.

Soon all the girls were sewing pockets into their dresses so they could carry the little Bibles and called themselves the Pocket Testament League. They gave out New Testaments to anyone who promised to read them, including a policeman, one of many in the community to receive Christ.

See? Papa God can use any of us—even a little girl—in mighty ways. Helen Cadbury Dixon passed away at ninety-two in 1969. Will you join me in sharing a Cadbury bar—and Helen's story—with someone who needs to hear it today?

Almighty Yahweh,
Use me, like You used
Helen, to share the sweet
message of Christ.

Traditions

*We will not hide these truths from our children; we will tell
the next generation about the glorious deeds of the Lord.*
PSALM 78:4 NLT

"Now, walk Jesus down the toothpick path but don't let Him slide off Battlecat."

"Okay, but if G.I. Joe is playing Peter, can he bivouac behind the couch after the rooster crows three times?"

Bizarre as these comments sound, they were part of our family Easter traditions while our children were growing up. In order to make the Easter story more real to them, we acted out the entire week preceding Easter with their toys, beginning with Jesus' Palm Sunday entry into Jerusalem and ending with His glorious resurrection.

On Good Friday, we'd set aside an hour to open up the picture Bible and assemble our props, which included three crosses made of pencils rubber-banded together and stuck point down into a sturdy shoebox (Calvary). The box doubled as the tomb so that when the crosses were removed after the crucifixion, Jesus was tenderly wrapped in Granddaddy's white hankie and buried in the shoebox cave with a round pillow rolled in front.

We tiptoed reverently around the tomb until Easter morning, when the kids would race in to find the stone rolled away, a discarded hankie, and a triumphant Jesus sitting atop the shoebox, His little plastic arms raised high in victory.

Corny, you may say, but the kids loved this symbolic ritual honoring our Lord Jesus and it served to imprint these most important events, crucial to our faith, in their minds forever.

*Risen Savior,
I want my family traditions
to pass on the exciting truths
of Your power and mighty
miracles to my children and
grandchildren in ways they can
understand. Motivate me to find
creative ways to enlighten them.*

Legacy of Faith

*We will tell the next generation about the glorious deeds
of the LORD, about his power and his mighty wonders.*
PSALM 78:4 NLT

Yesterday we began talking about the importance of incorporating elements of faith in our Easter traditions. Here are some other ideas to consider.

My friend Gloria created a tradition of Gospel Easter Eggs. Each year they'd assemble neighbor children and their own three daughters to tell the story of a boy who recognized the true meaning of Easter in an empty plastic Easter egg (representing Jesus' empty tomb).

They filled plastic eggs for the children to hide containing other symbols of Easter—flowers symbolizing new life, nails for Jesus' crucifixion, a dirty rag representing sins, thirty cents signifying the silver paid to Judas. . .you get the idea. And so did the kids. Many learned about God's Son for the first time at this much-anticipated annual neighborhood event.

My friend Marianne wanted her children to respect the Jewish customs in which Jesus participated, so they established a traditional family Passover Dinner (Seder) held on Good Friday. Using reference books from the local Christian bookstore, they performed the ancient ceremony, pointing out to the children the symbolism of various facets of Christianity as well as Judaism.

Resurrection cookies are another terrific family tradition—hollow cookies that children help bake the day before Easter. The cookies are then sealed in the cooled oven overnight and opened the next morning to celebrate the miracle of the empty tomb.

So what Easter traditions do you celebrate? Which are you passing on to your children?

*Lord of New Life,
Give me the courage—
and energy—to create
a legacy of faith for
generations to come.*

Bunny Revenge

*"Self-sacrifice is the way, my way,
to saving yourself, your true self."*
MARK 8:35 MSG

Six weeks without chocolate? Are you *serious*?

He was.

Papa God whispered to my heart that He wanted to teach me more about personal sacrifice during Lent. But not chocolate! How could I possibly give up my lifeblood? My reason for living past 3:00 p.m.? Surely I misunderstood. Instead of chocolates, maybe He said to give up *socklets* or *wallclocks*.

I realized the purpose of Lent was self-sacrifice, reflection, and repentance. It's no personal sacrifice if the item I'm fasting holds no special meaning to me. Like being melted into my very soul with its luscious Godiva tentacles caressing the comfort center of my brain. Sigh.

I struggled through the Lenten season wrestling the overwhelming hourly urge to indulge my secret vice. Well, maybe not so secret. When you're denied something, it screams your name. Occasionally I screamed back.

Still, I'm happy to tell you I held firm. I constantly reminded myself if Jesus could suffer and die for me, I could give up this one little thing for Him. Every time I opened my chocolate stash drawer and breathed in the heavenly aroma, I'd remember His sacrifice for me.

Closing the drawer was the hard part. Forty days is an eternity.

I clung to the promise of Easter morning when I would celebrate Jesus' victory over death and my personal victory of self-sacrifice by wreaking revenge on my chocolate Easter bunny in one gigantic gulp.

But when Easter morning dawned, strangely, the craving was gone. Instead, I was filled with humble gratitude from my season of undistracted reflection. And that's all the reward I needed.

*Beautiful Savior,
I'm deeply grateful for
Your sacrifice for me.
So. Deeply. Grateful.*

Little Biddy Buddy

These trials are only to test your faith.
1 PETER 1:7 TLB

A week before Easter, our friendly neighbor presented my kids with a downy yellow chick. This was not a swell idea; we already had two cats, a dog, and two hamsters.

"Don't worry," she whispered in response to my horrified expression. "Easter peeps never live very long; the kids will play with it a few days then nature will take its course."

Wrong.

Mr. Peepers ignored the kids and followed me around the house like a feathered toddler. I truly expected his first squawk to be "Mom!" He became my little biddy buddy.

He spent his spare time (when he wasn't following me into the shower or sitting beside me on the couch) roosting on a basketball like an oversized orange egg.

Hmm. Reckon that's why they call 'em roosters?

Well, Mr. Peepers grew into the largest breed of rooster in the southeast, leering down his beak at the cats that had tormented him as a peep. He outgrew his sleeping accommodations—two laundry baskets wired together in the garage—and the friendly neighbor wasn't so friendly when awakened at 5:00 a.m. by *ERR-ER-ERRRRR.*

Reluctantly, I found a farmer with lots of chickens who agreed to take him, promising *never* to consider the Kentucky Fried route.

So I buckled Mr. Peepers into his seat belt and drove him out to the country. I thought my heart would explode when he chased my departing car down the farmer's long dirt driveway.

Sniff.

The farmer said Mr. Peepers eventually adjusted and became quite popular with the cute chicks. That's my boy!

Lord of Levity,
Remind me that one day I'll
laugh at my current trials.

Biggest Fan

*They all joined together constantly in prayer,
along with. . .Mary the mother of Jesus.*
ACTS 1:14 NIV

This verse is the last time Mary is mentioned in the Bible, but in these few words, she leaves a legacy for mothers throughout time.

Much had happened in the thirty-three years since the birth of Jesus. Mary and Joseph fled for their lives with newborn Jesus; when they later returned to Nazareth, four strapping boys were added to the family: James (who wrote the New Testament book, James), Joses, Simon, and Judas. Plus a few daughters, but sadly we don't know their names (Mark 6:3).

Jesus scared His parents spitless when He disappeared while on vacation at age twelve.

Mary rejoiced when the child she'd diligently raised in the Law of Moses—fully believing Him to be the Son of God—astounded everyone at a wedding with His first miracle at age thirty (the last round was on Jesus).

She proudly watched Him heal the sick, forgive sins, love the unlovable, and cast out demons for three years. Mary's boy turned the world upside down.

Then she endured His arrest on false charges, torture, trumped-up trial, and crucifixion. She grieved, heartbroken, at the foot of the cross, as her beloved son labored for His final breaths.

But on Easter morning, her shattered heart was gloriously mended when Jesus rose from the dead, just as He'd promised. She no doubt stayed close until He ascended to heaven. Afterward, according to today's verse, Mary lived out her life as a disciple of her own son, the Savior of the world.

Mary's our role model of a supportive mother. Protective. Prayerful. Present. His biggest fan.
Girls, we have big shoes to fill.

*Light of the World,
Like Mary, help me always
be my child's biggest fan.*

Chillin'

Happiness makes you smile;
sorrow can crush you.
PROVERBS 15:13 CEV

A group of us girlfriends put on the Ritz and strutted our cheesiest bling at a Broadway-style stage play at our local Performing Arts Center. Boy were we stylin'—although I might've looked, well, a teensy bit gangsta in my new seven-dollar black pinstriped suit with matching vest and Dick Tracy hat (YAY for consignment shop treasures!).

No matter. Hey, I can do Bonnie and Clyde if it means chillin' with my peeps.

Girlfriends are our link to levity when reality becomes too intense, our safety nets when we're free-falling. They're the distributors of grace when we're fragile, tears when we're broken, and warm hugs to begin fitting the pieces back together.

Aristotle said, "The anecdote for fifty enemies is one friend."

Preach it, ancient Greek bro!

Everyone needs a soul sister who offers unconditional love and acceptance. A safe place where we can store our secrets and be sure they won't leak. Someone to travel the life road with—speed humps, potholes, sharp turns, sheer drops, and mountaintops. And best of all, a BFF (Blessed Friend Forever) to tip cows with at midnight. (If you're Southern, you'll get that because you probably did it last week; if you're not, google it. And accept my condolences for missing out on a real hoot!)

Did you know that fun is actually contagious? A British medical journal concluded from social experiments that happiness transferred between people can last up to a year. A year! So it's true—when you smile, the whole world really *does* smile with you!

Creator of Female Hearts,
You know that I need to
connect with my chicas. . . . You
made me that way! Motivate
me to make girlfriend time a
priority this very week.

Seeds of Faith

"Let the children come to me. . . .
For the Kingdom of God belongs to
those who are like these children."
LUKE 18:16 NLT

I love being the preschool Bible Story Lady at our church. One day our lesson was about the woman at the well, who was loved and accepted by Jesus when she felt ostracized by others. . . a difficult concept for three-year-olds, right?

I explained how she drew her well water at noon when it was hot and nobody else was around because she was left out of many village activities.

To help these precious little ones understand, I likened it to me being born with a nasty thing called a hernia that kept me from running or sliding or playing with other children until the day the doctor did an operation to fix it when I was three. Until then, I felt sad like the woman at the well because I couldn't do things I wanted to either.

At that point I stopped my story, intentionally creating a cliff-hanger by telling them I'd finish my hernia story after we sang a song.

As I reached to switch on the music, an adorable little blond girl suddenly blurted out, "Wait—can't you finish the story now? We want to know what happened to your *Narnia*!"

Okay, so maybe the details got a little skewed, but the point is, everyone needs to know about Jesus' love. Love for a lonely, sweating, friendless, miserable woman at a well; love for a sad little girl with a Narnia.

Friend of the Lonely,
Children are fertile ground
for planting seeds of faith that
will take root and blossom the
rest of their lives. How can I
fertilize those seeds?

Not Just a Pretty Face

*Like a gold ring in a pig's snout is a
beautiful face on an empty head.*
PROVERBS 11:22 MSG

I double-checked the credits. Sure enough, the actress I remembered from the seventies was the one in the modern movie, although she barely resembled her younger self. She hadn't aged well at all.

The next day while filling my gas tank, I glimpsed my own reflection in my car's side window, suddenly empathizing with that poor actress. In the revealing sunlight, every wrinkle, pore, blemish, and saggy jowl glared back at me. Aack! I hadn't aged all that well either.

I'm immensely thankful that I don't make a living by my appearance. How draining it must be to have to look beautiful all the time. Some have done it for decades: Christie Brinkley, Raquel Welch, and Sophia Loren come to mind. Timeless beauties, by anyone's standards. But at what cost?

So what is beauty by Papa God's standards?

I believe it's that intangible, indescribable, radiant beauty that shines from within. We've all known people who had it, people who don't necessarily possess society's standards of physical beauty but leave us basking in their luminosity nonetheless...Mother Teresa, Corrie ten Boom, and my grandmother, Nellie Ruth Rogers.

As we journey through life, never knowing what surprises (or wrinkles or bags) the next bend in the road will bring, we can rest assured that we'll always be beautiful to our heavenly Father, who personally engineered our unique aging blueprint.

And He's the only one who really counts.

*Breather of Life,
Thank You for giving me the
opportunity to grow older.
Help me remember what a
marvelous blessing it is.*

Walking With

"Do to others as you would like them to do to you."
LUKE 6:31 NLT

RC said he'd walk with her. And he meant it.

He was talking about my niece, Andie, a university student majoring in English who'd registered for an all-day writing retreat. You see, Andie has lifelong physical disabilities, due to cerebral palsy, that make walking difficult. And her eyesight is extremely limited, so she needs assistance finding her way around anywhere new.

Knowing all that, RC graciously volunteered to be Andie's buddy for the retreat, walking with her the entire day.

In this sense, *walking with* means the stronger partner subtly paces himself to the stride of the weaker. Without condescending in the least, he sees to the needs of his companion. The weaker partner relaxes in his protective covering and feels secure. She is then able to lean into the care of the stronger and absorb his strength as her own.

Much like Papa God walks with me. And with you.

Something else you should know about RC: he voluntarily drives four hundred miles nearly every weekend to walk with his widowed sister-in-law during her battle against breast cancer.

You know, it's an incomparable blessing for us to walk with someone in this life. I believe Papa God sent RC as an example of how to do it right. Of how to do it like Papa God does it. Of how He wants *all* of us to do it.

Jehovah Rohi (Our Shepherd),
Show me today whom to walk
with in Your footsteps.

Man-Eater

Every good and perfect gift comes down from the Father.
JAMES 1:17 CEV

Our new pet was the size of a powder puff. Freckles, a dwarf rabbit, lived in her cage on the porch until my daughter decided she looked lonely and began chaperoning field trips into the house. Of course Freckles never wanted to leave, which resulted in a daily family bunny chase.

Everyone would eventually give up except my husband, Chuck, who viewed the hunt as a challenging new indoor sport. It brought out the caveman in him. He'd systematically stalk and corner Freckles, pounce on his prey, and then heroically deposit the squirming rodent in her cage.

But Freckles began viewing Chuck as her mortal enemy and transferred that animosity toward any human with hairy legs and a deep voice. Whenever any unsuspecting postpubescent male entered the room, she'd launch into man-eater mode and attack, sinking her sharp front teeth into tender ankles and begin chewing her way north.

She was nearly unstoppable. . .like Bugs on drugs.

We finally gave Freckles to a single mother with a daughter, and she lived happily testosterone-free ever after.

Like Freckles, we all sometimes bite the hand that feeds us. Self-sufficiency becomes our man-eater. We neglect earnest prayer and rely on our own faulty judgment, which we delude ourselves into believing was responsible for the smooth sailing we now enjoy.

I think about Freckles when I begin to take my blessings for granted. When I'm blessed with trouble-free times, when everyone's well and getting along, the pantry's stocked, strangers at the door *aren't* bill collectors.

How soon I forget where it all came from.

Giver of All Good Gifts,
I need You all the time,
in times of abundance
as well as drought.

Becoming a Happy Have-Not

"He has. . .lifted up the humble."
LUKE 1:52 NIV

I arrived at the tennis courts ten minutes early. Twenty minutes later, I was still the only one there. Odd. Did the gang change days and not tell me? Nah, they wouldn't be that thoughtless. They were my friends.

So I practiced my serve until my serving arm felt like boiled spaghetti. Still no one there. Humph. My bottom lip began to protrude like my sulking preschool grandson's. My widdle fee-wings were hurt. My so-called friends had changed *something*—day, time, planet—and left me out.

I felt like a have-not in an exclusive club of haves. A humiliated have-not at that.

I packed up my rolling tennis bag and trudged up the hill to the parking lot like a disgruntled bag lady. "Hey," a voice called from the pickleball court I was passing. "We're a player short. Would you like to join us?"

Angels sang. Harps played. Someone wanted me! I was no longer an outie. I was now an innie! Maybe not a have, but at least a *happy* have-not.

The only caveat was that I'd never played pickleball. But I wouldn't let a minor detail like that stop me—that lovely group of long-suffering people patiently taught me. And once I got the hang of it, I had a jolly good time.

Feeling wanted makes all the difference in the world, doesn't it?

Hmm. I wonder how many people I'll see today who secretly feel like humiliated have-nots?

> *Lover of Haves AND Have-nots,*
> *Motivate me to reach out*
> *to others and take a personal*
> *interest in their lives. To make*
> *sure they feel wanted and not*
> *like a humiliated have-not.*

Late Bloomer

Jesus said. . ."There are no 'ifs' among believers.
Anything can happen."
MARK 9:23 MSG

I once was offended when a journalist called me a "late bloomer." I thought it was a not-so-veiled reference to my long-standing affiliation with the Church of the Better Late Than Never.

Can I help it that every event I attend starts early? I used to blame my tardiness on the kids, but after they grew up and moved away, I had to start blaming the dog. He takes way too long to brush his teeth.

I soon realized that I actually *am* a late bloomer: someone who took a bit longer than most to blossom into full potential. I didn't start writing until forty-five years and two other careers had zipped by.

You know, it's really a compliment to be a late bloomer. It's quite a club!

Geoffrey Chaucer wrote the epic *Canterbury Tales* in his late fifties. Socrates learned to play musical instruments at age eighty. Roget compiled his *Thesaurus* when he was seventy-three. Laura Ingalls Wilder wrote the Little House series between ages sixty-four and seventy-six. Ben Franklin helped draft the Declaration of Independence in his seventies. Mother Teresa received the Nobel Peace Prize at sixty-nine.

And you? Are you a Late Bloomers Club member too?

No matter what age you currently are, there's bound to be *something* you've always wanted to try but never have. Think about it. What's stopping you—fear of failure? Money? Risk? Embarrassment?

Bah. Mere excuses.

I'm signing you up for a lifetime club membership right now so you can start watering and fertilizing. It's never too late to bloom where Papa God transplants you!

Sovereign God,
Regardless of my lateness,
cultivate me in new soil and
bring forth an unexpected,
beautiful blossom.

What's in a Name?

"You shall not take the name of the LORD your God in vain."
EXODUS 20:7 NASB

"This is all your fault," my unsmiling neighbor leveled at me as we picked up moss, limbs, pine-cones, and other debris strewn across our yards.

"*My* fault?"

"Storm's named after you, isn't it?"

Wasn't the first time I'd heard my name taken in vain since the arrival of Tropical Storm Debby. She arrived in a snit and hung around annoying Florida all week with pounding rain, high winds, new sinkholes, closed roads, canceled plans, and nasty headlines that somehow made me feel responsible:

GO AWAY, DEBBY!

DAMAGE IN DEBBY'S WAKE

DEBBY SCARY, EVEN FROM A DISTANCE

I felt like everybody in the state hated me. I heard people all over muttering my name in hard, angry tones. I knew it wasn't personal, but it sure felt like it.

And then a thought occurred to me. . .is this how God feels when people take His name in vain? When in fury she damns someone to hell; when the hammer accidentally whacks his thumb; when she casually throws around OMGs left and right?

In today's society, we've gotten so desensitized to hearing God's name used disrespectfully, we hardly notice anymore.

But He notices. And no doubt winces every time.

Lord God Almighty,
Help me remember that I'm
made in Your image; that
means my feelings mirror
Yours. Just like me, You feel.
You love. And You hurt when I
dis Your name. Please increase
my awareness of how respectful
I am of Your holy name.

Loose Cannons

When there are many words, transgression is unavoidable,
but he who restrains his lips is wise.
PROVERBS 10:19 NASB

I'd just finished my little speech at the women's banquet and was trying to catch my breath before manning the book table at the back of the room. A beautifully coiffed, expensively dressed, sixty-something woman whose lips were smiling but eyes were not approached me. She was, as my granny used to say, "well preserved."

"Oh Debora," she said in a louder-than-necessary voice. "I think it's simply mah-va-lous that you lost forty pounds last year!" She glanced around to see who was listening.

"Let me ask you something. . ." She paused, her manner sending up a red flag of impending danger in my head. Then the cannon fired.

"How long do you think it'll be before all that loose skin starts to shrink up?"

Aack!

There seems to be one in every crowd. Someone who just can't find it within themselves to encourage rather than discourage. Someone who thinks their candle will shine brighter by blowing out yours.

Yes, just like you, I've been insulted. . .mostly unintentionally. Early on, I learned that a simple smile in response goes a long way. It really doesn't hurt a bit and nobody's the better when bitterness is exchanged. I've actually made some lasting friendships when choosing to overlook certain comments.

And you, dear friend? How do you handle loose cannons?

Master of Self-Control,
Teach me restraint. The next
time someone decides to point
out I'm a human river of wrin-
kles, help me not coldcock them
with my underarm Dumbo flaps.

Marriage Creed

*Bear with each other and forgive one another if any of you has
a grievance against someone. Forgive as the Lord forgave you.*
COLOSSIANS 3:13 NIV

"Yesterday my husband said I need to decide whether I want to be married or single."

I nearly choked on my water as we took a break between tennis games. Alana wasn't a close friend, but we played occasionally. Alana didn't appear distressed that her marriage was in trouble; she casually shared the ultimatum she'd received as she toweled off her pretty face.

"I won't tolerate anyone telling me what to do. If he wants a divorce, he can have it. I'll just get a boyfriend. Or maybe two. We've been married thirteen years, and I've always had a backup plan. Separate finances, my own car. I kept my house in my name when he moved in. . .just in case."

"But what about your son?" I tried not to look shocked. "Doesn't he need both of you?"

"He'll be fine." Alana brushed off my concern. "We'll just split him right down the middle." With this Solomon-esque statement (as a nonbeliever, I'm pretty sure she'd never read that biblical account), Alana made a cutting motion with her hand down the center of her body.

Alana's callous attitude about her marriage floored me. Sure we all get annoyed with our spouses sometimes, but we lean on marriage creeds like today's verse when things get rough. Bear with one another. . .forgive as you're forgiven. Spiritual qualities only Papa God can provide when we're scraping the bottom of the patience barrel.

How about you? What marital creed do you live by?

*Bonder of Hearts,
Help me bear with my man and
learn to forgive the grievances
that come between us. Just as
You bear with and forgive me.*

Peeved

As they were leaving Bethany, Jesus was hungry.
MARK 11:12 NIV

Nothing was going right: looming deadline, dinner to make, kids treading on my last nerve. Peeved, I picked up a stray shoe and flung it against the wall. What would Jesus do with all this stress?

Well. . . What *would* Jesus do?

I shouldn't be surprised when Papa God directly answers a question, but I always am. He sent me to Mark 11:11–23 to read about a time Jesus was stressed to the max. He'd just entered Jerusalem, pressed by crowds on all sides. Noisy, smelly, jostling people everywhere.

When Jesus arrived at church, a place He usually found comforting, He was disgusted at the retail circus His Father's holy house had become. He exited the city, no doubt getting as far away from the offensive debacle as possible.

Next morning, Jesus roused His boys early and led them back to Jerusalem, probably exhausted from a sleepless night rehearsing the verbal lashing He was planning to lay on the temple crooks.

Jesus wanted breakfast, but McDonald's was closed. His stomach probably growled like a grizzly. But wait. . .yonder was a fig tree.

When you or I are tired, stressed, and hungry, we take it out on something. Well, Jesus did too. Now here's the clincher to this story: Jesus, who knew what crop was harvested when, must have realized it wasn't fig season. But when confronted with the figless fig tree, Jesus blew a gasket. "No one is going to eat fruit from you again—ever!" (Mark 11:14 MSG).

Why would Jesus curse this innocent fig tree?

Stay tuned tomorrow.

*Papa God,
Thank You that it's okay for
me to ask hard questions.*

Stress Mess

"Embrace this God-life. Really embrace it,
and nothing will be too much for you."
MARK 11:22 MSG

(Continued)

Stress. That's what I believe prompted Jesus to curse the fig tree. The susceptible human side of Him was stressed to the teeth—traveling, fatigue, hunger, knowing He was going to die soon yet must still perform unpleasant confrontations like trashing the temple.

He needed a release valve.

Now you might ask at this point, "But what about the God side of Him? Wasn't Jesus man and God at the same time?" Good questions.

From my *her*spective, Jesus could have allowed His God side to overshadow His human side and cruised through the last week of His life on earth as an above-it-all deity. Just like He could have called legions of angels to remove Him from the cross or block His pain receptors so He didn't feel the agony of whips, nails, and thorns piercing His skin.

But He didn't. He chose to feel it all. . .to agonize through it all. . .for us.

And I believe He allowed His human side to react with frustration to the fig tree for you and me—to show that He did indeed feel what we feel today during times of futility, stress, disappointment.

That He fully grasps firsthand our urge to throw something, clench fists, and gnash molars.

That's why today's verse—Jesus' very words in the tsunami of a stress mess—is so meaningful. He *gets* what you're going through, girlfriend. He understands. Totally. And He's tossing you a life preserver to stay afloat in the torrent of your stress mess.

Dearest Savior,
I'm so glad You chose to
feel what I'm feeling. Today
I choose to embrace Your love
and peace to keep from
drowning in my stress mess.

Gender Bender

*Barak said to her, "If you go with me, I will go; but if you
don't go with me, I won't go." "Certainly I will go with you," said
Deborah. ". . .the LORD will deliver Sisera into the hands of a woman."*
JUDGES 4:8–9 NIV

I love the story of Deborah in the fourth chapter of Judges. In an estrogen-oppressing patriarchal society, Deb was a game changer. A gender bender.

Deborah, a wife (4:4) and mother (5:7), was thick with Papa God. He often spoke to her and through her, which earned her the title of prophetess. In a day when women were merely servants and window dressing, Deb burst through the glass ceiling to become a judge, national leader, and trusted military advisor. General Barak so depended on Deborah's guidance that when facing a seemingly impossible-to-win battle, he uttered today's rather unmanly scripture.

Something really cool about the prophecy at the end of today's verse—Deborah wasn't talking about herself. She was referring to *another* woman who would rise from the ranks of the invisible gender to become a behind-the-scenes hero.

Jael was her name. A quiet, stay-at-home mom who intentionally flew beneath the radar. Until the day destiny burst through her door. After Deborah's army routed the powerful enemy, opposing General Sisera fled for his life. . .right into Jael's kitchen, begging for food and refuge.

Jael calmed him, fed him, tucked him into bed, and then hammered a tent peg through his forehead.

Gulp.

Sounds harsh, I know, but Jael did what was necessary to bring peace to her country (5:31) and was heralded as courageous.

Two different women. Two different styles of leadership. Both effective. Both God-honoring. What's your leadership style?

*My Deliverer,
However You choose to use
me—high profile or low—
use me to honor You.*

Beneath the Words

"He who has ears to hear, let him hear!"
MATTHEW 13:9 NKJV

My mother is the Malapropism Queen of the Universe.

Malapropism? Means to unintentionally substitute words, resulting in twisted—and often hilarious—meanings.

So I grew up being told to put my dirty shoes in the toilet or fold the dry leeches. Amid frequent reminders to vacuum the yard or hang up my teeth, I learned out of necessity to listen for the meaning *beneath* the words instead of only the words themselves.

Rather like deciphering verbal hieroglyphics.

Naturally, as we age, my sister and I are now Malapropism Princesses rivaling for the Queen's throne. Sis grabs corn on the cob with thongs and I spoon up gravy with a paddle.

Our kids and grandkids view it as a game and simply nod when we ask them to get the cheese from the dryer or empty the telephone. They know hearing sometimes requires listening beneath the words.

Listening beneath the words is essential in the Christian life too. But why do we so often falter in following Jesus' admonition in today's verse? The Gospels alone record ten instances of Jesus repeating these important words.

Of course He's talking about spiritual ears, not physical ears. Although we have no earlids (like eyelids) to cover our physical ears, we often manage to block incoming messages to our spiritual ears as if we're wearing earplugs.

We don't want to miss the point here... As Christ followers, we've been gifted with spiritual ears to hear beneath the stories in the Bible. But we won't hear anything unless we intentionally *listen*.

*Whisperer to My Soul,
Help me unclog my spiritual
ears today and listen for the
meaning beneath Your words.*

Heat Wave

Rejoice with those who rejoice,
and weep with those who weep.
ROMANS 12:15 NASB

Shortly after I'd begun submitting articles for publication, I was speaking with a friend in the lobby of my church. Bubbling with excitement over my third published magazine article, I'd just begun filling in the glorious details when I noticed a hovering acquaintance eavesdropping.

"Excuse me," Miss Buttinsky said, doing just that. "Did I hear you say you're pursuing writing—as in getting *published*?"

"Why, yes," I replied, naively expecting congratulations for my accomplishment.

"Hey, what exactly qualifies *you* to be a writer?" she asked with a look on her face that brought back memories of my irritated mother asking ten-year-old me if my filthy room was clean yet. Without waiting for my reply, she continued. "Did you major in journalism?"

"Um. . .no. . ."

"Well, were you an English major?" The wannabe writer's words were crisp and well enunciated.

"Not exactly." Geesh, it felt like a heat wave was rolling through the room.

"So how, then, are you qualified to be a writer?" she asked point-blank, crossing her arms and cocking her head.

Flabbergasted, I glanced at my friend, who was staring back at me with her mouth hanging open. How was I supposed to answer that?

With sudden divine inspiration, I said to Miss Buttinsky, "You're absolutely right. I'm *not* qualified to be a writer. But you know something really funny? There are three editors out there who THINK I am!"

Lord of Empathy,
Teach me not to discourage others
but instead brighten someone's
day with encouragement
and compassion.

Mauve

Exercise self-control.
1 PETER 1:13 NLT

I was exasperated. I'd looked all over for mauve towels to replace my old ratty set. I didn't want to spend much money since we planned to remodel the bathroom within a few years, so I set out to find some inexpensive towels that were a cut above horse feedbag quality and matched the mauve and silver wallpaper (yes, I said *wallpaper*) that had adorned the bathroom walls for a decade.

Never much of a home decor fashionista (bet you already figured that out, huh?), I soon discovered mauve was out. Way out. Like Mars out. And it had apparently been out for a *l-o-n-g* time.

Visiting the one store I hadn't yet tried, I entered the towel department with fingers crossed. No mauve in sight. And no staff to ask for assistance.

Then a store clerk whooshed by. By whooshed, I mean he obviously wasn't on the lookout for customers needing help. He marched like Buddy the Elf on a mission with a clipboard tucked under his arm and a look of serious consternation on his face.

Or maybe it was constipation.

Anyway, I sort of jogged after him. "Excuse me," I threw at him like a cowpoke lassoing a stampeding bull. "Could you please tell me if you have any mauve towels?"

"Mauuuuve?" The distasteful word slimed off his tongue like rancid mayonnaise. He stared at me as if I'd just belched out loud. Then one eyebrow shot up. "Actually, I believe we do have some in the economy section." He sighed and reluctantly turned to lead me there, muttering, "Although I can't imagine why."

Stay tuned for tomorrow's thrilling conclusion.

*Ever-Patient Lord,
Give me self-control when I
encounter snooty people today.*

The Color of Grace

*Set your hope fully on the grace that will be brought
to you at the revelation of Jesus Christ.*
1 PETER 1:13 ESV

(Continued)

I followed the clerk to an obscure shelf where a stack of mauve towels cowered behind more popular colors. Thanking him, I turned and shook open the folded top towel with a *whap*. Spotting several pulled threads in the terrycloth, I refolded it, set it aside, and reached for another.

After only two of the first four towels passed inspection, I became aware of the uptight clerk hovering behind me.

"Ma'am, what ARE you doing?"

"Checking for picks." I tried to keep my tone friendly, although his was anything but.

"Picks?"

"Yes, flaws. . .imperfections. Like this right here." I pointed out the pick, assuming he'd remove the damaged merchandise from the floor.

Snatching the towel from my hands, he scowled and whipped a ruler out of his back pocket. "If there are any flaws, it's because people keep unfolding them." He dropped to his knees, spread the towel on the tile floor, and folded it into a precise square, measuring each fold with his ruler. He then reshelved the towels for the next unsuspecting customer.

Clutching the two good towels, with face flaming, I fled to the checkout then to my car. Still quivering with indignation, I angrily started the engine. David Crowder's voice blared from the radio, hitting a God-smack homerun. "Hap-pi-ness, there's grace! Enough for us and the whole human race."

My defensiveness melted. "Okay, Lord. I get it. You're reminding me that happiness is a choice. We can give others the same grace and patience You give us, or we can stay irritated and unhappy."

*Abba Father,
Today I choose grace.
And happiness. And any
color besides mauve.*

Bigger Than Fear

"Having hope will give you courage.
You will be protected and will rest in safety."
JOB 11:18 NLT

Tossing, turning, sleepless nights: What woman doesn't know these intimately? Our thoughts race with the what-ifs as we sculpt features onto our faceless anxieties, effectively giving fear laser eyes, supersonic ears, and a cavernous mouth.

The monster we've created first whispers legitimate concerns into our heart's ear but ends up shrieking alarming possibilities that *could* happen.

Remember the *I Love Lucy* episode when Lucy decides to bake her own bread? As she mixes and kneads the dough, a tiny pinch of yeast doesn't seem like enough, so she dumps in more. Then she leaves the pans of dough to rise. When she returns, huge blobs of gooey, sticky bread dough have ballooned over the sides and oozed to the floor.

That basically describes the what-ifs: uber yeast.

Only a pinch of runaway, negative, worst-case scenarios can balloon into heaping, globbing, overwhelming terror. When fear jumps its creek bed and begins flooding the banks of your life, it's time to build a DAM:

- **D: Damage control.** Identify the fear that's sabotaging you; name it aloud.
- **A: Attach a bit.** Like a bit controls a horse's direction, steer your thoughts toward preselected, reassuring scripture that Papa God is in control.
- **M: Manage your fear.** Make good choices in what you allow to influence you, such as what you read, movies you see, people you listen to.

How precious is Yahweh's promise that He'll give us courage to say NO to anxious thoughts intent on terrorizing us. He's our hope and protector. And He's bigger than fear.

....

....

....

....

....

....

....

....

> *Yahweh Yireh*
> *(The Lord Will Provide),*
> *What a relief that anxiety*
> *flees in Your presence. Give me*
> *sweet rest with You tonight.*

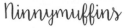
Ninnymuffins

To Him who is able to do far more
abundantly beyond all that we ask or think.
Ephesians 3:20 NASB

Here I sit in my chocolate-stained computer chair, pondering how I got here.

Fifteen years ago I was immersed in my tidy little life as an occupational therapist, mother, wife, and tennis addict. A literary ninnymuffin, I hadn't written anything deeper than Christmas newsletters for thirty years.

Then one day in 2002, in a dentist's office of all places, I prayed about how to fill the void in my life when my youngest chick flew the coop. A still, small voice whispered to my soul, "It's time."

I understood—time to follow your childhood dream of writing to inspire others.

And so the adventure began.

I've never looked back, not through reams of rejection slips. Not through the infernal wait-wait-waiting of publication purgatory. Not through $1.57 royalty checks or endless phone conversations about speaking gigs that never materialized.

I started out as a cyber-ninnymuffin. I knew nothing about websites, widgets, or WordServe. But I learned. I also learned that the most incredible moment in a writer's life is when someone shares how Jesus touched her heart through your words. It's then you break down completely, awestruck and humbled that you were used as His instrument. That you're the pen but He's the ink.

And I learned the incredible depth of today's scripture. . .*far more, abundantly, beyond* our greatest expectations. That's what our God does for ninnymuffins.

So how is Papa exceeding your expectations, dearest ninnymuffin?

Fulfiller of Impossible Dreams,
Show me the incredible breadth
of far more. . .abundantly. . .beyond
my wildest expectations. Please
make this humble ninnymuffin
Your instrument today.

Bird Flew

Satisfy us in the morning with your unfailing love.
PSALM 90:14 NIV

I happened upon a pair of cardinals on my morning prayer walk. They were so busy shopping for breakfast—pecking the ground—they didn't notice my quivering dog straining at his leash.

The little mister, in his flaming crimson suit, became aware of us first. He skittered closer to the female, who was preoccupied with her shopping list. When she still didn't look up as he hopped around in a distressed "Hey, Edna, pay attention, will ya?" circle, he flew away.

He flew away. What a coward. Desert your woman at the first hint of trouble. Humph. I was totally indignant on her behalf, but she just kept pecking away at her chores, oblivious to his abandonment and the lurking canine danger.

I began channeling to my feathered sister, "You deserve better than him, honey. What a jerk!" when the little twit suddenly squawked from an overhead branch so loud it made me jump.

Ladybird immediately flew straight to his side. I can only surmise he'd hollered something like, "Edna, get your tail feathers up here RIGHT NOW!"

Oh. He wasn't leaving her. He was *leading* her. The same way Spouse sometimes leads me when I won't listen the first time he makes a sound suggestion.

The way Papa God sometimes leads me when I'm too busy to hear His voice.

Oh. Maybe I should try harder to pay attention in the first place to those who love me and are trying to look out for my best interest, instead of staying immersed in my to-do list.

Oh.

> *Ever-Protecting Father,*
> *Even when it sometimes feels*
> *like I've been abandoned,*
> *thank You for leading me*
> *in ways I can't see.*

Loose Lips

He who restrains his lips is wise.
PROVERBS 10:19 NASB

My wedding ring should have been a mood ring. The first two decades of my marriage were a roller coaster of happiness and frustration.

I was determined to fix the flaws in my husband, whether he wanted to be fixed or not. I simply pointed out things he could improve upon whenever I noticed them. Which was just about every day.

For some reason, it didn't work. What I saw as being helpful, he saw as nagging.

Then I ran across today's verse. What a novel concept for me: keeping my wise and helpful suggestions for spousal improvement to myself. Why, I was sure the Master Potter couldn't mold my husband into a vessel of excellence without my clay-stained fingers creeping up from beneath the table to assist.

But to my surprise, when I backed off, my husband's unique qualities became much clearer, and I could better appreciate the fine, godly man with whom I'd been blessed.

Sorta like keeping your fingers out of the batter so you can later enjoy more delicious triple chocolate brownies warm from the oven.

What a difference it made in our relationship when I managed to swallow those critical words before they incited a skirmish, undermined our mutual trust in each other, and eroded our sense of intimacy.

Hurtful words are like daggers; the wounds they inflict bleed and fester and require a long time to heal. Some never do.

Master Potter,
Help me keep my fingers out
of the clay as You mold my
husband into the man You
desire him to be. And please. . .
teach me restraint.

Anemic Gifts

"My power is strongest when you are weak."
2 CORINTHIANS 12:9 CEV

One Sunday, I was standing quietly in the back of our church during worship, having my own little private praise fest.

A well-dressed man came to lean against the wall nearby. I didn't know him, but he was obviously in distress. Stifled sobs alerted me that he was struggling to control his emotions.

I squirmed. This was miles out of my comfort zone.

Spiritual giant that I am, my first thought was, *Lord, why did You send him back here? Nobody will see that he needs help.*

Then the truth dawned. *Oh, no—not me! Send somebody who really* can *help.* At that point in my walk with Christ, I was extremely uncomfortable praying aloud. I avoided it like the plague.

For the next sixty seconds, I fought the urge to flee. In the end, obedience conquered fear. Barely. I nervously stepped closer to the man with the broken spirit and asked if I could pray for him. He nodded, removed his glasses, and wiped his eyes on his starched sleeve.

It was a pretty anemic prayer, but I think we both felt the Holy Spirit right there in our little circle of two. Power—not coming from me—surged. The man appeared to be encouraged as he thanked me, smiled, and walked away holding his head a little higher.

Today's verse took on new meaning for me. I'd been elevated to a higher spiritual plane because of my *inabilities* and complete dependency on Papa. He had filled in the holes of my inadequacies just as He'd promised.

Almighty God,
Teach me that it matters
not what my gifts and abilities
are, only that I choose to be
obedient and use them when
You call. . .anemic or not.

Hidden Strength

You are no longer ruled by your desires,
but by God's Spirit, who lives in you.
ROMANS 8:9 CEV

Do you struggle with mindless munching? Boy, do we writerly types. It's far too easy to reach out with a free hand and shovel something into our mouths while we think through a tough passage.

Chewing helps brain function, right? Hey, calories consumed unconsciously shouldn't count.

I read a hilarious account by author Karen Linamen about the time she tried to break herself of mindless nibbling by filling the munchie bowl on her desk with doggy kibble instead of chips. Later, while engrossed in a story, she suddenly realized a handful of kibble was poised to enter her mouth. Ick.

She returned the kibble to the bowl, a bit nauseated but feeling victorious over her bad habit. And so quickly too!

At the end of the day, Karen stacked her papers and rose to leave her desk. Her eyes locked on the empty bowl glaring accusingly at her. Where had all that kibble gone?

Gross.

Pass the Pepto Bismol.

Even if mindless munching isn't your fault du jour, I'm betting there's *some* desire that fuels a bad habit you just can't shake. We all have 'em.

The good news is that we don't have to be ruled by our desires. We have complete and total access to the strongest will in the universe: the Holy Spirit. And He trumps *everything* else. Even doggy kibble.

Papa God,
Thank You for Your Spirit
living in me, hidden strength
when mine's not enough.
Which is most of the time.

The Lesson

Ask God to bless everyone who mistreats you.
ROMANS 12:14 CEV

Today in preschool children's church, our lesson is: when someone is mean to you, you don't have to be mean back.

Restless Danny begins his usual migration pattern around the room while everyone else sings and does hand motions with me. My sweet little grandson Blaine arrives late; my assistant directs him to the only empty chair in the room—the one Danny just vacated.

Suddenly, Danny notices Blaine sitting in his chair. He charges. Blaine hits the floor. Hard. I helplessly watch as my little buddy is pummeled by a bully in training pants.

Blaine blinks back tears. Danny climbs into the chair.

I want to throttle this rotten kid.

"Helloooo, Deb. Remember the lesson? When someone's mean to you, you don't have to be mean back."

But Lord, Danny deserves it.

"Doesn't matter. I wasn't mean back when they beat Me up and shredded My skin with whips. Aren't you trying to become more like Me?"

I guess.

"So now it's time to forgive Danny."

Maybe. After I announce, "Here's a prime example of our lesson today, class. This is a bully. A mean, bad, horrible little boy."

"But I love Danny."

Danny. Must. Be. Punished.

"He made a mistake. Don't you ever make mistakes?"

I think I'm about to right now.

"No, you won't. Because you love Me. And I love you. And we both love children who are learning to love Me too. Now forgive him."

It's too hard.

"Of course it's hard. That's why I'm here. I'll help you. Let's forgive him together."

*Help Me Get It, Lord:
When someone is mean
to me (or my loved ones),
I don't have to be mean back.*

One Word

I will praise the Lord while I live.
PSALM 146:2 NASB

I was asked to speak at a multiethnic international Christian women's event where different languages were spoken. Because multiple interpreters were often speaking at once, it was occasionally chaotic, sometimes cacophonous, always interesting, and never more fun.

Forbearance was abundant. Everyone there wore their patience and kindness like a beautiful necklace.

Something stood out to me as we expressed our Jesus-joy in worship. We were all praising Papa God in different languages, sometimes singing words we couldn't pronounce, with meanings we didn't understand, or listening to the Bible read in a foreign tongue.

Yet we had one thing in common.

It was one word that meant the same in every language. We all began saying it in unison while smiling from ear to ear when it became apparent that regardless of our nationality, each of us shared this unique phrase of worship: *Hallelujah.*

By definition, *hallelujah* expresses praise, joy, and gratitude. And by dingies, we expressed all those things, wrapped tightly up in one says-it-all word: *Hallelujah.*

Until that day, I'd always thought *hallelujah* was just another faith-speak term like "Praise the Lord" or "Have mercy!" But that word is special to me now, because I know that whenever I say it, thousands of my soul sisters and brothers across the globe are saying it too. Our hearts are bound together in one timeless, bottomless, boundary-less expression of praise to our Papa.

Hallelujah!

*Most Righteous Father,
I lift heartfelt praise,
worship, and gratitude to
You today. Hallelujah!*

Blindfolded

The LORD gives sight to the blind.
PSALM 146:8 NIV

I was enjoying the peaceful scenery of cows, horses, and the occasional pygmy goat (aren't they cute?) driving through rural Florida. Then I saw her. Standing beside a fence bordering the highway, all alone. A blindfolded horse.

I was puzzled why this filly had been singled out. None of the other horses in the field wore blindfolds. They moved around freely, navigating their own paths.

Is she being punished? Does she stubbornly refuse to obey her master? Or maybe she has a longtime dream to run free and has escaped one too many times?

She struck me as a forlorn figure, standing there droopy and spiritless, sporting the plaid eye cover she was powerless to remove, lost in broad daylight. Her caption begged to read *Where do I go from here?*

I could so identify with that blindfolded horse. I've walked a mile in her horseshoes. And so have you.

We all go through periods when our vision is occluded for any number of reasons and we become lost in broad daylight. Our internal GPS (God-Powered Satellite) shorts out, and we don't have a good feel for where we are or a clue about which direction to head next.

The blindfold starts to chafe and itch. Sometimes it even creates a miserable pressure sore; but we're helpless to rip the blindfold off. We only have hooves when it requires hands.

Maybe you're in that field now, feeling alone and blindfolded. I know Someone who can help. You know Him too. Someone who can lead you out of the lonely pasture and far away from that confounded blindfold.

*Restorer of Sight,
Won't You please remove
my blindfold? Restore my
vision. Lead me.*

Liberated

They all joined together constantly in prayer.
ACTS 1:14 NIV

Remember the blindfolded horse from yesterday? I've been thinking about her standing in that field, fearful to move anywhere without guidance. . .just. . .waiting.

Waiting is sooo hard, isn't it? We wait for medical test results, for the new job to come through, for forgiveness from that friend we offended, for the illness to finally end, to be smitten with true love, for the gratitude we feel we deserve but have never received.

So many things to wait for.

Today's scripture is a wonderful biblical lesson on how to handle waiting. Like the blindfolded horse, Jesus' lost-in-broad-daylight disciples were anxiously waiting for direction after Jesus had ascended into heaven. They were alone. Nothing had gone as they expected. They didn't know what to do.

Sound familiar? Sure does to me.

So based on this passage, here's our new waiting plan:

- Reach out; connect with others. Don't alienate yourself—you need their support.
- Keep busy; no standing around swatting flies with your tail.
- Pray, pray, and pray some more. Join hands with Papa God; you'll be able to feel the gentle tug on your bit when He begins to lead you to your next destination.
- Wait for Papa, not His answer. Focus on His nature, His loving attributes, His *person*. Learn to experience and appreciate Papa's presence, not what He can do for you.

The Holy Spirit soon infused the disciples with new vision and purpose at Pentecost. No more blindfolds!

That lost horse in the pasture needs her master to remove her blindfold.

So, my friend, do we.

Beloved Master,
I'm completely in Your hands.
In Your perfect timing,
liberate me from my blindfold
and give me direction.

Hearts Touching Hearts

"Daughter, your faith has healed you. Go in peace."
MARK 5:34 NIV

They entered the Mother's Day "Mother-Daughter" banquet in pairs. . .from little girls dressed in pretty hair bows, holding tiny purses like Mommy's, to women in midlife, assisting their elderly mothers with their walkers.

I felt out of place and, truthfully, a little lonely standing there all by myself.

Entering the banquet hall, I randomly sat at a table occupied by two ladies. In voices clearly meant for my ears, they spoke—with each other, not me—about needing *all* the chairs for their group. When I rose to join the buffet line, they quickly leaned my chair forward, indicating it was taken.

I felt my face flush with embarrassment. I considered fleeing for home. But I felt a gentle tug from the Lord to stay. So I squared my shoulders and looked for another seat.

To my utmost delight, I was adopted by a family of four generations. These lovely, generous ladies welcomed me, a stranger, as if I belonged. What a blessing I received witnessing a conservatively dressed mother with her arm around her multiple-pierced, tattooed daughter, singing praises together to their Savior.

I watched a young mother peacefully cradling her thumb-sucking toddler, who was learning what real love looks like.

And a grandma offering comforting arms to another elderly lady who stood quietly weeping during "Amazing Grace."

My heart swelled with emotion. No wonder Papa asked me to stay. He wanted me to see and feel hearts touching other hearts in ways that only mothers and daughters can.

Lord of Peace and Healing,
Show me today how to touch
those I love with Your love.

Deep and Wide

"Whose daughter are you?"
GENESIS 24:23 NLT

As Mother's Day approaches, I'm reminded of the myriad of emotions each of us experiences on the day set aside to honor mothers. Last year at our church women's banquet, I observed the wide range of those emotions.

There was the teen helping her non-English-speaking grandmother in the bathroom, the two sharing a private joke in the elder's native language.

A young mother emulating the patience of Papa God as she tenderly comforted her distraught daughter while gathering napkins to sop up her spilled lemonade. She was teaching her child, by example, how mercy jumps from the pages of the Bible to application in every life.

Smiles crinkled a great-grandmother's leathery face as she watched her toddler progeny stretch to tippy-toe and gaze with large round eyes at the wonder of a burning candle, rosebud lips forming a silent "oooo."

Then there was the teenager sitting alone, disappointment reflected in her sad expression and slumped posture as she stared at her silent cell phone. Someone had let her down on this day she'd hoped to spend with the woman who had given her life.

It brought to mind my friend who'd admitted in a voice heavy with regret, "My mother was merely the vessel that carried me for nine months. Nothing more."

Yes, on Mother's Day, the spectrum of emotion runs deep and wide based on our past and present relationships with our own mothers, our children, or those that haunt us most. . .the relationships we wish we'd had.

But despite it all, we know whose daughter we are.

*Heavenly Father,
I'm so glad You are my Papa!
I will always and forever
be Your little girl.*

Surviving the Hood

"May the Lord reward your work."
RUTH 2:12 NASB

It's no secret: raising kids is hard work. I believe Papa God has a special reward waiting in heaven for moms. . .something akin to a twenty-four-year deluxe spa treatment with Godiva smorgasbord.

In the meantime, some tasty morsels to nibble on from my mom-sisters:

- "My children suck the marrow from my bones." (Lynn)
- "Giving birth to a child is the beginning of a long good-bye." (Sarah)
- "Don't you wish we could freeze-dry our kids until they're twenty-five then add water?" (Cheryl)
- "If you wouldn't want someone calling you poopy-face, don't call anyone else poopy-face." (Debbie explaining Matthew 7:12 to her twins)
- "I'm a parenting survivor!" (Carol at her son's high school graduation)
- Think you're busy? According to Guinness World Records, the greatest number of children born to one mother is sixty-nine (an eighteenth-century Russian peasant). She had twenty-seven pregnancies: sixteen pairs of twins, seven sets of triplets, and four sets of quads. I'm betting her tombstone said "Rest in Peace. Finally."
- "You're only as happy as your unhappiest child." (My granny)
- "The shortest route from newlyweds to newly-deads is through kids." (Lisa)
- When my friend Eddie asked her son, married one year, when he planned to have kids, he answered, "I'm not ready to share my fries like you always did, Mom."

I'd like to end this tribute to the hood (motherhood) with encouragement to continue diligently praying for your children and grandchildren: "Pour out your heart like water before the face of the Lord. Lift your hands toward Him for the life of your young children" (Lamentations 2:19 NKJV).

....

....

....

....

....

....

....

> *Lover of My Babies,*
> *Thanks for the ride.*
> *It's bumpy sometimes,*
> *but You're my seat belt.*

Blabber Control

*"Because you won't believe me, you'll be unable
to say a word until the day of your son's birth."*
LUKE 1:20 MSG

Don't mess with Gabriel.

Zechariah learned that lesson well. He'd been taking his priestly turn in the temple when suddenly a big, frightening, shiny *being* appeared out of nowhere. Zech almost lost his lunch.

"Do not be afraid," the angel said (Luke 1:13 NIV).

"Why in the world not?" would've been my reply. Probably should've been Zechariah's too, for he scoffed at Gabriel's message of impending fatherhood in his old age.

Seriously? Gabriel's expression must've shrieked. *You're arguing with an ANGEL?*

Today's verse played out as Gabriel sucked all the words out of the doubting daddy, not to return until nine months later when baby John was christened and everyone turned to daddy Zechariah to settle the name dispute.

What must've gone through Zechariah's mind during those silent months? He couldn't discuss the situation with his flabbergasted, elderly, pregnant wife. He had to mutely watch her belly swell while his pregnant, unwed teenage relative from Nazareth sprang a surprise visit.

He could only listen as Elizabeth and Mary gushed with joy and praise over the miracles happening within them.

And once the baby was born, Zech had to wait and wonder for eight long days if he would ever get his voice back.

Sometimes we too endure long stretches of silence. All praise is sucked right out of our doubting selves and we feel spiritually mute. We wait and wonder if we'll ever get our Jesus-joy back.

Then it happens. Like Zechariah, our praise is miraculously reborn and we can't seem to shut up.

*Lord Jesus,
Praise is the kind of blabber
control issue I don't mind
having. Fill 'er up and spill 'er out.*

Bless Who?

Bless the LORD, O my soul.
PSALM 103:2 NKJV

Notice anything unusual about today's verse?

Don't we usually ask for the Lord's blessings on us, not vice versa? In a surprising twist, Psalm 103 discusses *us* blessing *Him*.

So how can we—the meager creation—bless our Creator? If blessings are good gifts, what can we possibly give Yahweh, who owns everything?

Papa Himself clues us in (look up these verses in your Bible):

- **Heart attitude**. Psalm 103:2–5: Praise Him for the marvelous things He does—forgives sins, heals wounds, pours His love and compassion over you daily, offers eternal life, and wraps you in His beauty and strength.
- **Emulate Him.** Proverbs 3:27: Love like He loves. Uplift and treat others kindly.
- **Praise Him.** Psalm 103:22: Enjoy the works of His hand, His marvelous creation. Thank Him *aloud* and profusely praise Him (Psalm 104:1, 35) for the good things in your life (yes, darlin', there ARE good things; dig deep!).
- **Make Him proud.** Jeremiah 31:3: You're His little girl, a beloved daughter of the King. Hold your head high and be as proud of Him as He is of you.
- **Give Him your very best.** John 12:3: Years ago, when I read in Philippians 4:18 that sweet-smelling sacrifices are pleasing to God, I began wearing my best perfume for worship. The Old Testament refers to Yahweh enjoying the smell of temple meat sacrifices too, but since Eau de Sirloin is hard to find, I dab on my sweetest scent as a sacrificial blessing to Jesus, patterned after what Mary did in the John passage above.

So, sister, how can you bless your Savior today?

....

....

....

....

....

....

....

> *Elohim (Mighty Creator),*
> *I want more than anything*
> *to bless You and bring a*
> *smile to Your loving face.*

Not Just Any Arrow

He has...made Me a select arrow;
He has hidden Me in His quiver.
ISAIAH 49:2 NASB

The eve of my forty-ninth birthday waned melancholy. I'd just received yet *another* "sorry, we'll pass" from a book publisher, making my collection of rejection slips big enough to papier mâché a piñata. Maybe a life-sized rhinoceros. Okay, a whole herd.

What really bothered me was the nagging suspicion that I'd misheard my calling. That the Almighty had said "fight a crook" or "bite a snook" instead of "write a book."

I randomly opened my Bible to today's verse, a supernatural IM just for me. Papa was sending me encouragement, reminding me that I'm a *select* arrow. Special. Exclusive.

A customized weapon designed to pierce the outer shells of His intended targets.

He was saying that no other arrow's quite like me; no person has the exact same background, experiences, and perspective. I'm the ONLY one who can accomplish the task He has prepared especially for me.

For now, I'm concealed, hidden in His quiver until the right time to use me in battle. Only at that specific time will I be most effective for His glory. Until then, I must remain content to wait among the other arrows, each to be selected in its own time to fulfill Papa God's designated destiny.

I felt as if I'd been wrapped in a warm blanket of assurance that my time would come. And sure enough, eventually it did.

So what about you, dear friend? What are you waiting in Papa's quiver to be selected for?

Master Archer,
Thank You for carving me
into a select arrow. Use me
at the appointed time and
place to glorify You. In the
meantime, help me wait in
Your quiver patiently.

Making Memories

If you bite and devour each other,
watch out or you will be destroyed by each other.
GALATIANS 5:15 NIV

Your boy kicks the game-winning goal; your little girl shines at the dance recital—these are the makings of wonderful lifelong memories. But what if your kid drops a teammate at the cheer-leading competition or strikes out with bases loaded?

Disappointing moments are also part of the childhood experience, the stuff of not-so-pleasant memories. How we deal with them can make or break the spirits of our children. Demonstrating unconditional love after a poor performance mirrors the unchanging love of our heavenly Father despite our shortcomings.

When my daughter's disastrous turnover during a high school basketball game incited the wrath of her coaches and teammates, I tried to think of something to lift her discouraged spirits. Unable to come up with anything profound, I propped a handmade sign on her bed that read "You played your heart out. We're PROUD of you!"

When she arrived home from the game, she went straight to her room. I peeked inside. She was clutching that sign to her chest, silent tears dripping down her face. She cherished that simple symbol of her value to us and kept it displayed prominently on her wall for years.

Encouraging our kids after a loss teaches them that their worth in God's eyes—and ours—isn't dependent upon their skills or accomplishments. Just because they lose doesn't mean they're losers. A Christlike attitude and demonstrating Papa's grace even under pressure—not the score of a game—determine who's a winner.

Loving Father,
Help me remember that my role is
pivotal in forming the childhood
memories of my kids. I want my
actions and attitudes to reflect
Your mercy, grace, and fun.

Stubborn

"You're not in the driver's seat; I am."
MARK 8:34 MSG

While driving to an appointment down a narrow country road, I hit my brakes for a fat black-and-white duck waddling toward me down the center line. Undaunted, she just kept bringing it. (I assume female gender here because she acted as illogically as I do.)

I laid on my horn. She stuck her stubborn beak in the air and parked her feathered derriere on the asphalt.

What's wrong with this chick? Here's a two-ton van versus a five-pound bird and she thinks she can win? Steel and chrome versus webbed feet and feathers? C'mon!

It occurred to me, as we stared each other down, halted at an impasse because neither was willing to give an inch, that this had happened before. How many times am I rendered immobile by silly obstacles that I allow to halt the pursuit of my goals? Itty-bitty speed bumps that somehow swell to disproportionate size and loom over me like the Alps?

The roadblock may seem like an immovable precipice, but in reality, it's the size of a duck.

In this particular battle of the wills, I learned that horns won't work, opponent size doesn't matter, time is not a factor, and rank is irrelevant. But there *is* a way to remove the obstacle. It takes persistence. That and willingness to exit the comfy air-conditioned car in 95-degree heat, nudge the foul fowl with a stout stick, and herd her off the road loudly squawking her annoyance.

There's no future in playing chicken with a duck.

*Life Mapmaker,
Teach me to be
persistent in herding
life's stubborn ducks
off my roadway.*

Chocolate Sermon

*Above all else, guard your heart,
for everything you do flows from it.*
PROVERBS 4:23 NIV

One of my favorite power-of-chocolate stories is the post-WWII account by Corrie ten Boom in her book *Amazing Love*. Several years after Corrie was released from notorious Ravensbruck when the war ended, she was invited to share Christ in another concentration camp, this one containing Ravensbruck women guards who were now themselves prisoners.

The shoe was on the other foot.

But miraculously, Corrie wasn't revengeful. She had already forgiven them for their part in the deaths of her beloved sister and father and found God's peace in her heart. She only wanted to reach these bitter, hardened women with the message that Jesus came into this world to offer people joy in *all* circumstances, a lesson she had experienced firsthand.

But the ex-guards wouldn't listen.

When Corrie asked the camp superintendent why, she was told the Germans considered themselves much more "highly cultivated" than this simple Dutch woman and her unsophisticated message. They looked down on Corrie with disdain.

So Corrie hit her knees and prayed for a common thread that could connect her with these resistant women. "I am not cultured or profound enough theologically for these women, Lord. Won't You please give me a message?"

The answer was surprising: chocolate.

Corrie had in her possession a box of chocolate, a rare commodity in all of Germany at that time, not to mention a concentration camp. The next day, she brought it out and watched the women's faces light up. Sour expressions became smiles, and all at once they were friends.

Stay tuned tomorrow for the heartwarming ending.

*Prince of Peace,
Show me the common thread
with that certain woman
You're calling me to touch
with Your love today.*

Chocolate Amen

"By this all men will know that you are My disciples,
if you have love for one another."
JOHN 13:35 NASB

(Continued)

What an unexpected luxury Corrie's chocolate was to those women prisoners! It was the common thread she'd been searching for. This time she spoke, and they listened.

"No one has questioned me about this chocolate," Corrie said. "No one asked whether it has been manufactured in Holland. . .or what quantities it contained of cocoa, sugar, milk. . . You have eaten and enjoyed it."

Holding up her Bible, she continued. "It is just the same with this Book. If I read about the Bible in a scientific, theological, or scholarly way, it does not make me happy. But if I read that God so loved the world, He gave His only begotten Son for me, then I am really happy."

Barriers dropped and Corrie saw a yearning dawn in their eyes, hunger for a deeper love than they'd ever known. A love beyond comprehension.

The following year, Corrie was visiting a hospital when an ill, emaciated woman reached for her hand. "Last year I was a prisoner in Darmstadt. . .when you preached on chocolate," the dying woman whispered. "That was the moment of my conversion. Since then I have not read *about* the Bible, but *in* it. Now I have to die, but I am not afraid."

Who'd have thought there was such power in a confection?

Sister, you know as well as I that the power wasn't in the chocolate but in the One who used it for His glory.

And I've got another chocolaty good story for you tomorrow.

Sweet Lord,
You had something amazing
in mind when You created
chocolate, didn't You? Show
me whom to bless today with
some brownie-love.

Chocolate Evangelism

*"In prayer there is a connection
between what God does and what you do."*
MATTHEW 6:14 MSG

The female prisoner was escorted by two uniformed guards into the rehab clinic where I worked as a hand therapist. Her bent head draped long dark hair over her face like a curtain. As if the bright orange jumpsuit weren't shameful enough, steel handcuffs and a chain between her leg shackles jangled as she shuffled toward my treatment table.

She was accused of murder.

She was only fifteen.

Maria couldn't bring herself to look me in the eyes that first day I treated her hand, filleted during an unspeakable crime. She was tearful, tense, untrusting. Like a frightened little girl.

During Maria's next visit, I noticed her eyeing the jar of chocolates on my desk. I offered her one, knowing she got few sweets in jail. She hastily unwrapped the treat, as if it might be snatched away before she could pop it into her mouth. I slipped her another.

Tentatively making eye contact through the protective shield of hair, she thanked me in a small voice. I smiled. She quickly lowered her eyes.

But the seed of friendship had been planted, a trusting relationship which bloomed through Maria's gut-wrenching trial, sentencing, incarceration, and a lifetime of me praying for this girl who became dear to my heart.

Chocolate cracked open a door that was eventually flung open wide when Maria asked Christ to be her Savior behind bars. Chocolate was the lumber Papa God used to build a bridge to a far, faraway heart.

Hey, how about one more chocolate evangelism story tomorrow?

*Worker of Miracles,
Chocolate is one of Your
finest bridge builders.
The hammer's in my hand;
show me the first nail.*

Chocolate Connection

*"Please take my gift. . .because God
has dealt graciously with me."*
GENESIS 33:11 NASB

Although the young Hindu woman sat at my therapy table, she wasn't really present. I'd been treating Uma's elbow tendonitis for weeks and still an invisible barrier divided us.

As with all my patients, I'd tried to extend Papa God's love to Uma, but my efforts had bounced off a stone wall. Although she dressed in beautiful saris and matching head scarves fashioned from exquisite fabrics, her cheerless demeanor and defeated body language suggested depression.

I couldn't make an emotional connection to show her I cared.

Then one day Uma arrived for therapy swathed from head to toe in fine cream-colored fabric lined with thin brown stripes. With my signature impulsive leap of tongue before brain, I gushed, "Oh, you look like a giant Hershey's Hug!"

By Uma's sudden grin, I knew we'd found common ground at last. I loaded the table with my stash of Hershey's Hugs and Kisses (NOT coincidence they're called that!), and during the following weeks, surrounded by growing piles of foil wrappers, Uma gradually opened up.

Her husband's traveling job necessitated her functioning as a single parent. All her relatives were in India. She felt exhausted, overwhelmed, and lonely.

What a golden opportunity to share the hope and joy of my Jesus!

Uma confessed that she'd begun to question tenets of the faith into which she'd been born and expressed an interest in learning more about Christianity.

How 'bout that—a Jesus hug generated by a chocolate Hug!

*Master Designer,
Thank You for this sweet,
creamy, luscious common
denominator that connects
women at a deeper level.
A heart level. A happy
tummy level.*

A Victorious Life

Precious in the sight of the
Lord is the death of his saints.
Psalm 116:15 kjv

Chuck and I were stunned when the call came.

"You need to come *now*," my nephew said, his voice breaking. "It doesn't look like she'll make it through the night."

Chuck's sister Suzi, a longtime believer, had seemed the very picture of vitality when she'd unexpectedly received a diagnosis of metastatic lung cancer only six weeks before. The family was devastated. It's true: we're all just one phone call from our knees.

We surrounded Suzi's bed, caressing her hands and sponging her forehead in attempt to soothe her restlessness. An hour passed painstakingly slowly.

Suddenly, Suzi threw back her head and lifted wide, clear eyes toward the ceiling directly above her bed. Her restlessness calmed. We all followed her gaze upward. We saw nothing, but Suzi was mesmerized.

We recalled Suzi's mysterious midnight encounter three days earlier. Suzi, her husband Pat declared, had begun conversing aloud to an unseen bedside visitor, whom she identified with complete confidence as Jesus.

Suzi's conversational cadence and pauses for responses Pat couldn't hear made him believe that the presence of the Son of God was unquestionably in that room.

The next morning, Suzi related that Jesus said it wasn't yet her time. She needed to stay and fight a little longer, but in the end, she would be victorious.

And victorious she was, as she peacefully drew her last breath.

What immense comfort to know that as precious as Suzi was to us, she was even more precious to her Creator, who welcomed her home with opened arms.

Conqueror of Death,
Help me see that the end
of life to us is merely the
beginning of eternity to You.

Seasons

Everything on earth has its own time and its own season.
ECCLESIASTES 3:1 CEV

I love the true story about the grandmother who exited a grocery store to find four men piling into her car. The men fled when she pulled a pistol from her purse and waved it in the air, screaming, "I have a gun, and I know how to use it!"

While loading her groceries into her backseat, she noticed a six-pack of beer and a football. Then she spied her car two spaces away.

Arriving at the police station to report her mistake, she encountered four pale men reporting a carjacking by a mad elderly woman with curly white hair, packing a large handgun.

Aging happens to us all. In fact, we've been aging since the day we were born. We just didn't notice the seasons whipping by until we hit late summer.

Face it, in this life the only thing that stays the same is change. And the only person who *likes* change is a baby with a wet diaper. In the vernacular of our kids, flux sucks.

Yep, the far side of the hill creeps up on you when you're still panting and sweaty from clawing up the front side. Suddenly the ground falls out from under you and you're skidding down the back slope. Hormones disappear, long-lost pounds reappear, memory disintegrates, and the face staring back at you from the mirror looks alarmingly like your mother's.

But it's just for a season. We too can become packing grannies if we keep attitudes of expectation, wonder, and excitement about the future.

*Lord of All Seasons,
Help me keep great
expectations about what
You have in store for me
around the next bend
in my life road.*

The Almighty vs. the Mighty All

We have no reason to be afraid....
The LORD is on our side.
NUMBERS 14:9 CEV

For more than five years, the praise band guitarist sacrificed personal time for rehearsals and playing for multiple church services each week. During the church's year-long search for a new pastor and worship leader, he was the visible face of stability—like glue holding together a fraying rope. Soon after the arrival of new leadership, he was asked to relinquish his position in the band. The new worship leader also played guitar. Two were one too many. He quietly disappeared.

Ouch.

Rejection hurts. And sadly, it sometimes happens within the body of believers.

The Bible has a lot to say about rejection. One meaningful story is found in Numbers chapters 13 and 14. Caleb and Joshua, the only two of the twelve spies sent to case out Canaan who didn't diss the power of God and cave in to fear of taking the land, were soundly rejected by their own people because they didn't fall in line. They didn't conform to popular opinion. They chose to listen to the Almighty instead of the mighty all, who were so infuriated they grabbed stones to pelt the two to death.

Jehovah personally stepped in to rebuke their rejecters, and then He rejected *them* from the Promised Land. Caleb and Joshua were rewarded with long life and entry into Canaan.

What's the takeaway here? Trust. Belief that if we stand for what's right, we may be rejected temporarily here on earth, but in the scope of eternity, we'll be lavishly rewarded by Papa God, the only judge who really counts.

Lord of Justice,
Today, help me be strong
enough to do what's
right and lean on trust.
Even in the face of rejection.

Guilty

GOD's business is putting things right.
PSALM 11:7 MSG

We arrived in Barcelona, traveling with Bob and Sandi, friends also celebrating their thirty-fifth wedding anniversary. (We knew each other in college and married two weeks apart so we could be in each other's weddings.)

After a lovely dinner in an outdoor café Paris-style, we retired to our high-rise hotel rooms in the heart of the city.

I settled down to a book in bed while Chuck fiddled with his computer. Suddenly, accompanied by a sound like a truck falling through the roof, the lights died across the entire hotel floor.

In the tarry darkness of the hotel room, I heard a faint "uh-oh!" from my fella.

"Chuck," I ventured, "what exactly do you mean by 'uh-oh'?"

Guilty silence.

"Chuck?"

"Um. . .I think maybe I did that."

"You did what?"

"Blew out the electricity when I plugged in a charger that didn't want to fit."

We could hear people braving the dark halls, bumping into handrails and each other, anxiously asking in heavily accented English, "What happened?"

Our friends knocked on our door, confused and discombobulated like everyone else. Chuck quickly ushered them in and secured the door like James Bond hiding allies from Russian spies.

When they heard what happened, Bob burst into laughter and Sandi burst into song, "That's the night that the lights went out in Georgia; that's the night that they hung an innocent man. . ."

Chuck bravely confessed when the authorities arrived to restore power. But for the rest of the trip, his faux pas was resurrected by that infernal song serenaded by our friends: "That's the night that the lights went out in Barcelona. . . ."

Creator of Fun,
I'm thankful today for
friends who make me laugh.
Even at my own expense.

Come as You Are

He saved us through the washing of
rebirth and renewal by the Holy Spirit.
TITUS 3:5 NIV

I poured a cup of water over my head in the 93-degree heat after sweating out two sets of tennis. Dripping, stinky, and exhausted, I checked my messages.

Aack! It was the rehab clinic where I worked as a hand therapist. "Patient scheduled 11:00 a.m. today."

WHAT? It was my day off! And it was 10:45.

"I can't work today," I sputtered into the phone. "I'm not in work clothes. . ."

"Just come as you are," the secretary responded. "Nobody will notice."

Sure. I surveyed my sweat-soaked tennis togs. I couldn't have looked less professional. I doused my nasty self with body spray but only succeeded in reeking like a high school girls' locker room.

But off to work I go. Heigh-ho, Heigh-ho.

Naturally none of the other therapists had an extra lab coat or even a sweater to camouflage my inappropriateness. When I called the patient from the waiting room, he eyed me warily.

"I. . .um. . .thought we were doing Halloween early (it was August)," I said lamely. "I'm supposed to be Serena Williams."

The invitation to "come as you are" can be risky. No telling what disgusting messiness you might find if people take you up on it.

Yet Papa God extends that very invitation to each of us when He calls us to Himself. *"Come as you are. . .with your ugly attitudes, stinky sinfulness, slimy pride, pathetic helplessness. Come on, dear child, and I'll clean you up and make you fresh as new-fallen snow."*

No matter how you started, you'll end up beautiful.

....

....

....

....

....

....

....

Lord of Transformations, *I'm so glad that Your* *supernatural body wash* *works inside and out.*

Holding It Together

Christ gives the body its strength, and he uses its joints and muscles to hold it together, as it grows by the power of God.
COLOSSIANS 2:19 CEV

My friend Kim has a contagious laugh, a weakness for strays, five terrific kids. . .and cancer. After battling the beast for seven years, Kim's doctors are trying a new medication. Her blood counts are looking up, but the side effects are dragging her down.

Pain. Kim suffers severe, debilitating musculoskeletal pain in joints all over her body. Her feet hurt so badly, forty-something Kim says, "I shuffle like an old lady picking her way through a minefield."

One night in desperation, she asked Papa God how she could possibly be joyful in this horrendous situation. He spoke to her heart, *"Find it in My Word. . .NOT in your life."*

Okay, she told Him. Maybe tomorrow. She'd just taken a pain pill and climbed into bed.

He asked whether she was going to be obedient or not.

Says Kim, "So I crawled out from beneath my heating pad and gimped across the room to lug my ten-pound Bible back to bed with my only good hand."

Out of the entire Bible, she turned to Colossians, where today's verse leapt off the page and into her heart.

Whoa. Joints and muscles? Really? Could it be any clearer that Papa God was speaking directly to Kim? Papa took her directly to His personalized message that He's there, He's aware, and He cares about her special needs.

Kim still suffers. But she finds supernatural joy in knowing that her Savior loves her and is tenderly "growing" her spirit as He strengthens her body.

Lord Jesus,
You understand suffering
firsthand. Please keep holding
me together. Even when it hurts.

Help Me Help You

*Do not withhold good from those who deserve
it when it's in your power to help them.*
PROVERBS 3:27 NLT

During the marriage conference, Chuck and I intentionally sat with different couples at every meal. By the end of the week, we'd gotten to know—as well as one can over rubbery chicken and chocolate pie—many on a deeper-than-casual level.

On the final conference day, I felt a goose nudge from Papa God to give away the four copies I'd brought of my then-new *Too Blessed to be Stressed 3-Minute Devotions for Women*. "You know," I told Chuck, "after hearing their personal stories, I think Kim, Suzan, Cindy, and Janice would benefit most from the books. But I don't want to hurt anyone else's feelings. I'll just let the conference leader draw names."

So later that day, the leader pulled random names out of a thoroughly shaken bag: Kim. . .Suzan . . .Cindy. . .(at this point, Chuck turned to me, eyes popping and mouth hanging open). . .Janice.

What d'ya know? Papa God is such a hoot. And I mean that in utmost respect.

When we reach out to do good to people with whatever means we have (my books, your yummy fudge or babysitting services or listening ear), He'll reach out to help us. That's right. Jehovah will—to misquote Jerry Maguire—help us help them.

But we don't always see His hand moving. Maybe because we don't *expect* His help so we're not looking for it. Or perhaps we don't offer OUR help as often as we should.

Either way, it's in our power to change.

*Helper of Helpers,
You've placed certain things
within my power to help others.
Or not. Goose me to use my
power for good.*

Spiritual Cellulite

*Workouts in the gymnasium are useful,
but a disciplined life in God is far more so.*
1 TIMOTHY 4:8 MSG

Did you hear about the nutty nutrition professor who ate only junk food for eight weeks on a "convenience store diet"? Instead of balanced meals, Mark Haub of Kansas State University consumed Doritos, Little Debbie snacks, and Oreos, but strategically limited his intake to 1,800 calories daily.

The result? Girl, you're gonna screech. *He lost twenty-seven pounds.*

The long-term health detriments of such a diet would be horrific, but the point is that quantity—regardless of quality—of calories is what counts in weight reduction. Bottom line: if you burn up more calories than you swallow, you lose weight. Whether those calories come from carrots or carrot cake.

Discipline is the key in keeping fit spiritually as well. It's good when we vow to make changes on both spiritual and physical planes: to read our Bibles daily, pray more, make healthier eating choices. But if we don't make a specific plan and then diligently work that plan, it won't happen.

You don't simply wish for dinner and then sit back and wait for it to magically appear, do you? No, you must *do* something to make it happen. Plan your menu, do the shopping, prepare the food, and then pop it in the oven. Otherwise you'd end up with a growling tummy and empty plate.

Likewise, to become spiritually healthier, we must DO something to make it happen. Become proactive. Take the spiritual cellulite by the horns.

No one ever said discipline is easy, but the end results are absolutely worth it.

*Spiritual Trainer,
Strengthen me in my
discipline to build spiritual
muscles of steel as well as
physical buns of steel.*

Cotton Ball Worries

*Praise be to the Lord, to God our Savior,
who daily bears our burdens.*
PSALM 68:19 NIV

I walked into the elevator as two southern belles exited, deep in drawled conversation. The elevator doors had no sooner closed behind them when the gal in the corner with the distinctive Jersey twang rolled her eyes at her slick chick chum.

"Who says dhat—'Can you *carry me* to da store tamarrra?' Like you're a sack o' patatas. Whey'd dey learn English—in a baan?"

I spent a long moment pondering what was wrong with asking someone to carry you to the store. I am and always have been, after all, a hick from the Florida-Georgia border long before it was a smash band.

Oh. *Carry me.*

The proper verb should have probably been "take" me to the store, but I've heard "carry me" my whole backwoods life, so it seemed perfectly normal to me. Like saying, "I used to not" or "Quit that directly or I'm gonna slap you upside your punkin' head, bless your lil heart."

It wasn't until college that I was enlightened about the. . .shall we say *charming eloquence* of regional colloquialisms and realized that literally carrying someone to the store would pretty much do us in. Carrying around ANYTHING for very long gets plum exhausting.

Just try holding a cotton ball over your head for ten minutes. That fluffy half ounce soon feels like a cement half ton. Worry is like that. If you don't learn to lay down your burdens, that cotton ball worry will eventually break your back.

*God Who Cares,
Make me aware of the cotton ball
worries I'm carrying today. Show
me how to lay them at Your feet
and not snatch them back up.*

Unload

*"Come to me, all you who are weary and burdened,
and I will give you rest."*
MATTHEW 11:28 NIV

Remember the cotton ball worries from yesterday?

Since I've felt kind of droopy lately (both physically and emotionally), I stopped to think about what I might be carrying around with me that would drag me down so. Didn't take long.

Unforgiveness. For sure. I've been wearing it this week like a fifty-pound sack of manure strapped to my back. Got so used to it, I forgot it was there.

You know, by not forgiving, we carry people and wounds around with us, weighing us down with our invisible burdens.

Harboring resentment is like chugging down strychnine and expecting the other person to die. Your anger doesn't hurt your offender. It hurts you. It wounds you and those who care about you. . .those who feel helpless and hopeless watching bitterness gnaw away like ravenous sewer rats at the *you* they love. Rats that will never be satiated.

I've heard it said that apologizing doesn't necessarily mean you're wrong and they're right. It just means you value relationships more than your ego. And isn't that the way Papa God wants us to prioritize?

Yep. Sometimes I need an elbow in the gut to jar my need-to-forgive muscle. It occasionally gets stuck in the fat of complacency and needs a little jolt to get moving again.

So that's my job for today: exercise that flabby forgiveness muscle, unload the manure, and reclaim my Jesus-joy.

How about you, dear friend—any invisible burdens weighing you down?

*Lord Jesus,
There You are, standing there with
Your arms opened wide, waiting
to take my burdens with Your
nail-scarred hands. Here they are.
Thank You. Really. Thank You.*

Balancing Act

But you, Lord, are a shield around me,
my glory, the One who lifts my head high.
PSALM 3:3 NIV

When I speak to women's groups on the topic "Too Blessed to *Stay* Stressed," every single hand in the building shoots up when I ask, as part of the Stress Test, "Who doesn't feel appreciated for all the tasks that you do?"

Yep, most of us feel as though we get much more criticism than praise. Or perhaps we remember the criticism more clearly and have trouble deleting its repercussions from our perception of ourselves.

It's a shame, really, because in reality, we often receive praise that we barely notice at the time and hardly ever deposit in our self-esteem tanks:

"Great dinner, Mom!"

"That looks very nice on you."

"I wouldn't trust this important project to anyone else."

"You're my BFF!"

Yet the implied admiration, honor, and respect are wiped out by one flippant negative remark:

"Don't be ridiculous."

"Seriously—you don't get it?"

"My grandmother has a skirt just like that."

"Which diets have you tried?"

So many times we're deathly afraid of receiving criticism—even helpful, necessary criticism that would help us refine, revise, and perfect our skill set. We erect an inner steel wall and brace ourselves for flaming arrows.

Then when we actually do receive praise, we brush it off.

Am I talking about you, girlfriend? How well do you take a compliment?

Life's a balancing act; learning to accept and internalize praise and downplay criticism is an important part of rehearsal.

Affirming Father,
Help me accept praise today,
even in its mildest form. As Your
prized creation, I am worthy of
praise. I lift my head high.

My Main Man John

*Therefore that disciple whom Jesus
loved said to Peter, "It is the Lord!"*
JOHN 21:7 NKJV

I've often pondered why John was labeled "the disciple whom Jesus loved" (see also John 13:23, 19:26, 20:2, and 21:20).

Wouldn't you like to be known as "the girl whom Jesus loved"? I certainly would. So how do we achieve that status? Let's take a look at John's life for clues. John was:

- **Attentive.** He soaked up Jesus' teachings and took them to heart. John must've taken copious notes, as one of only four (Matthew, Mark, Luke, and John) assigned by Papa God to document the life of the Son of God, Savior of the world.
- **Loyal.** He was the only disciple who stuck by Jesus during the confusion and horror of His trial and crucifixion. Although helpless to stop the proceedings, John recognized the importance of being there. And Jesus noticed.
- **Willing.** Jesus entrusted the care of His beloved mother, Mary, to John as He hung dying on the cross. He knew He could count on John for anything.

As I consider these three qualities, I measure them against myself. When it comes to my faith:

- Am I attentive?
- Do I listen with my spiritual ears?
- Do I seek to dig deeper into the Bible?
- Do I loyally stick with Jesus through the rough seas of my life. . .and the patches of calm when it appears I'm in control?
- Am I willing to do anything Jesus asks of me? *Anything?*

Tough questions. But questions we each need to ask ourselves if we're sincere about becoming a disciple-whom-Jesus-loved.

*Precious Jesus,
Above all, I want to be remembered
as the girl You loved and who
loved You back. Attentively.
Loyally. Willingly.*

Help!

*"Please, I don't talk well. I've never been
good with words. . . . I stutter and stammer."*
EXODUS 4:10 MSG

As if having CP, being totally blind in one eye and legally blind in the other isn't enough, my niece Andie has developed a speaking stutter. She finds this quite distressing when meeting new people. She fears they will immediately jump to the conclusion that she's cognitively impaired and treat her that way.

When Andie entered college and took classes that shoved her in front of the class for presentations and speeches, I asked if stuttering was a problem. "Surprisingly, no," she replied. "I've never stuttered once during public speaking class. It's a God thing. I prayed for help, and He reminded me that I have this perfectly good memory. So I memorize my presentation. I don't stutter when reciting."

Now consider Moses' reaction (today's verse) when he was assigned Official Yahweh Spokesperson before the most tyrannical king in the world. So typical of Papa. He chose a broken person to do His biggest work.

When Moses argued (yes, he actually *argued* with the Creator of the universe!) to send someone else, you've gotta love Papa's retort: "Who do you think made the human mouth? . . . Isn't it I, GOD? So, get going. . . . I'll be right there to teach you" (Exodus 4:11–12 MSG).

Moses was a stutterer like Andie. He too asked for help, but not with the same goal in mind. Whereas Andie wanted help to complete her assignment, Moses wanted help getting out of his.

How about you, sister? Are you bucking an assignment from Papa rather than seeking His help to get through it?

*Great Deliverer,
Some of Your assignments
scare me spitless. I'm broken,
You know. Help! I'm confident
You'll get me through this.*

Human Doing

Commune with your own heart...and be still.
PSALM 4:4 KJV

My entire life, I've been cursed with the gene of hyperproductivity. In my vocabulary, *rest* is a foul four-letter word. Lounging around makes me twitch.

Until I was twenty-five (the year I had my first baby), I never watched TV or home movies from my couch. I was upside down doing handstands, ironing, or exercising so I could "achieve something during my downtime."

I gave up sitcoms years ago because I drove everyone crazy jumping up ten times during a show to rush off to complete some project in microwave speed and hurry back, shouting, "What did I miss?"

Hyperproductivity really is a curse.

I no doubt inherited this trait from my mother, who was never one to let the dandelions grow beneath her feet. Still a bustling generator of chronic performance today at eighty-seven, she has two gears: full speed ahead and crash. The latter occurs only when she runs out of gas.

I must constantly be accomplishing something. The drive to do overwhelms my ability to simply be. My constipated calendar attests that I'm a human *doing* instead of a human *being*.

But I long to experience the mellow contentment of simply sitting back and *being*. Of living in the moment and feeling the wonder of life itself. Of communing with my Creator in the stillness of the darkness; of taking the time to watch a sunset, no matter how many things have yet to be checked off my daily to-do list.

Do you too struggle with hyperproductivity? Are you a human *doing* rather than a human *being*?

Holy Still, Small Voice,
Please calm me with Your
holy stillness. I yearn for it.
Please grant me a still
moment today to simply be.

Leftovers

*"The Son of Man came to look for
and to save people who are lost."*
LUKE 19:10 CEV

As guest speaker in a high school English class not long ago, observing students took me back to my own awkward adolescence. Some things hadn't changed.

Students still clustered in cliques, the loudest and most obvious of which were the jocks. Long-boned, muscular boys squeezed into too-small desks, their team jackets branding them as elite.

They were flanked by jock wannabes and groupies who said nothing original but merely echoed the utterances of their heroes and laughed hysterically at every dumb joke. Fighting excruciatingly hard for every scrap of attention thrown to them by the *players*, they appeared happy simply to be allowed in their presence.

Then there were the ditzy gigglers surrounding an outfitted cheerleader like spokes of a wheel. The cheerleader, with one eye on the jocks and the other on her reflection in the window-pane, kept up a nonstop monologue, punctuated by too-loud laughter or exclamations of disgust accompanied by animated facial expressions.

But my heart was moved by the leftovers—those who sat alone in corners. A musician kept beat with his pencil drumsticks to the music in his head. An empty-eyed kid stared at nothing. A mousy girl hunched over her desk, head down and eyes veiled by a curtain of straggly hair. One grim-faced girl clad in gothic black methodically twisted a silver stud protruding from her eyebrow. The nerd adjusted his glasses and focused on his computer.

All together but each so very alone.

My spiritual eyes were jarred open to the glaring condition of the raw human soul: lost without Jesus.

*Saver of the Lost,
Help me see around
me today—really
see—those who need
an introduction to You.*

Critter Lessons

Lord Almighty, blessed is the one who trusts in you.
PSALM 84:12 NIV

One summer afternoon, I rushed outside to investigate a commotion and found to my dismay that my calico Ruthie had cornered a squealing baby squirrel in my garage.

As I stepped between Ruthie and her intended lunch, the silly squirrel scampered up my leg like a tree trunk.

Now I understood how my thigh might be mistaken for an oak tree, but I was completely mystified by how to deal with a terrified rodent clutching said thigh while a hungry cat prepared to sink her sharp teeth into both of us.

I scooped up the squirrel, cupping him tightly in my hands, and fled into the house, intending to soothe him before release.

But the little fellow refused to be comforted, striving instead to break away from the comforter. I had proven myself as his savior, but he would not trust me enough to allow me to take care of him.

It occurred to me that I'd been showing no more faith than the little squirrel.

I recognized Christ as my Savior, but I couldn't turn the care of my precious daughter over to Him. She was leaving for college the following year, and I was already up nights worrying about the multitude of bad things that could happen to her.

My Savior had proven His loving-kindness to me many times, but I continued to struggle with trust every time something of great personal value was on the line.

Convicted by my squirrelly reluctance to trust the One who'd saved me, I stopped right then and there and released my motherly concerns to Him. What sweet relief!

Trustworthy Father,
Teach me to consider Your
track record and trust
You with my valuables.

Satisfaction

We are the clay, you are the potter;
we are all the work of your hand.
ISAIAH 64:8 NIV

During the past decade, I've come to view writing and speaking as the job the Lord has prepared me for my entire life.

I never saw it coming. But He did.

He filled me with a love of reading from infancy and provided thousands of library books for me to digest growing up. He made my mother insist I take piano lessons for twelve years although I begged to quit every other day. He infected me with the acting bug in college so I took classes to become comfortable on stage.

I never knew why I was doing those things, but Papa God did. It was all preparation.

Now I write books, speak to groups, and perform catchy little songs to my own recorded music. I'm reduced to tears when someone tells me something I wrote spoke to them as a message from the Lord. I still cannot believe I'm so blessed to be used as His instrument, a pen in His hand. It's what I've prayed as far back as I can remember—to be used by Him as He sees fit.

The same prayer you no doubt pray.

And I'm sure if you look back, you'll see that the events of your life were preparation for your ministry. Or perhaps you're still preparing. Regardless, He wants you to share the gifts He's been honing in you.

The pleasure derived from fulfilling your customized ministry is warm, satisfying, and real, not from pride but from the assurance that you're smack-dab in the middle of the path He's prepared you for.

Master Potter,
Prepare me. Mold me.
Use me. There's nothing more
satisfying. Not even Godiva.

Angels

*Angels are merely spirits sent to serve
people who are going to be saved.*
HEBREWS 1:14 CEV

The strange old man unnerved me. I was ten and naive, but even I knew there were bad things out there threatening little girls.

My family had stopped at a rural Georgia gas station en route to my granny's house about 9:00 p.m. I'd headed to the dimly lit outdoor restroom, obscured from everyone's view.

Everyone except the whiskered geezer standing in the shadows. . .watching me.

I hoped he'd be gone when I exited, but there he was, closing in as I reached to shut the door. He grabbed my hand and began rubbing his warm thumbs across my palm, muttering garbled words I couldn't understand.

My hand. How had he known?

Three enormous warts on my palm had plagued me for months, embarrassing me with their hideousness and hurting whenever I gripped anything. We'd tried all sorts of cures, but nothing had worked. I'd even prayed for God to intervene.

Whoa. Could this be His answer?

The grizzly old guy stared into my eyes, and oddly, I wasn't afraid. Weirded out but unafraid. He kept rubbing my palm until Mama showed up. She'd no sooner appeared than the man dropped my hand and lumbered away, still murmuring.

"Who was *that*?" she asked. I had no clue.

Well, believe it or not, those horrid warts dropped off the next day one by one. . .never to return.

I wonder sometimes if he was an angel. Like the ones in today's verse that Papa sends to serve believers. And consider this verse: "Some people have entertained angels without knowing it" (Hebrews 13:2 NIV).

Maybe even whiskered ones.

*God of Angel Armies,
I'm immensely grateful
for Your celestial servants
taking care of me.*

Barney

Encourage one another and build each other up.
1 THESSALONIANS 5:11 NIV

As I hurried toward the church exit, I noticed the grieving woman standing alone in the corner, dabbing her eyes with a tissue. I knew she had recently lost her mother to cancer, but the lengthy church service had made me late for my son's baseball game. I just couldn't stop now.

Resolving to give her a call later in the week, I pressed on with my urgent agenda.

The following Sunday as I sat in church, I had a God-smack moment. My good intentions had completely slipped my mind and a full week had gone by without following through with this woman in obvious pain.

It happened to be the same day we took a Biblical Personality Test; I was categorized with a "Barnabas" disposition. *Who?*

A little research revealed that Barnabas, one of the first converts to Christianity at Pentecost, was known for his selfless generosity, dedication to spreading the Gospel, and ability to settle disputes. Though his name was Joseph, the apostles called him Barnabas, which translates, "Son of Encouragement" (Acts 4:36).

Say what? Must be a mistake. How could I possibly be considered an encourager? *Me*—the person so consumed with her own schedule that she overlooked a suffering woman desperately needing comfort?

But you know what? Instead of sloughing it off as a misdiagnosis, I determined to prove myself worthy of being called an encourager. And I learned that encouraging others isn't just for those with "Barnabas" tendencies. Today's Bible verse speaks to *all* believers.

Including you, my friend!

User of the Flawed but Willing,
Give me Your strength in
courage to encourage that
discouraged person You
bring into my path today.

Getting in the Game

Pray without ceasing.
1 THESSALONIANS 5:17 KJV

Effective conversation is like a tennis match. You hit the ball over the net then your partner hits it back. Unless someone drops the ball, you keep going back and forth, back and forth.

Prayer is like that too. We speak to Papa God and He speaks back to us through various means, scripture being a primary one. He speaks, we listen. Then we speak and He listens. Back and forth like a yellow ball over a net.

It's a love match.

So why is it that on some days "Help!" is the only word He hears from us? We don't even use all 140 characters of our prayer-tweets.

We sometimes tell ourselves praying is enough. We just don't have free space. . .or energy . . .or motivation to spend time in the Word. But you know what? It simply doesn't work if you constantly feed balls over the net and never wait for your partner to return them.

It has to go both ways for conversation to take place. Otherwise it's a monologue.

That means, of course, that prayer and daily scripture reading go hand in hand. Like peas and carrots. Peanut butter and jelly. RC and moon pies (for us southern belles).

Prayer is designed to be a 24-7 dynamic, organic communication with a living, loving Savior whom we grow to depend upon as much as the air we breathe. Not just an occasional occurrence but a lifestyle. Woven into the fiber of our very being.

Prayer is not just spiritual punctuation; it's every word of our life's story.

*Infinitely Patient Lord,
Help me transition from a guilt-prayer squeezed in late at night before zzzz'ing out to a pray-without-ceasing lifestyle.*

It's Your Serve

"Call on me and come and pray to me,
and I will listen to you."
JEREMIAH 29:12 NIV

Yesterday we talked about prayer being like a tennis match. You hit the ball over the net; Papa God hits it back. Over and back. Over and back.

You know, the truly amazing part is that Papa God wants to play with us at all. I mean, He certainly doesn't have to. He's big and powerful enough He could just rush the net and smash, smash, smash every shot. But instead, He chooses to rally with us.

Doesn't it blow your mind that He wants to hear our deepest thoughts, feelings, disappointments, yearnings, wishes, and dreams? Even with the entirety of creation demanding His attention, the Almighty takes a personal interest in you. . .and me.

Whew. Hard to wrap your head around, isn't it? What a compliment. What an honor.

Yet we sometimes consider prayer a chore. One more thing to check off our to-do list. We get so preoccupied with living that prayer is reduced to rhino-in-the-road desperation tweets to NeedGodNOW.com.

I've found it enormously helpful to keep a mobile prayer pad with me everywhere I go. I find it especially handy in my car—my rolling cathedral—so I can pray instead of screech at red lights and traffic jams.

I highly recommend it for morphing road rage into prayer and praise.

If you do use a prayer pad, be sure to record the answers to your prayers so you'll never again doubt that prayer is the nerve that moves the muscles in the hand of God.

Okay, dearest prayer partner—it's your serve!

Loving Communicator,
I can't thank You enough for
hearing. . .for responding. . .
for never dropping the ball.

I Choose Laughter

If we are "out of our mind," as some say, it is for God.
2 CORINTHIANS 5:13 NIV

"Good afternoon, Mr. Maloney," I chirped cheerfully. "I'm here to do your therapy." He was sitting in the chair beside his bed, eyes half-closed, listing slightly to the starboard. This is the normal posture of eighty-year-olds at 2:00 p.m.

My job as the occupational therapist in a skilled nursing facility was to keep my patients' limbs limber and functioning so they could return home after rehabbing a stroke or debilitating injury.

I grabbed Mr. Maloney's arm and began exercising it as I always did—first the shoulder then the elbow, followed by the wrist and fingers. *Hmm.* He seemed a little stiffer than usual. Mr. Maloney stared straight ahead as he always did, not bothering to respond as I chattered away, giving him a good workout.

In the middle of a sentence, I noticed something strange. His chest was not moving. I stopped ranging him and spoke louder. "MR. MALONEY—ARE YOU OKAY?" I stuck my finger beneath his nose. No air moving in. No air moving out.

Uh-oh.

I dropped his arm like a hot potato and stepped back. He was unresponsive for a good reason. Mr. Maloney wasn't just mostly dead.

So I did what any good therapist would do. "Okay. Um. I'll go get the nurse now," I informed dearly departed Mr. Maloney. "And there will be no charge for today's therapy."

*Lord of Heaven and Mirth,
When I have the choice to laugh
or cry, help me choose laughter.*

Valley of the Shadow

The earth and everything on it belong to the Lord.
PSALM 24:1 CEV

I slammed my hands over my ears as the infernal phone kept ringing. Maybe if I ignored the bill collectors, they'd go away. *I HATE this,* I thought, my heart pounding. *I feel like a criminal. Will it ever end?*

It'd been a rough three years for us, beginning with the arrival of our second baby during a period our health insurance had lapsed. Out-of-pocket expenses were staggering. Chuck was still recovering from a long-term illness, and his full commission income combined with my part-time salary just wasn't enough.

I felt like I was walking through the valley of the shadow of financial death.

You're acquainted with that ominous dark fear too, aren't you? The kind that seizes your heart when official-looking men with clipboards appear at your door. Or when your kids don't understand why they can't go places and do the same things their friends do.

It's no secret that we live in volatile economic times. Many people have lost their jobs, their livelihoods, and their financial security.

Did you know that finances are important to Papa God? There are over two thousand Bible verses about money and possessions—*over two thousand*!

When discussing money and what it buys, we must first recognize that what we think we own isn't really ours. According to today's scripture, we're just caretakers. Although the bank account, trust fund, or mortgage might display our name, we're not the real owner. Papa God is.

With that thought in mind, stay tuned tomorrow for more on the same subject.

*Lord of My Finances,
Help me recognize that
honoring You means viewing
the possessions You've entrusted
me to manage not as mine,
mine, mine, but as totally
and completely Yours.*

Just Stuff

God is not unjust. He will not forget
how hard you have worked for him.
HEBREWS 6:10 NLT

Yesterday we talked about fear related to finances. Ready for more?

Have you ever wondered why we're so afraid of losing what we have?

I believe it's because deep down inside, we don't believe the Lord is actually in control, and if we don't defend what's ours, no one will. We have a hard time wrapping our heads around the concept that we are merely the managers of His possessions.

His possessions, not ours.

In my book *Fear, Faith, and a Fistful of Chocolate,* I shared the story of my friend Georgia, whose husband was out of work five long years. Georgia and her two sons learned to do without as their bank account shriveled. They lost their house, car, and college fund.

Yet their basic needs were continually, mysteriously, miraculously met. The tax refund that just had to be a mistake. . .but wasn't; the donated car; the bare acquaintance who regularly stopped by with loaded bags from the restaurant she worked in; the neighbor boy who appeared with like-new, outgrown sneakers for Georgia's eight-year-old right after he'd worn a hole in his only pair.

Through it all, Georgia continued to faithfully serve the Lord with the meager resources she had. She volunteered her time to help the needy at a homeless shelter when she had nothing else to give.

Georgia was a responsible manager of the possessions—however small—she had been given. And eventually, Papa God immensely blessed her with more—a home her family could call their own and a thriving business.

Let's talk some more about learning to trust the Lord with our finances tomorrow.

Master Provider,
Help me remember it's just stuff.

Not Over Yet

"Father, I thank You that You have heard Me."
JOHN 11:41 NKJV

The past few days, we've discussed trusting Papa God through financially hard times. Here are some tools I've found invaluable in my own battle with financial fear:

- **Don't give up hope**. He will continue to be faithful to us no matter what. "If we are not faithful, he will still be faithful. Christ cannot deny who he is" (2 Timothy 2:13 CEV).
- **Separate your needs from your wants**. Sometimes we get confused and pray for a Mercedes when what we really need is a bicycle. "You can be sure that God will take care of everything you need" (Philippians 4:19 MSG).
- **Sweeten your bitter words.** You might have to eat them one day. Don't dwell on the unfairness of your circumstances. "Fix your thoughts on what is true, and honorable, and right" (Philippians 4:8 NLT).
- **Remember what God has done for you.** He gave you the ultimate sacrifice: His Son on a cross. Salvation. Eternal life. Quote John 3:16 to refresh your recall.
- **Keep communication lines open.** Talk to your heavenly Father—even cry out your frustrations. Then dry your tears and thank Him for the blessings you do have. For a sharper perspective, visit a surgical ward or a homeless shelter.
- **Keep your eyes fixed on Jesus**. Keep honoring your Savior, even if you don't feel like it. Go to church, hang with believers, study your Bible, listen to Christian music. . . because feeding our faith starves our fears. "Look straight ahead, and fix your eyes on what lies before you" (Proverbs 4:25 NLT).

*Most Generous God,
Teach me that when it comes
to battling fear, it's not over till
I WIN!*

Offbeat

"Don't be afraid.... Take courage! I am here!"
MARK 6:50 NLT

People have all kinds of fears looming over their heads. Some may sound too weird to be taken seriously, but listen, their fears are as real and threatening to them as your fear of snakes—or heights—or Madonna cone bras—is to you.

These are some rather offbeat but nevertheless real fears people have that lean a bit to the bizarre:

- Pentheraphobia: Fear of your mother-in-law. Yikes! NOT a recipe for a long and happy marriage.
- Arachibutyrophia: (Ten points if you can pronounce this one!) Fear of peanut butter sticking to the roof of your mouth. No kiddin'. Symptoms include excessive sweating, itching, and even convulsions when peanut butter is nearby.
- Cathisophobia: Fear of sitting. Not just for hemorrhoid suffers, this disorder is sometimes rooted in excessive childhood punishment.
- Novercaphobia: Fear of your stepmother. This one was likely founded by a little Cinder girl with an affinity for glass footwear.
- Deipnophobia: Fear of dinner conversation. I would imagine this disorder runs rampant in those who believe no one will think you're stupid until you open your mouth and prove it.

Yes, fear can take many forms, rational or irrational. What fears are plaguing you today? Remember, fear of something is what gives it power. It only takes a spark of worry to ignite a blaze of anxiety.

He Who Is BIGGER Than All My Fears, Help me nip the buds of little fears, because little fears beget bigger fears. And remind me that fear is addictive once I've acquired a taste for it.

Rhymes with Bag, Hag, and Nag

I praise you because I am fearfully and wonderfully made.
PSALM 139:14 NIV

Is it just me or does it bother anybody else to wear a dress brazenly labeled "Sag Harbor"?

Now I realize Sag Harbor is an actual New York location, and I'm sure it's quite beautiful. But what on earth was the manufacturer thinking when he (I'm assuming masculine thinking processes here) denoted to a line of women's clothing a title that reminds us *mature* ladies so blatantly of our shortcomings?

Sag is a bad, bad word that discloses in one cruel syllable the havoc gravity wreaks on an aging body.

It's the monster that rears its ugly head when I bow my head to pray and my facial skin puddles about my chin.

It accurately describes the general positioning of my bust, upper arms, and buttocks in relation to the rest of my body. *Sag.* Yuck. Although it's a real geographical site, why would we want to label ourselves with that hideous word?

Might as well launch a line of Buttzville (New Jersey) panties. Or Needmore (Alabama) push-up bras for complementing our Hooker (California) evening dresses. Or how about a Big Ugly (West Virginia) tee to go with your Toad Suck (Arkansas) sandals for a smashing fashion statement?

Okay, back to the basics of today's scripture—praising our Creator for how we are made: wonderfully. And fearfully. (So true. Three-way mirrors scare the bejeebies outta me!)

Maybe you and I need to be reminded now and then that regardless of our appearance, we can be altogether lovely.

Gracious Provider,
Today I'm especially thankful
for this earth suit You've
fashioned for me. I praise Your
wonderful works and humbly
ask that You help me get over
that hideous "s" word.

Blindsided

*The day of the Lord's return will come
unexpectedly, like a thief in the night.*
1 THESSALONIANS 5:2 NLT

My neighbor's husband shook her awake at 6:00 a.m., whispering that a strange man was asleep on their screened porch and she should stay put until the police arrived, while he tiptoed back downstairs to keep an eye on the intruder.

Right.

Of course, Cheryl snuck downstairs and peeked around the corner. (Wouldn't you?) Sure enough, a snoring stranger was draped across the couch on the other side of the sliding glass door; he'd evidently started to break in but was blindsided by Mr. Sandman.

When the police arrived, the story emerged that the guy's van was parked several blocks away, filled with stolen items he'd pilfered from neighborhood cars during the night. Then he got greedy and turned his attention to a residence. Cheryl's residence. But the late hours caught up with him; with Cheryl's comfy sofa right there calling his name, he decided to take a little nap.

Robbery is such an exhausting profession.

Great candidate for the Stupidest Criminal Award, don't you think?

But a good reminder that the day you meet Jesus face-to-face will surprise you like a thief in the night. And I don't mean one snoozing on your davenport.

None of us know when. We only know that at some point, our life on earth will end and eternity will begin. We want to be ready, not blindsided.

*Creator of Forever,
Help me pack my spiritual bags
for my divine appointment with
eternity. Whether it's today,
tomorrow, or in fifty years,
I wanna be good to go.*

Dreams

*"I, the LORD, would reveal myself in visions.
I would speak to them in dreams."*
NUMBERS 12:6 NLT

When I was a young high school tennis player, I dreamed of greatness. . .Wimbledon, the French Open, Arthur Ashe Stadium. Then I realized that meant LOTS of practice.

Bummer.

So I never did become a great tennis player, but I did become a memorable one, or so I'm told by my opponents, although I think they're referring to my psychedelic socks. If you can't be revered, you can be you-nique, right?

Some dreams just aren't meant to be fulfilled. But others are. Like Old Testament Joseph. He had a dream that his family would one day bow down to him. Then horrible obstacles arose—he was stripped of everything and sold into slavery far, far away.

Joseph's dream must have seemed ludicrous as he toiled day after drudging day, enduring ridicule, imprisonment, and beatings. But he kept hoping, kept trusting God to exonerate him.

Ironically, it was a dream that bailed him out of jail and kick-started his new life as ruler of Egypt. Ruler but not even a citizen. Ha! Only Jehovah could do that.

I wonder if Joseph thought about that first improbable—no, *impossible*—dream when his brothers eventually groveled before him. Just as God had predicted. Joseph was so ripped with emotion, he couldn't speak. His dream had become reality.

I'm glad Papa God still makes dreams come true today, aren't you? Not flimsy, unrealistic dreams like whomping Venus Williams, but dreams that He plants in our hearts that never fade away.

These dreams are meant to be lifelong. And if Papa God wills it, He fulfills it, girlfriend. Against all odds.

*Divine Dream Weaver,
Fill me with hope and
vision that the dreams
You plant in my heart
will one day come true.*

Better, Not Bitter

He [Jesus] said to him, "Follow me!"
JOHN 21:19 NIV

My friend Marianne was the child of a deaf mother. She remembers pondering disabilities and concluding that the one sense she could never live without was sight.

And now she's going blind.

Marianne was diagnosed with macular degeneration at age fifty-six and began a gradual decline that resulted in the loss of her job, her ability to drive, read, and perform the vast array of crafts she once loved.

Does she rail at the Almighty for her misfortune?

"Not at all," Marianne says. "I'm not bitter, I'm better. God allowed my blindness in order to grow me. Of course it's not been easy, but I've learned to glorify Him in my dependency. I have an amazing relationship with God now that I never would have."

Marianne cites today's verse as her source of motivation to follow the Lord no matter what obstacles she faces. "He didn't just say, 'Follow me when things are great and you have all your faculties.' He said, 'Follow me even when you're at your worst.' That's when we learn to truly depend on Him for every need."

And that kind of dependency transforms the second letter in *bitter* to a whole new attitude.

How about you, dear friend? Have you suffered a loss—perhaps not the loss of one of your senses but something devastating nonetheless? Something that nudged you toward frustration, lingering anger, or even bitterness toward God?

I know I have. I believe everyone will at some point in their life.

My prayer for you today is that in your dependency on Papa, you'll transform bitterness into betterness.

---

*Yahweh Shalom
(The Lord Is My Peace),
Show me the clear path to
following You, even when
I'm at my worst.*

Selfie

Search me, God. . . . See if there is any offensive
way in me, and lead me in the way everlasting.
PSALM 139:23–24 NIV

My friend Ruth and her husband bought a selfie stick to take photos of their fiftieth anniversary trip to Europe. If you're not acquainted with this handy dandy little device, you simply place your phone/camera on an adjustable clamp that extends beyond the range of the human arm. . . usually right into someone's face or stomach.

Attaching the stick requires a trained magician, because if not properly attached, the phone that cost your entire inheritance from Auntie Gertrude can fall off into a river, over a cliff, or into the depths of a ruined castle, never to be seen again.

Then, if you do succeed in attaching the camera, holding the stick beyond arm's reach is quite a trick—no wavering as you scramble for position while your arm grows two-ton weary. You often end up with unidentifiably blurred people blobs or the midsections of faceless folks.

But those selfies that do turn out? Priceless! You've now got an indisputable record of where you've been, what you've accomplished, and who was with you.

You know, spiritual selfies are a good idea too. From time to time, it's good for us to take a step back and reflect on where our faith has been, what we've accomplished in the name of the Lord, and all the ways Papa God was with us, even when we weren't aware of it in the moment.

So how about taking a spiritual selfie this week?

River of Living Water,
When I reflect on what You've
done in my life, I'm grateful and
humbled. Nourish new seeds of
faith in me and help me grow in
my spiritual dry patches.

Rockin' It

*"He [Saul] is a chosen instrument of Mine,
to bear My name before the Gentiles."*
ACTS 9:15 NASB

Saul, the avowed ringleader in chasing down and murdering early Christians—the most extreme form of rejection—was stopped in his tracks en route to Damascus to do that very thing.

Temporarily blinded by God's enlightenment, his viewpoint swiveled 180 degrees; Saul was suddenly thrust into the reluctant fellowship of those he'd previously stalked, ridiculed, and cast out.

Dubious believers turned the tables and initially rejected *him* after his conversion. The glove was on the other fist. You have to believe Saul's emotional eyes were opened (appropriate figure of speech, eh?) when he learned firsthand what rejection really felt like.

Horrible. That's what it feels like. You and I surely know that.

But Papa God's peeps were eventually won over by Saul's sincere devotion to Jesus and gradually accepted him into the fold.

Saul, renamed Paul (a new name for a new man), was specifically chosen by Yahweh to spread the Gospel to the Gentiles (that's you and me!), long rejected by early Jews as being unworthy of the good news.

He was picked *because* of his experience with rejection and the level of new understanding it brought him. Rejection had prepared him for his ministry.

Hey, could that mean that rejection, as painful as it is, could possibly have a place, a purpose, in *our* lives?

Hmm. Let's think about that more tomorrow.

*Yahweh Tsuri (Hebrew
for The Lord, My Rock),
Show me today that even
the most painful things I go
through have a purpose.*

Rejecting Rejection

Jesus stretched out His hand and touched him,
saying, "I am willing; be cleansed."
MATTHEW 8:3 NASB

Let's continue our conversation about rejection from yesterday.

Those suffering the hideous deformities of leprosy in ancient days were cruelly rejected by their peers. Leprosy, now called Hansen's disease, was spread by skin contact or nasal secretions. Symptoms included twisted limbs, clawed hands, skin tumors, collapse of the nose (cartilage), and loss of sensation due to extensive nerve damage. Rats often nibbled away lepers' toes at night and they never felt it.

Through no fault of their own, people succumbing to leprosy were suddenly untouchables. . . outcasts. Banished to live in isolated colonies where many died of starvation or inability to care for themselves due to their disabilities.

Yet some rejected lepers never lost hope. "And a leper came to Him [Jesus] and bowed down before Him, and said, 'Lord, if You are willing, You can make me clean.' Jesus stretched out His hand and touched him, saying, 'I am willing; be cleansed' " (Matthew 8:2–3 NASB).

Jesus stretched out His hand and touched him. Can we do any less?

Jesus taught us ultimate compassion by example. Against all social mores, He reached out and touched the raw, hurting person behind the untouchable facade. By doing so, He rejected society's rejection and brought healing and wholeness to ravaged bodies and shredded hearts.

Yahweh Yireh
(The Lord Will Provide),
Like You, I reject rejection by
offering a compassionate
touch to those silently suffering
the pain of being an outcast.

Fatherly Love

*A father to the fatherless...
is God in his holy dwelling.*
PSALM 68:5 NIV

It's time again for Daddy's haircut, a father-daughter ritual that dates back to my teen years when I was the primary barber for many in my little world, including Daddy, my dog, and the boy next door.

Decades later, as Daddy sits serenely on a stool, I notice his shoulders, once tall and straight, are now hunched and rounded. The thick black hair that graces the memories of my youth is thinning and gray.

As I drape the towel around his shoulders, I remember the protective giant I ran to in times of doubt or fear. The man who soothed me back to sleep after my nightmare-induced screams shattered the night.

Before daybreak, I'd follow him into the bathroom as he shaved and readied himself for work. He'd carefully spread a bath towel on the cold bathroom tile so I could curl up around his feet and listen to endless tales of knights and ladies, unwise home-building pigs, and a cinder girl who found happiness ever after.

Patience and quiet dignity were his way—very different from his fiery wife and two temperamental daughters. He was a calming balance for our family, speaking little but saying much through his steadfast love for us and his Lord.

As I gather a tuft of hair between my fingers and begin to cut, I feel overwhelmed by warmth, love, and gratitude for this man, who gifted me with a relationship like no other in life . . .a daughter's love for her papa.

*Dearest Papa God,
I'm humbled and grateful for
the blessing of a loving earthly
father; many women look to You
as their only example of a true,
loving father. Thank You for
filling that void.*

Unplugged

Leaving that place, Jesus withdrew.
MATTHEW 15:21 NIV

For the first decade of our marriage, five years prior to and five years after the addition of two children, we camped out every chance we got. We couldn't afford a pop-up, much less an RV, so we roughed it in flimsy tents that barely kept the outdoors out doors.

Hordes of mosquitoes and biting no-see-ums drove us inside our temporary domicile, and rivers of rainwater and sweltering summer heat drove us back out again. Dirt, flies, and lack of running water were just part of the experience. We were young. What did we know?

My city-born husband never quite got the hang of the whole wilderness experience, though. I remember many a rustic camping trip when he trekked to the communal bathroom (the only electricity available) in the dead of night lugging his juicer and bushel of raw veggies. Campers exiting the men's room would slap their thighs in hilarity as they told their wives about the crazy dude juicing carrots in the last stall.

After enduring multiple rainouts, leaky air mattresses, and an honest-to-goodness hurricane (tents do NOT fare well in gale force winds, let me tell you), we finally decided the back-to-nature vacation wasn't for us and opted instead for civilization's hotel carpets and room service. I quickly acclimated to box springs, clean bathtubs, and climate control.

But you know what? I actually miss the campfires, stories shared under starlit skies, and especially the spontaneous private moments with Papa God. Those rare, unplugged times when there's nothing electronic blaring, beeping, or dictating our next move.

That's when Papa's still, small voice best breaks through the everyday static best.

*Lover of Quiet Hearts,
Help me find time today to
unplug so You can bring
peace to my chaos.*

More Than I Can Chew

I will thank you by living as I should!
PSALM 119:7 NLT

In my yard one summer afternoon, a strange rustling alerted me to a large flying insect tangled in the bushes. It looked like a cross between a moth and a bat, bright yellow, with a six-inch wingspan and a Vienna sausage-sized body.

At first I thought it appeared panicked because of its imprisonment, but then the real reason slithered out of the bushes. A garter snake, the size of an eight-inch twig, stalked his gourmet dinner. The fact that the entrée was five times his size didn't deter the little snake in the least.

Suddenly, the insect broke free from the bushes and began winging his way low across the lawn with the snake in hot pursuit. With amazing agility, the tiny snake sprang upward, latching on to the moth-bat's wing and hung on as he was dragged across the yard. Around and around they went, both working hard but getting nowhere.

I trotted up to the locked-in-combat duo and stomped my foot hard on the ground. The startled snake released his jaws-of-death grip on the moth-bat, which escaped into the treetops.

I got to wondering: How many times have I too bitten off more than I could chew? How often am I overly optimistic in my estimation of all the tasks I can handle?

Not being able to say no had long caused my plate to be increasingly piled high with responsibilities that kept me overstressed and struggling, not unlike the little snake.

Maybe this bizarre little scene was Papa's way of telling me to slow down and concentrate my efforts on what really matters.

Master Creator,
Help me learn to establish
priorities and to say,
when I need to, NO.

Homecoming Queen

Be kind to one another.
EPHESIANS 4:32 NKJV

My wheelchair was wedged tightly into the handicapped row near the stage; knee surgery the day before wasn't about to keep me from the Monkees concert. I smiled at the thirty-something fellow beside me. He smiled back, saliva dripping from the corner of his mouth. His wheelchair plate read TOMMY.

Tommy's arms were folded tightly across his chest; he couldn't speak, but boy could he laugh! His laugh was deep and contagious and made his whole body bounce.

We rocked out together through great songs like "I'm Not Your Stepping Stone," giggling like giddy kids. Suddenly the lights went down and glowing cell phones went up as everyone swayed back and forth, singing at the top of their lungs about a Daydream Believer and his homecoming queen.

It was a magical moment. I wasn't about to let Tommy miss it. I grabbed his hand, wrestled it as high as I could, and heaved both of us side to side. He howled with glee, bouncing in his wheelchair as drool flew everywhere.

When the lights came up, Tommy wouldn't release my hand. His mother appeared with tears in her eyes. "Tommy doesn't get out much," she said, smiling at her boy, who kept his eyes glued to my face. "Most people won't touch him, but tonight you treated him like everyone else. I've never seen him so happy. He's always been a daydream believer. . .and now you're his homecoming queen."

Wow. HUGE wow.

I'm beyond thrilled to be Tommy's homecoming queen. It's a title I'll wear with honor until the day I go live in my forever home with my Homecoming King.

My Beloved King,
Help me look for ways to
be kind to someone today.
Even little kindnesses
can mean so much.

Too Hard

"Is anything too hard for the LORD?"
GENESIS 18:14 NIV

My friend Rose was stunned. Until she received the doctor's call, she was clueless that anything was wrong.

Sure, she'd been exhausted lately, but she'd attributed that to being completely drained from losing her mother and mother-in-law within six weeks. And reeling from her father-in-law's recent cancer diagnosis.

Nothing had prepared her for the inconceivable news: she had stage 4 renal failure.

After ten months of a strict diet and tons of medicine, her body only grew weaker. She was put on the kidney donor waiting list and began dialysis. Scores of relatives and friends were tested, but none was a match.

All her own efforts failed. In a moment of revelation, Rose realized, "I'd been trying to do God's work, and I wasn't doing it well." Rose placed herself entirely in His hands.

Oh no! More bad news: the brother of Rose's former husband suffered a fatal aneurism at age 62. Even as Rose mourned Jerry's unexpected passing, she received word that Jerry's family had suggested donating his kidney.

To her.

In their deepest grief, Tom, Denise, Ashley, and Lindsey graciously offered Rose Jerry's gift of life.

But was it a match?

The transplant team rushed the tests. To the doctors' amazement, it was a *perfect* match.

"God's hand was on this the whole time, but I was too busy trying to solve the problem myself to see it," Rose admits a year after the successful transplant. "I've been given a second chance at life and I give God all the praise."

*Dryer of Tears,
Like Rose, I've been
trying to fix things myself.
I place _____ in
Your hands. Nothing is
too hard for You.*

Positive Thinking

I have no interest in what you have—only in you.
2 CORINTHIANS 12:14 MSG

I overheard this conversation in the bread aisle last week:

Tall, freckled redhead: "Hey Edna, I ain't seen your Ruthie since she was in kindygarden. What does she look like now that she's all growed up?"

Five-foot, two-hundred-pound, frizzy-haired woman: "Well, I reckon she looks a lot like me—petite, maybe a little chubby, wavy hair, and glasses."

I did a double take. I would NOT in a million years have described this woman as petite or a *little* chubby. She was built like a wrecking ball.

And wavy hair? Seriously? Think chia pet.

The more I thought about it, the more I realized that few of us would describe ourselves as others do. . .because we try to think of ourselves in a way that preserves as much self-esteem as possible. And that's a good thing. If we don't perceive ourselves in a positive light, who else will?

I think it's time to tweak the way I think of people, even in the privacy of my own head. I would much rather allow someone the dignity of being "slim" as opposed to "skinny," "big-boned" rather than "behemoth," "mature" instead of "old," "assertive" but not "pushy."

How about you? If I give you the benefit of the doubt, will you do the same for me?

Signing off,
Your highlighted (not graying),
flowing-haired (not split-ended),
healthy-appetited (not pudgy),
perky (not ADD),
au natural (no makeup today),
BFF (we're Blessed Friends Forever, right?),
Deb

*He Who Always
Sees the Best in Me,
Help me look for the best
in others all day today.*

Tree Stumps

*"I have come that they may have life,
and that they may have it more abundantly."*
JOHN 10:10 NKJV

Sadie Galego was born in 1900 in a small town in Maine where horse-drawn carriages were the norm. As a teenager, Sadie packed sardines for twenty-five cents per hundred cans. She went on to teach forty years in the same classroom, an old maid schoolmarm with a heart of gold.

After retirement, Sadie grew tired of the same ole same ole and became a world traveler, hopping on planes to see exotic places and experience new thrills. At age eighty-nine, she got married for the first time. . .to a man twelve years younger!

Yep, Sadie robbed the cradle. Or maybe the rocking chair. She and Frank had been friends for more than thirty years when they decided to marry and surprised their families with the good news hours before the wedding. They lived happily together in a retirement center until Sadie up and outlived her husband by eight years before passing away in 2009.

I would say Sadie lived an abundant life, wouldn't you?

Papa God intended our lives to be abundant. And living abundantly includes facing opportunities that may require taking risks.

Listen, sweetie, if you never try new things, you'll turn into a tree stump. And sooner or later the termites of atrophy will gnaw away at you until you're nothing but sawdust. Limp, lifeless, useless sawdust.

Now really, is that the kind of life you want?

Sadie didn't. She wouldn't settle for less than abundant. How about you?

*Master of My Heart,
Help me avoid a tree
stump existence and
embrace the abundant
life You desire for me.*

Risk-Taker

"I am about to do something new.
See, I have already begun!"
ISAIAH 43:19 NLT

Heard about the gal who plucked chickens for a living? Day after day she stood at a conveyor belt, pulling feathers off dead chickens. When asked if her job was boring, she replied, "Of course not! You get a brand-new chicken every thirty seconds!"

Not all of us have this plucky chicken-plucker's optimistic attitude about the same ole same ole. Yesterday we talked about living an abundant life; today let's chat more about taking risks.

There's something about trying new ventures that re-spunks and revitalizes our weary spirits, puts a little spring into our flip-flops. Doing something you've never done before awakens your inner child. . .that mischievous, giggly, freckled imp who used to love balancing atop the playground seesaw, launching herself down the slide headfirst, and flying through the air on a rope swing.

So where has that adventurous kid gone?

Nowhere. She's still here. More cautious than she used to be. . .she's peeking out from beneath all those blankets of insecurity you've heaped on top of her all these years. But she's alive and well. It's up to you to reach down, grab her hand, and pull her out so she can remind you what you used to know about risk-taking.

We mustn't be afraid to try something new. Helen Keller said, "Life is either a daring adventure or nothing."

Cinderella, who had never before been to a ball, was overheard marveling, "One shoe can make all the difference."

Noah had never even built a dinghy before he took on the ark.

Maybe it's time to ditch the chickens and take a chance.

Living Lord,
Inspire me to venture
from my comfort zone and
try something new today.

Chutzpah

*"Whoever acknowledges me before others,
I will also acknowledge before my Father in heaven."*
MATTHEW 10:32 NIV

As we toured the ruins of the once-thriving biblical city of Ephesus (in current day Turkey), I noticed several recurrent symbols carved into the doorposts of buildings or crudely etched into stone thresholds.

I was familiar with the fish, or *ichthus,* a clandestine symbol used by early Christians to avoid punishment for secretly meeting together. But the other symbol, one that resembled a spoked wagon wheel, stumped me.

As we walked the dry, dusty streets, I asked our guide about the circular symbol tucked discreetly throughout the city. In heavily accented English, she told us of the horrors endured by the first Christians of Ephesus in AD 60–70, after Paul's second missionary journey (Acts 18). The leaders and artisans of the prominent temple of Artemis were enraged that enthusiastic newfound Christians were poisoning their bustling idol business, so they were driven underground by legal persecution.

As she spoke, our guide began drawing in the sand at her feet with a long stick. She superimposed Greek letters on top of each other: I, X, O, Y, E (the closest I can simulate the Greek alphabet with this keyboard), which, roughly translated, means "Jesus Christ, God's Son, Savior."

When she finished drawing, what d'ya know? There was the wagon wheel we'd been seeing. It too was a secretive symbol of Christianity that was used to identify Jesus followers.

*Faithful Father,
I'm so grateful that I don't have
to keep my faith a secret. Give
me the chutzpah to acknowledge You before everyone I
encounter today. Everyone.*

Customized Mission Field

You will hear a voice saying,
"This is the road! Now follow it."
ISAIAH 30:21 CEV

Back in 2002, the magazine ad for the writing contest lit a spark in my innards. I'd always wanted to write since I'd read Catherine Marshall's *Christy* for the ninth time before my sixteenth birthday. It had planted a seed that one day maybe I could touch other hearts the way *Christy* had touched mine.

But what would I write about?

I told Papa God plainly that I was willing but unable. He'd have to whack me upside the head with an idea because I was clueless. To my astonishment, I awoke at 2:00 a.m. with a full-blown story outline in my head. It was about the series of miracles Papa had arranged for my family to acquire our beloved house.

I had serious doubts that anyone else would find it interesting, much less inspiring, but there it was. So I wrote and submitted my house story.

It didn't even place in the contest.

"Try again," a still, small voice told me.

So I wrote four other articles (just to help Papa out, ya know) and sent all five to different magazines. Guess which was accepted for publication? The house story, of course! And that was the beginning of my writing ministry.

All Christ followers are called to do specific tasks. Not just jobs or professions but *ministries.* Our jobs are our mission fields. Whether we're digging dirt with a good attitude or facing rude customers without biting back, He plans to use us to influence someone for all eternity.

Arranger of My Destiny,
Lead me to my
customized mission field.

Bosom Friends

A friend loves at all times.
PROVERBS 17:17 NASB

My friend Marianna received quite a fright.

She'd been in bed all evening, knocked out from pain meds due to day surgery, when she awoke, still woozy, checked her texts and saw: THIS IS DAD; HOW ARE YOU FEELING?

Gulp. Her father had been dead for twenty-five years.

The text was from me (Deb); the silly thing had auto-corrected.

Girlfriends. What would we do without them? Anne of Green Gables was right about girls needing bosom friends, friends who really hear us, friends whom we hold close to our hearts, knowing that they understand what we're going through.

Marianna is one of my bosom friends, my neighbor and heart-sister. We've become close through attending our neighborhood Bible study weekly for the past three years. We bosom friends have waded through many hardships together—illnesses, marital woes, financial troubles, and disappointment with the choices our children make.

But we've also rejoiced in personal victories together—new jobs, answered prayers, repaired relationships. And we've grown closer to Papa God and each other every step of the way.

So who is your bosom friend? What's preventing you from reaching out to start cultivating one today?

*Most Excellent Yahweh,
Please bring into my life
that special friend—a bosom
friend—who hears the song
down deep in my soul and
cares enough to harmonize.*

Shortcuts

Endurance builds character, which gives
us a hope that will never disappoint us.
ROMANS 5:4–5 CEV

Have you ever watched cantaloupes being harvested?

It's really quite mesmerizing in its beauty and simplicity. A truck straddles a row of low-growing fruit, moving forward at a snail's pace. Men stand atop the truck bed, catching cantaloupes tossed up to them by partners moving parallel in the field.

The tossers are incredible. In one graceful swoop, they lean over, pick a cantaloupe, and hoist the five-pound fruit up and over their heads in perfect arcs to the receivers on the truck. Then immediately bend back down for another. Down, up. Down, up. Down, up. Hundreds of times.

Over and over, the heavy orbs arc through the air into calloused, waiting hands. The receivers then turn and roll the melons into a crate headed to market. Catch, turn, catch, turn, catch, turn.

Everyone moves in perfect timing like a graceful, choreographed dance. Unexpected grace in an unexpected place.

Are you looking for a shortcut, my friend? Is something in your life so hard and wearying that you don't think you can endure one more toss, much less hundreds?

Sometimes there simply is no shortcut. We must go through the motions and endure the long, tedious journey. Because the repetition, the details, the *hardness* of it are essential to the process. The process that produces change in us. The process that makes the journey an essential part of our destination.

Refiner of My Heart,
Give me grace—Your grace—to
persevere in the hard places.

Make Your Bed

Peter said to him, "Aeneas, Jesus Christ heals you;
get up and make your bed." Immediately he got up.
ACTS 9:34 NASB

In her book *Stained Glass Hearts,* Women of Faith veteran Patsy Clairmont credits three unlikely words with saving her life. After suffering hundreds of debilitating panic attacks, Patsy was desperate. She was the equivalent of a breathing corpse. Something had to change.

One morning while she was hiding beneath her blanket, Patsy heard her Savior's still, small voice whisper to her tormented heart: *"Make your bed."*

Patsy felt powerless to address the mountain of problems in her life, but by golly, she could make her bed. And thereby couldn't continue wallowing in it. She had to get up and put one shaky foot in front of the other on the rocky road back to real life.

Surprisingly, I ran across those same three words in the Acts passage above. Aeneas had been a bedridden paralytic for eight years when the apostle Peter visited his hometown, Lydda.

The Bible doesn't say, but I'm sure Aeneas dreamed of his pre-paralyzed days when he ran through a field in the sunshine, walked to work, and tended his vegetable garden. He felt vital . . .productive. . .useful.

Then one day, like Patsy, he wasn't.

Get up. Make your bed.

In essence, return to the business of *living.*

Three simple words were astounding game changers in the lives of Aeneas and Patsy. How do they apply to us today?

Perhaps it has to do with motivation. With taking the first step away from stagnancy and moving forward, shucking our old normal and seeking a *better* normal. For what if complacency is robbing us of the "more" Papa wants us to be?

Great Restorer,
Help me be obedient
today to "make my bed."

Replenishing Joy

Weeping may endure for a night,
but joy comes in the morning.
PSALM 30:5 NKJV

My friend Darlene grew up in a community of believers, enjoying close relationships with her family, church, and Lord during her first eighteen years.

When she left for college, Darlene drifted away from the Christian life. Although her beliefs didn't change, her behavior did. You could no longer see Jesus in her actions or hear Him in her voice.

Years later, Darlene married Jerry, a handsome pilot, and bought land on a residential grass airfield. They built a hangar for Jerry's three airplanes and lived in a small apartment inside the hangar while their dream house was under construction.

One day Darlene heard a terrifying sound. . .Jerry's plane spiraling out of control as it went down near their airfield. He was killed in the horrific crash.

Darlene soon realized she was in deep trouble. . .a widow over five hundred miles from family with a house to complete and a business to run. Alone.

Faith was all she had left.

Darlene began actively seeking renewal of the relationship with Jesus she'd left behind. He was waiting with arms outstretched. She asked the Holy Spirit to guide her actions, words, and thoughts; and she found other dedicated minds and spirits in Bible studies, mentor relationships, and a local church.

Best of all, Darlene found joy again.

Have you ever drifted away from your faith? Or turned your back intentionally, perhaps due to disappointment, distrust, or pain?

Make no mistake, Jesus will *always* be waiting, with arms outstretched, to welcome you back and replenish your joy.

Ever-Faithful Savior,
I love that You offer me
Your joy, new every morning,
even after my darkest night.

Freedom

It is for freedom that Christ has set us free.
GALATIANS 5:1 NIV

Independence Day. For you, does that conjure up visions of a cocky Will Smith shouting, "I coulda been at a barbecue!" while lugging a nasty alien from his crashed spacecraft, dreadlocks dragging auspiciously behind? (Google the film clip for a good laugh!)

Or do you envision fireworks, parades, baseball games, and political speeches?

I suppose the phrase means different things to different people.

Most Americans associate it with the historic adoption of the Declaration of Independence, our proclamation of liberty from Britain on July 4, 1776. The day thirteen American colonies birthed "a new nation, conceived in liberty and dedicated to the proposition that all men are created equal." (Can't believe I still remember that from the fifth grade!)

Other countries have their own version of Independence Day; everyone once belonged to somebody, right?

But belonging to someone else, adhering to their rules and regulations, being told what to do and when grows old. People yearn for freedom. For autonomy. For independence.

Happens in the workplace, a bad marriage, with teenagers, and of course, with our founding fathers (and founding mothers; mustn't forget them!).

So let's spend some time today honoring their grit, sacrifices, and perseverance in acquiring the freedom we enjoy today.

Oh, a bit of interesting historical trivia: Thomas Jefferson and John Adams, the only signers of the Declaration of Independence who became US presidents, both died on July 4, 1826—the fiftieth anniversary of the date they signed.

Run that up the flagpole at your barbecue and see who salutes.

*Father of Freedom,
I love my country. Thank You
for the liberties I sometimes
take for granted: [Okay, start
listing them, sweet thang.]*

Weeding the Patch

"For God so loved the world that He gave His
only begotten Son, that whoever believes in Him
should not perish but have everlasting life."
JOHN 3:16 NKJV

Today's familiar verse assures us that *whoever* believes in the Gospel of Jesus Christ can hang out with Him for all eternity. Sounds pretty nondiscriminatory, right?

The trouble comes when we take it upon ourselves to assist the Almighty by weeding out the dandelions that don't fit into our tomato patch. We don't like anything or anyone that's different from our personal group of believers.

They make us uncomfortable.

But Jehovah doesn't want us all to be tomatoes.

I'd venture to say He actually loves the people we consider weeds. . .believers with pierced tongues, purple hair, gothic attire, eyeball to toenail tattoos, or even—*heaven forbid!*—bad breath.

I've been involved in a variety of Christian communities from the extremes of the frozen chosen to the wild and wacky woolen. Worship styles differ broadly among believers, making it easy to criticize those who, in our humble but accurate opinions, "Amen" too loudly or too often, drop to their knees or raise their hands, sing the wrong kind of songs, dress too casually, recite too much liturgy (or not enough), or worst of all, read from the wrong Bible translation.

In a perfect world, all believers would worship their Creator together, unified in bringing glory to God. But in our fallen world, diversity often breeds prejudice: Democrats detest Republicans; races struggle to get along; and religious extremists invoke fear.

How marvelous that the Most High always has and always will love dandelions as much as He loves tomatoes.

Creator of Tomatoes
AND Tomahtoes,
Help me see the dandelions
in my patch today through
Your eyes, not mine.

Breakdown

*It's good for a man to have a wife,
and for a woman to have a husband.*
1 CORINTHIANS 7:2 MSG

It starts out with romance and roses, a luscious wedding cake, gorgeous beaded dress, and the promise of endless joy-filled tomorrows.

Then something mysterious happens. Somewhere along the winding road of unity, erosion creates a few potholes, roadblocks, and maybe a detour or two. The marriage vehicle blows a tire and crashes into a YIELD sign. The disillusioned bride and groom are left standing on the side of the road asking, "What happened?"

In all honesty, it befalls all of us at some point.

But we don't have to abandon our wrecked car and hitchhike. Nope. We can change the flat, repair the damage, fill 'er up with brand-new fuel, and climb back in to continue our lifelong journey to happily ever after.

How?

For the next three days, we're going to explore the story of a biblical gal, found in 1 Samuel 18 and 19, who started out in a sizzling romance but refused to stoke the relationship fires and let the embers go cold. I believe there's a lot we can learn from her mistakes.

Michal (she was actually a princess, King Saul's daughter) had been secretly in love with David, her father's political archenemy and quite the hottie, for some time. David was the early version of a rock star, revered by pretty much everyone. . .except Saul. David was the up-and-comer, favored by God and man; uptight Saul feared for his crown and rightly so (he eventually lost his kingship to David).

More tomorrow. . .

*Mighty Yahweh,
Thank You for thinking of
marriage. Where else could
I be gifted with Godiva and
still scratch where it itches?*

Risking Everything

So Michal let David down through a window,
and he fled and escaped.
1 SAMUEL 19:12 NIV

(Continued)

Michal stood helplessly by as her father promised her older sister to David (Michal's poster boy) in marriage. But wait—yay! Pop reneged.

Then, when a servant ratted out Michal's secret crush, she was used as a pawn by dear ole Dad to coerce patriotic David into avenging the king's enemies. Saul hoped David would be killed in battle, but when David instead became a military hero, Saul was obligated to give Michal to David in marriage.

Ah, the man of her dreams was finally hers.

At first, Michal loved David passionately—enough to deceive her father and risk provoking the schizoid whose nasty temper could have easily resulted in her own death. She helped David flee for his life in a daring midnight escape.

After Michal facilitated her true love's flight to freedom, her revengeful jerk of a father married her off to another man in David's absence. David too took at least two other wives while he was constantly running and hiding from Saul.

Honestly, I can't imagine why anyone would want to have more than one spouse. . .too many socks to keep off the floor.

Anyway, during the years following, Michal must have lost all hope of ever seeing David again. Living with him in a real marriage looked impossible. Her father, the all-powerful king, seethed with hatred toward David and ruthlessly hunted him down, vowing to rip him to shreds.

Princessing definitely has its downfalls.

Stay tuned for more. . .

King of All,
As a daughter of the one true
King, I'm glad I can rest securely
in Your love and not worry about
my tyrannical father trading me
like a baseball card.

Gag the Nag

*When she [Michal] saw King David leaping and dancing
before the Lord, she despised him in her heart.*
2 Samuel 6:16 niv

(Continued)

After Michal's forced remarriage, we don't know if she shifted her allegiance to the new husband or if she kept pining away for David, growing more and more disconsolate over the unfairness of life.

I suspect the latter.

Time passed. Lots happened before David was finally crowned king of Israel in Saul's place and Michal was returned to his household. But she was now just "one of the girls" instead of his adored one and only. To make matters worse, she was barren, a source of shame in that culture, while David's other wives spit out babies like watermelon seeds.

Michal grew bitter and haughty in spirit. She and David had little quality time together, and when they did, she allowed her critical tongue to fan the flames of discontent.

Michal's ungratefulness dictated her thinking, attitude, and behavior. She became a nag. She started whining and wouldn't shut up. Her affection for her once-beloved husband turned into contempt. She criticized him openly and ridiculed him for celebrating before the Lord.

The Bible doesn't say what finally became of Michal—except that she remained childless until her death—but it's a sure bet her relationship with David spiraled downward. I'm guessing there weren't many more opportunities to make babies with the man she continually criticized.

I believe Papa God includes Michal's story in the Bible as an example for our own marriages. Michal didn't ask for all the lousy things that happened to her, but she refused to redeem her circumstances by managing her attitude.

More tomorrow. . .

*Exalted One,
Empower me to redeem
my circumstances,
stop criticizing my husband,
and gag the nag.*

Crank It Up

*Love never gives up, never loses faith, is always hopeful,
and endures through every circumstance.*
1 CORINTHIANS 13:7 NLT

(Continued)

So what are the elements that contributed to Michal and David's relationship erosion?

- Separation—physical and emotional.
- Allowing situations over which you have no control to make you bitter.
- A runaway, critical tongue.
- Focusing on what you *don't* have rather than being grateful for what you do.

Do you recognize any of these in your own marriage?

In retrospect, these are all elements that I too have been guilty of allowing to creep into my marriage during our difficult patches—times when our marital vehicle ran off the road. I feel sure that the key to our marriage finding its way back on track repeatedly for nearly forty years is found in number four above. It can be nutshelled into one word: *gratitude*.

If we seek a spirit of gratitude and make it a priority to renew our grateful attitudes daily, numbers one through three will become nonissues. Those potholes we talked about in "Breakdown"—emotional distance, bitterness, and destructive criticism—will be paved over with humbleness, patience, and generosity of spirit.

And our marital Edsel won't break down nearly so often.

Best of all, we won't be tempted to ditch the old boring model and upgrade. If we just put forth a little more elbow grease and polish up the tarnished chassis, we may actually begin to respect and admire it just like when it was new and shiny.

> *Generator of Fresh Attitudes,
> Help me crank up gratitude
> within my marriage today:
> to focus on constructing rather
> than destructing. It's awfully
> hard to stab my man while
> I'm holding his hand.*

Priceless

How priceless is your unfailing love, O God!
PSALM 36:7 NIV

I mop the sweat from my forehead with my sodden wristband. Summer tennis has its downside.

Ah, but its upside—sunshine, much-needed exercise, and that dear little buttercup by the net post growing in a sea of pavement. That little sweetie has overcome the odds to sprout in a toenail-sized crack.

I comment on the buttercup's inspiring tenacity to the three guys sharing my court. Their responses flabbergast me.

Man #1: "How did that thing get there? I'll yank it up when we switch sides."

Man #2: "Got weed killer in my trunk."

Man #3: "Oh, man. It's gonna drive me crazy until we rip it out."

Now, I understand experience colors their view—these are all men who've been trained for years by society (and their wives) to seek and destroy any extraneous entities defacing their immaculate lawns. And I realize that buttercups are, by most standards, considered weeds.

But my childhood memories are rich with dewy buttercups dotting the fields by my house, perfect for holding under my sister's chin to confirm her affinity for butter and gathering in a lovely bouquet to express everlasting love to my mama. To me, they're exquisite flowers straight from Papa God.

These guys, however, will not be swayed. Weeds: Rip. Kill. Destroy.

So we must agree to disagree. It's a matter of perspective: vexation versus inspiration, pesky weed versus purveyor of pleasure, worthless versus priceless.

Sort of like how we categorize people, isn't it? Based on our limited experience, we consider them either weeds or flowers, worthless or priceless.

Perhaps our perspective needs tweaking.

*Father of All Mankind,
Today, let me see others
through Your eyes: no
weeds, only buttercups.*

Hot Mess

I'm a mess. I'm nothing. . .make something of me.
PSALM 40:17 MSG

Ever feel like an unfocused, disjointed, hot mess when it comes to praying? You're not alone, sister. Here's the sound track from my typical 5:00 a.m. prayer walk:

Tell me again why we're up so early, Lord.

Really, would it have caused an earthquake for me to sleep another half hour? The whole world's on snooze. Except me. And that raccoon by those bushes. Look, is that a bloom? Can't tell IN THE DARK! Been so warm the plants think spring has sprung. Shoot. I didn't even get to wear my new sweater this winter. It's really cute with the black leggings.

Okay. . .um. . .please bless my parents, kids, and grands today. They. . .oh, man—I forgot I'm babysitting tonight. Listen, Papa, can You keep the sick baby from coughing all over me? Got a speaking gig coming up; can't afford to get croupy. Hey, remember that birthday when I had that nasty cold and hocked up a wad of phlegm onto my birthday cake when I blew out the candles? Ha! What a hoot. . . .

Wait. Focus.

So. . .I give You my writing today, Lord. . . . Will ya look at that—did my neighbor get a new car? I could use a new car too, ya know. Maybe a light color so I don't have to wash it. . . .

Yep. My prayer time can be pretty pathetic; I picture Papa God rolling His eyes, setting the phone down, and preventing another war while He waits for me to get to the point.

I admit I need a little work.

So. . .how focused are your prayers?

Most Patient God,
Mold this hot mess into a
powerful prayer warrior.
And can You make mine silver?

The Quilt

*Do not forget the things your eyes have seen or let
them fade from your heart.... Teach them to your children.*
DEUTERONOMY 4:9 NIV

I was devastated. I'd searched everywhere, but my grandmother's quilt was nowhere to be found. Having just returned from her funeral, my heart was in tatters.

Granny had pieced the quilt together with mismatched snippets of fabric cut from old tablecloths, curtains, even my mother's baby clothes. I remember the day she gave it to me, caressing the faded fabric with her age-gnarled fingers. "It was made with love a long time ago," she'd crooned in her Georgia drawl. "Now that you're getting married, I want you to have it."

I accepted the gift but wondered what in the world I would do with the hodgepodge thing. It certainly didn't match the decor of my brand-new apartment. I was twenty-one, and the old had little priority among the building blocks of my new life.

Years passed, and the aging quilt was often thrown into closets or stuffed under beds. The kids played on it under a tree in the yard and used it as a beach blanket. It kept us warm at ball games and protected us from the elements on camping trips.

The quilt became quite frayed, but it never occurred to me that it mattered. I took for granted that the old comforter would always be there, just like Granny.

But one day the quilt disappeared. Soon after, Granny passed away at age ninety-four.

At last I understood what a priceless link to my heritage it truly was. I *needed* that quilt. But how would I ever find it?

Continued tomorrow...

*Master of My Past,
Present, and Future,
Help me value the links that
tie generations together.*

Preserving Precious Memories

*We will tell the next generation the
praiseworthy deeds of the Lord.*
PSALM 78:4 NIV

(Continued)

Tears dropped onto my bare foot as I curled up in my armchair. I yearned to hold my grandmother's quilt, that invaluable link to my past. But it was lost. All because of my own carelessness.

Why had I not realized the value of preserving my connection with the one whose name and faith I share? (Granny was Nellie Ruth; I'm Debora Ruth.) I prayed for Papa God to somehow reunite me with the quilt, painstakingly sewn by hand with bits of my heritage.

Months later, while rummaging through a crate of long-forgotten camping equipment in the attic, I discovered Granny's quilt. My heart flooded with memories and my eyes flooded with tears as I clutched the musty material. "I've missed you so much!" I told the quilt, really speaking to the woman whose careworn hands had fashioned the priceless keepsake.

When Papa God restored the lost quilt, I learned a valuable lesson: transgenerational ties are important and should be protected and cherished. In fact, as I write these words, I'm gazing at Granny's quilt now displayed in a place of honor on the wall of my writing cave (office).

You may think it's my overactive imagination, but when I admire the delicate workmanship and run my fingers over the faded cloth that my grandmother lovingly fashioned into a fabric story of my life—and hers—I feel the warmth of her smile. She's right here beside me once again.

What family keepsake binds your heart with the loved ones of your past?

*God of Generations,
Many thanks for those who
came before me, passing
down not just my knobby
knees but faith in You.*

Prune Smoothies

We will not compare ourselves with each other....
Each of us is an original.
GALATIANS 5:26 MSG

Forty-something Josie got fed up with her thinning eyelashes and paid an ex-aesthetician to fit her with a beautiful new set of falsies (eyelashes, not boobies).

"I only wanted to look pretty," Josie said, shaking her head. "First she glued my eyes shut while applying the eyelashes. Then when she finally got them unstuck, my eyes were flaming red from the adhesive. When the eyelashes hardened, the darn things were so long they kept hitting my glasses so I couldn't blink. They were like spikes sticking out of my eye sockets. I felt like a Goth drag queen."

Yep, the aging process causes thinning of some body parts and thickening of others. We don't know whether to pad them or pound them.

Aging is a peculiar thing. . .just when you begin to grow into your skin, it outgrows you. And the extra has nowhere to go except hang there all crinkled up like a discarded Snickers wrapper.

My lifelong bestie Jan and I were discussing this when she grabbed the sides of her face and pulled back as if she were adjusting a drooping Edgar suit (remember that audacious *Men in Black* scene?). "See," she exclaimed, "I still look good!"

This launched an animated discussion about the merits of alligator clips behind the ears.

My aging motto is: if you can't fix it, decorate it. I learned this principle from a broken-down mailbox in my neighborhood. When draped with cheerful fall flowers, the depressing, decrepit thing took on a cheerful, uplifting personality.

Hey, what works for broken-down mailboxes can work for broken-down bodies too!

Yahweh,
As I ripen, please keep
everything working.
Those prune smoothies
are a real drag.

Shadow of the Hawk

In God I trust and am not afraid.
PSALM 56:11 NIV

My woodsy backyard is home to many critters. Once, a very noisy skirmish between the possum clan and fox tribe drew Spouse from his nice warm bed at 3:00 a.m. to call a truce by whacking a baseball bat against the metal door. Sadly, a casualty of war ended up beneath our porch drawing flies. Pew-eee!

Death is part of nature's cycle, I know, but I don't want to smell it beneath my floorboards. Or witness it either.

Which is why I've developed a strong aversion to hawks. They come by the squadrons, stalking the innocent baby squirrels and sweet birdies that call my yard home.

My furry friends will be scampering about, playing chase or frolicking merrily when they suddenly freeze. A dark shadow passes over the yard as a hawk soars overhead. Suddenly the lightning-quick carnivore swoops down and snatches a hapless victim.

So my woodland friends have learned to fear the shadow of the hawk.

Many people live in the shadow of a hawk too. . .not the feathered kind, yet a very real predator looming overhead, casting a fearful shadow that immobilizes momentum and steals joy.

Hawks can be unemployment, illness, rejection, loneliness, conflicts, pain. . .even the unknown future. Anything that makes us constantly worry that one day that hawk will swoop down and snatch our security away.

Know what? I'm tired of cowering in the shadow of my personal hawks, aren't you? Let's focus on how to protect ourselves when the shadow of the hawk darkens our path.

*Divine Protector,
Sign me up for a spiritual BB
gun. Or maybe a cruise missile.*

The Fifty-Sixth Cake

My God will meet all your needs.
PHILIPPIANS 4:19 NIV

I was excited to be speaking at a gala women's event celebrating chocolate. Woo-hoo! Gonna get my bad choco-self *down*!

Many prayers had petitioned Papa God to move at this community outreach event, and apparently He'd already begun—a week ahead, four hundred tickets had been sold. Fifty fancy chocolate layer cakes were ordered from a local bakery to double as table centerpieces and dessert.

Now these were not just Betty Crocker potluck cakes. . .they were luscious, three-layer, culinary works of art, adorned with ornate chocolate curlicues and doodads that make saliva spurt like a fire hose.

Two days before the event, a passel of ticket sales came in; another five cakes were rush-ordered. Pickup was scheduled only hours before starting time.

On D-Day, as Leah, the designated cake-picker-upper, drove to the bakery, she received a frantic call. Ten more last-minute tickets had been purchased. Another table would be added. Another cake would be needed.

"But there's no way they can make another cake that fast," Leah responded. "Those fifty-five cakes were custom-made just for us. I'll have to get a plain chocolate cake. Pray they even have one."

Alas, the display case was chocolate-less.

In near panic, Leah explained the situation to the white-aproned lady behind the counter. "Is there anything you can do?"

"Why, I believe there is," she said, a big smile spreading across her face. "I'm the baker. Wait right here."

Within seconds, she reappeared holding a beautifully decorated cake *exactly* like the other fifty-five.

"Something told me I should make an extra cake."

*Jehovah Jireh (Our Provider),
Help me trust You to meet all
my needs today, big and small.
And chocolate.*

Lost Hearts

Why is my heart so sad? I will put my hope in God!
PSALM 43:5 NLT

Seven tear-filled days had passed since we'd made the agonizing decision to put our beloved dog Dusty to sleep. Age had taken his sight, hearing, and health, but it could never steal his devotion. Nor mine. I was a disaster.

I prayed for Papa to heal my heartache as I drove dinner over to a sick friend's house.

The traffic was bumper-to-bumper. Suddenly I noticed a matted-fur bush atop four legs weaving through the busy lanes of traffic. Cars swerved, but it was only a matter of time before one didn't.

I hit my brakes. The fur bush stopped too. I looked down. He looked up.

"Are you lost?" I asked through my open window.

What must've been a tail wagged. Two liquid brown eyes studied me through thick tangles of fur matted like dreads. He cocked his head as if considering, and then a light sparked in his eyes. I'd swear he smiled. I opened my car door, and he leapt into my arms as if he'd been looking for me all along.

I knew at once he was a lost, lonely soul who'd recognized the same condition in me. I was submerged in dirt, brambles, and wet doggy kisses. It was love at first snuggle.

The vet later said that judging by his protruding bones; filthy, overgrown coat; and thickly calloused paws, he'd been on his own for a long, long time.

I have no doubt that divine orchestration united two lost hearts. Isn't that just like Papa God?

Dryer of Tears,
Thank You for replacing
mine with joy.

Blessed Friends Forever

And be kind to one another.
EPHESIANS 4:32 NKJV

Awhile back, when our extended family was at our mountain cabin (I'm talking *f-a-r* from civilization here), my eighty-five-year-old mother fell, sustaining a deep cut on her forearm. It bled like a stuck pig and wouldn't stop.

It was the middle of the night, no stores anywhere, and the only wound dressing available was a Spiderman Band-Aid.

After a whole paper towel roll failed to stymie the blood flow, my clever sister Cindy went closet foraging and found a long forgotten box of Kotex—you know, the big, fat, old-fashioned '70s kind. Thankfully, the mountain mice hadn't made a nest with them in the drawers like they sometimes do with shredded Kleenex.

Worked like a charm!

So well, in fact, by the next morning we were able to downgrade to a panty liner Scotch-taped to Mama's arm. Classy, right?

I mentioned our little medical misadventure to a couple of girlfriends via email in the morning, and that afternoon, up drives the UPS truck, traversing tight mountain ledges to deliver a handy dandy first-aid kit, compliments of my dear friend Gloria.

Now who in the world is that stinkin' thoughtful?

A BFF (Blessed Friend Forever), that's who.

Gloria's above-and-beyond act of kindness touched me deeply. It inspired me to bless others with little acts of kindness too. After all, aren't BFFs here to take care of each other?

*Ever-Loving Savior,
Help me bless at least
one person today
through an act of
kindness in Your name.*

Clueless

Anything you do against your beliefs is sin.
ROMANS 14:23 CEV

Checking my email, I was floored to see a message from an old friend I hadn't heard from in ages. Although we lived on opposite sides of the country, Linda had been one of my bridesmaids, and we'd upheld and supported each other through the early challenges of marriage and raising children.

I had long puzzled about the abrupt halt of communication when Linda suddenly stopped responding to my cards, calls, and emails with no explanation.

"Linda, is that really you?" I typed. "Where've you been?"

Linda confessed that she'd been nursing wounds from a comment I'd made that hurt her feelings five years ago. *Five years!*

I was stunned. I hadn't a clue that I'd caused the rift. What a waste of what might have been a thriving, vital relationship that could have benefited us both. Misunderstanding and resentment had stolen joy and blessings from something **as rare** and precious as friendship.

How very tragic. How very sad.

Pride tried to rear its ugly head to convince me that unintentional sin isn't really sin. But no. I knew that I had wrongly wounded Linda, and wounds bleed the same whether they're inflicted intentionally or not.

So I asked forgiveness from Linda for my careless words; she graciously gave it. And we started afresh.

Could it be time for a fresh start in one of your relationships too?

*Prince of Peace,
Spotlight the unresolved sins in
my life, especially the ones I'm
clueless about. I want to stop
the bleeding of wounds I've
unintentionally inflicted. Today.*

Magical Mystery Words

How priceless is your unfailing love, O God!
PSALM 36:7 NIV

The anonymous text appeared on my phone out of nowhere: I LOVE YOU.

At first I was confused. . . . Was this a joke? There was no name attached, only an unfamiliar phone number. *Hmm.* How sweet. How bizarre. Maybe they meant to send it to someone else and mistakenly snagged me.

Or maybe not.

I LOVE YOU.

Like a magnet I simply couldn't resist, I kept pulling out my phone to gaze at those three magical words. Someone was mightily blessing me today—but who?

I was amazed at the effect this powerful and mysterious declaration of affection had on me. All day long I felt warm and fuzzy. I found myself grinning for no reason. My shoulders de-slumped. My beige world turned Technicolored.

Wow. I was worthy of someone's love. Someone who was not obligated to say it like a family member or bestie. Someone who chose to drop the l-bomb for no apparent self-serving reason and then remain unknown.

Someone who just wanted to bless my socks off by gifting me with the highest verbal affirmation known to mankind: I love you.

Then it became strangely unimportant to learn the source of this unexpected joy. Even if it was a mistake, it wasn't. It was a love note from someone acting as Papa God's tangible texting fingers on earth, reminding me how valued and cherished I am.

Ohhhh, yeah. Something we *all* need to feel, especially on those joy-sucking dully-funk days.

*Greater Love Than
I Can Fathom,
Bring someone to mind
today who'd benefit from an
anonymous love note. Use me
as Your tangible fingers on
earth to remind them just how
cherished they are.*

Flattened

*On the seventh day, they got up at daybreak and. . .circled
the city [Jericho] seven times. The seventh time around. . .
Joshua commanded the army, "Shout! For the Lord has given you
the city! The city and all that is in it are to be devoted to the Lord."*
JOSHUA 6:15–17 NIV

Jen, age fifty, was devastated when she was diagnosed with stage 4 liver cancer. She'd suffered no major symptoms. So that day in the doctor's office, she felt as if she'd been flattened by a dump truck.

A believer, Jen prayed for a special sign from God that He hadn't abandoned her. She needed to feel His presence in a tangible way during this fight for her life.

Not long after, Jen's family went boating in the Gulf of Mexico. The boat anchored a mile offshore so Jen's son and his friend could swim. Jen sat on the side of the boat, dangling her feet into the calm blue water.

Out of nowhere, a dolphin appeared and circled the boat seven times, rising up to look Jen in the eyes and allow her to pet him each time. Jen knew this beautiful animal was bringing Papa God's special message. She was not alone, not now, not ever. Whether at sea, in a hospital, or in heaven, her heavenly Father would be right there by her side.

Not a dry eye on that boat.

Perhaps your eyes are leaking too. Can you identify with Jen's need for assurance? Even in non-life-threatening circumstances, we all need to know with certainty that Papa has our backs.

Rest assured, my friend. He does. He does.

*Steadfast Lord,
Like today's verse, I am Jericho.
Circle my walls so that when
they come tumblin' down, all
that I am will be devoted to You.*

Life Savers

Happy are those who are strong in the Lord.
PSALM 84:5 TLB

It started with one short, pithy, powerful scripture I really wanted to remember. I sticky-noted it to my bathroom mirror.

The next week I found another.

Today, *forty-two* sticky notes cover my mirror, and this is the second batch! I had to take the first fifty down when Spouse complained that he could no longer see his face in the mirror to brush his teeth.

I call them Life Savers—oh-so-sweet verses, each only twenty words or less, that have become absorbed by my mind and melted into my heart.

Scores of women I've shared my Life Savers with at my speaking events say it's the most uncomplicated, user-friendly system for scripture memorization they've seen. So I'd like to share it with you too, sister.

Here's how it works: each month you'll meditate on one new Life Saver. The first day of the month, you memo that Life Saver on your i-device and jot it on sticky notes to post in all the places you'll be sure to notice. . .your mirror, car console, your Godiva stash.

Then every time you see your "Flavor of the Month," repeat it aloud three times; the flavor comes through best when you wrap your tongue around it. Consider the meaning of each word. Savor the Saver. Suck the joy out of that spiritual treat until it's completely digested and permanently implanted in your innards.

You'll be amazed at how many times Papa uses that very verse to speak *to* you and *through* you. And the best part is, God's Word will be with you for the rest of your life.

Let's share some Life Savers tomorrow. . .

Keeper of Your Word,
Fill me with its sweetness.

Sweet. Totally.

I have hidden your word in my heart.
PSALM 119:11 NLT

Okay, ready for some of my Life Savers? Collect your own; Papa God has hundreds of flavors to choose from!

- "God is greater than our worried hearts" (1 John 3:20 MSG).
- "Where there is no wood, the fire goes out" (Proverbs 26:20 NKJV).
- "'I will watch my ways and keep my tongue from sin; I will put a muzzle on my mouth'" (Psalm 39:1 NIV).
- "'I will not sacrifice to the LORD my God. . .offerings that cost me nothing'" (2 Samuel 24:24 NIV).
- "Guard against corruption from the godless world" (James 1:27 MSG).
- "Kindness should begin at home" (1 Timothy 5:4 TLB).
- "Don't hit back; discover beauty in everyone" (Romans 12:17 MSG).
- "Be decent and true in everything you do" (Romans 13:13 TLB).
- "A gentle tongue can break a bone" (Proverbs 25:15 NIV).
- "You know me inside and out, you hold me together" (Psalm 41:12 MSG).
- "I begged for your help, and you answered my prayer" (Jonah 2:2 CEV).
- "'Is anything too hard for the LORD?'" (Genesis 18:14 NIV).
- "I love you, GOD—you make me strong" (Psalm 18:1 MSG).
- "He knows the secrets of the heart" (Psalm 44:21 NIV).
- "I'm so grateful to Christ Jesus for making me adequate to do this work" (1 Timothy 1:12 MSG).
- "Don't fret or worry. Instead of worrying, pray" (Philippians 4:6 MSG).
- "Encourage one another and build each other up" (1 Thessalonians 5:11 NIV).
- "Let your living spill over into thanksgiving" (Colossians 2:7 MSG).

My Rock,
Help me always remember
that God's Word = God's
strength; when I store Your
Word in my heart, Your
strength will be there, too.

Preconceived Ideas

Humble yourselves before God.
JAMES 4:7 NLT

The call from the women's center was surprising: "We've got a homeless woman here who lives in her car. She's written a book and wants to pursue publication. Since you're an author, could you speak to her?"

I cringed. "Well, I'm kind of busy right now with two speaking events to prepare for and a book proposal my agent wanted yesterday."

No reply.

Enter conscience. I *had* volunteered to help the charity "in any way I can." Sigh. Time to put my conviction where my mouth is.

So regardless of my preconceived notion that this would be a waste of valuable time, I met with Lyndy in a church lobby to discuss her manuscript in air-conditioned comfort.

Having fallen on hard times, Lyndy was a bit rough around the edges but articulate and educated. She'd painstakingly typed her book on a computer at the public library.

Lyndy's tension was palpable as she handed me her manuscript; fear and distrust clouded her eyes. I thought at any minute she might snatch the bundle of papers from my hands and bolt for the door. But after I'd read the first chapter and assured her it was fascinating and well written, her smile was absolutely radiant.

Despite my initial selfishness, I was blessed to be able to encourage this aspiring writer who had received only discouragement from life.

We hugged as kindred spirits when we parted ways, me to my nice home in a safe neighborhood and her to her rusty car packed with all her earthly possessions.

Yet I was the one most humbled.

*Upholder of All Your Children,
Please forgive my preconceived
ideas that prevent me from
discovering and delighting in
Your divine surprises.*

The Past Has Passed

*Rahab the harlot. . .Joshua spared. . .for she hid the
messengers whom Joshua sent to spy out Jericho.*
JOSHUA 6:25 NASB

She was the unlikeliest of heroes—a prostitute, a woman who sold her body to lusty men in the darkest of shadows.

Scum, we would say today.

Yet Rahab was the very person the Almighty chose to save the keisters of the Israeli spies in the Promised Land.

And He didn't stop there. Rahab, a Gentile harlot (that's *two* strikes against her!) became the mother-in-law of Ruth and was a vital link in the lineage of King David, and later, Jesus Christ Himself.

Did you catch that? Rahab, nasty past and all, was an ancestor of the Savior of the world! Papa God could have chosen *anyone* to occupy that place of honor in history, yet He chose a broken, used-goods, majorly flawed hooker.

How utterly like Papa God.

Rahab was inducted into the Faithful Hall of Fame (Hebrews chapter 11) along with some major league heavy hitters: Noah, Abraham, Sarah, Moses. Lowly little Rahab, despite her shameful past, was held up as a sterling example of faithfulness right alongside the sluggers.

How about that—a former call girl is our role model!

How astoundingly freeing! Especially for those of us who may be ashamed of our past or feel that we've strayed too far from God to ever be useful to Him. Papa loved Rahab for who she *was*, not what she *did*.

Rahab is proof that the Creator of the universe can—and will—use anyone for His higher purposes. *Anyone.* Even you and me.

*Living God,
How I love makeovers!
Rahab is the epitome of life
makeovers. If a lady of the
evening can do it, so can I!*

Humor Thy Father and Mother

"Please. . . Bless my family;
keep your eye on them always."
2 SAMUEL 7:29 MSG

As a child, I was as round as I was tall. I loved butter sandwiches and sugar on my cheese toast. As a twelve-year-old, I hit a gargantuan five feet three inches and dwarfed my teensy relatives at family reunions (Granddaddy was five feet even and begat four daughters even shorter than him).

I was a moose in a mouse family.

To tip the scales at one hundred pounds was unheard of for the females in our extended family, and I vividly recall my mother's horrified gasp when I scored an eye-popping 106 pounds at a doctor's appointment in the sixth grade.

So Mama became my food conscience. "Put that down!" and "You don't need that" were her mantras. She commented on every bite that entered my mouth until I finally left for college and indulged my newfound freedom by surpassing the freshman fifteen by ten pounds.

Every time I visited home for the next thirty years, Mama never missed an opportunity to slide in an editorial comment, "Oh, sweetheart, these pants belonged to Cousin Elsie. She passed, you know. They're *w-a-y* too big for your sister or me; I thought you could wear them. . . ."

Then, miracle of miracles, at age fifty, I finally bit the bullet instead of Godiva, and by the grace of God shed forty pounds.

When Mama saw me after my transformation, her jaw dropped. Her first words were, "Oh my goodness! You look terrible! You need to eat!"

Sigh. Sometimes ya just can't win.

Creator of Wacky Families,
You chose my relatives for me.
Good thing I like fruits and nuts.
Please help me keep my sense of
humor and just keep loving 'em.

Practice Makes Perfect

Practice hospitality.
ROMANS 12:13 NIV

Derelict shanties lined the Sibun River as it wound through dense tropical jungles in the Caribbean country of Belize. James, our native guide and inflatable boat caravan leader, pointed out manatees, crocodiles, and howler monkeys during our meandering twenty-mile trek.

When we needed a bathroom break, James led us to a dock where we tied our boats and followed him down a dirt path to a small wooden shack. A gracious dusky-skinned woman threw open her cracked front door and welcomed us in.

Directed to a dingy commode listing heavily in a bare closet, we skirted piles of laundry and personal belongings littered everywhere. Our host pointed to a sweaty, T-shirted man pounding with a hammer.

"Please forgive mess," she said, smiling. "House needs repair."

Repair? I thought loftily. *You should just knock it down and start over, lady.*

Then it hit me. This woman wasn't ashamed of her home. In fact, she was proud to share what little she had to meet our need. And she did so willingly, with pleasure.

My thoughts shifted to my own unwillingness to open my door to guests unless my house is picked up and tidy. Which, truthfully, is rare. I've neglected opportunities to host others simply for the sake of hospitality—without ego, without pride. To share my home, the gift Jehovah gave me, such as it is.

Does this mean I should give up housecleaning? Yes, please.

Actually, no. It means that I need to follow this hospitable woman's example and do what today's verse says.

*Adonai (Lord),
Hospitality isn't my strong
suit. But You know that.
That's why You said to practice.*

Grinding Grudges

*"First forgive anyone you are holding a grudge against,
so that your Father in heaven will forgive your sins, too."*
MARK 11:25 NLT

Caryl and her husband sold their home to people who moved in but never made payments and destroyed nearly everything in the house before disappearing. The financial liability fell back on Caryl's family; they were soon forced into bankruptcy.

Forgiveness didn't come easy. These people caused deep hurt. They'd carelessly inflicted damage that would continue to cause Caryl's family major financial problems for many years to come. The normal human response would be resentment and bitterness. And maybe a little lust for retribution. Understandable, right?

But Caryl knew her responsibility as a believer was to forgive. Even when the offender didn't ask for it. Even when they didn't deserve it. Even though she didn't *feel* forgiving.

Sometimes we hang on to grudges like an old, elastically challenged bra. Although the droopy thing has lost all semblance of support and allows our bosom buddies to sag to our navels, we've gotten used to it and just keep flopping around in it. We don't realize how beautifully things could be looking up if we only got rid of that ugly, ineffective garment and donned a new one.

"Forgiveness is not a feeling," Caryl says. "It's an act of obedience to God. It's not pretending you weren't hurt; it doesn't condone what they did. It's deciding to not hold it against them any longer. Forgiveness is freeing. It releases you. It released me."

*Master of Mercy,
Give me the freedom that
comes with forgiving someone.
The prisoner that really
needs to be set free is me.*

I've Got a Name

"I have called you by your name; you are Mine."
ISAIAH 43:1 NKJV

Spring 1974: I was a carefree high school junior riding in a senior's Mustang. Marshall said he had something important to share. . .something life-altering. But it had to be done in his car.

As we motored through the piney woods of north Florida, Marshall plugged a Jim Croce tape in his 8-track (these were caveman days) and the silence was stabbed (clever reference to Simon and Garfunkel, same era) by Croce's poignant lyrics, "I got a name; I got a name. . .they can change their minds but they can't change me. . .I got a name, I got a name."

Marshall's blue eyes sparkled with intensity. He'd finally found what he'd been searching for—validation. Affirmation. A sense of self. After years of trying on different personalities, he'd finally grown into self-worth that didn't pinch or chafe like an ill-fitting shoe. At last he felt secure in being the person God made him to be: himself.

I believe we all search for ourselves at different seasons of our lives, because "self" changes like maple tree leaves. The "You" of ten years ago isn't the "You" of today, nor is it the "You" of ten years from now.

Yet while you continually morph, your heavenly Father never changes. He stays the same loving, devoted Papa God who created you and calls you by name. He *knows* you. He's given you an intimate part of Himself: Jesus. You are special to Him. You are His daughter. In this, find security, sweet sister.

*El Olam (The Everlasting God),
How precious it is that among
all the millions who've ever
lived, You know my name. You're
my Papa; I'm Your daughter.
I feel Your love today.*

Sphincter-Pucker Moments

*We will not fear when earthquakes come
and the mountains crumble into the sea.*
PSALM 46:2 NLT

One crisp fall day in the Smokies, I took a spin on my four-wheeler, Sir Lancelot.

As I approached the paved road on the crest of a steep hill, I braked Lance to a rolling stop. Glanced right. . .nothing coming. I craned my neck left to peer around the curve as Lance rolled slowly into the highway.

Suddenly a deep rumble rattled my teeth, and I jerked back right to find the metallic grill of a semitruck bearing down on me.

Fear snatched my breath away. I jammed the accelerator so hard, Lance leapt straight up in the air like a crazed rodeo bull and bucked us both into a heap on the far shoulder of the road. There I sat in a horrified stupor as the truck, horn blasting an almost-too-late rebuke, disappeared around the curve.

I don't think my sphincter muscles will ever recover.

Papa God gave us the emotion of fear for good reason. It serves a useful purpose—to motivate us, move us forward, and keep us from making mistakes. Fear sometimes even saves us from ourselves.

How often would we have skipped school growing up without the disciplining fear of failure? How rotund might we become without fear of regaining those twenty pounds we worked so hard to lose? Why else would we faithfully squash our bosom buddies flat with mammograms without the possibility of that frightening *C* word invading our bodies?

It's when fear becomes controlling that it debilitates. When it alters our course from the splendid women Papa intended us to be and makes us settle for a wimpy, whiny imitation.

*Mighty God,
Give me Your courage
in my sphincter-pucker
moments. I hate dribbles.*

Hear Ye, Hear Ye

Marriage is to be held in honor among all.
HEBREWS 13:4 NASB

Communication in marriage is essential to staying together. Studies show that communication is 7 percent words, 38 percent tone of voice, and 55 percent nonverbal.

After four decades of marital blitz, um, I mean bliss, Spouse has perfected the art of selective hearing. His receiver doesn't always pick up my broadcasted waves and vice versa, so we sometimes accuse each other of faulty amplifiers when it's actually a tower problem.

So I've learned to use as few words as possible, relying heavily on voice tone and body language.

"Nothing" when uttered in reply to his "What's wrong *now*?" actually means "SOMETHING!" The clue is the icy eyes, crossed arms, and clenched lips.

"I don't care!" with a head toss and averted eyes means "You bet your Superman boxers I care!" and he knows he'd better pursue this line of questioning if he wants more than watermelon for supper.

"Just one more minute" means ten if pertaining to logging offline, twenty if applying makeup is involved, and a literal sixty seconds if the trash needs to go out.

Hands on hips and a wagging chicken neck are a sure indication that "Fine!" is creative hyperbole when spewed at the end of an argument. It really means "You're wrong, I'm right, and I refuse to discuss it any longer."

Eyeball rolling is a very effective nonverbal cue. It indicates patience is running thin and he needs to quickly figure out what "Nothing" is before it becomes "Fine!"

Whew. It's all so tiring. Isn't it a relief that Papa God cuts through the fluff and hears our very hearts?

Lover of My Soul,
I so value Your acute hearing.
Thank You for always tuning in.

Blooming

There will be an abundance of
flowers and singing and joy!
ISAIAH 35:2 NLT

Three years ago I planted a beautiful orange hibiscus in my flowerbed. That was the last time I saw it bloom.

Not to say it hasn't grown, not at all. One look at the seven-feet-tall lush plant would make you believe it's thriving. But it *never* blooms.

I don't get it. Sure, I haven't much of a green thumb—it's kinda brownish black—but hey, isn't blooming what flowers are supposed to do? Horticulture 101?

I noticed that my neighbor's hibiscus blooms nonstop all summer. I asked how come, and she said they fertilize regularly and prune the plant back to bare six-inch stalks each winter. Pruning is essential for blooming.

Well. Who knew?

This morning I walked outside after a rainstorm to find my gigantic healthy but barren hibiscus lying on the ground. It had grown so tall its lanky stems couldn't withstand the additional weight of rain collecting on the leaves, and it gave way beneath the strain. *Splat.*

As I stood there shaking my head at its pitiful plight, I realized that people are a lot like hibiscus. We may grow and look like we're doing fine, but if we're not spiritually fed regularly, we won't bloom. We may appear healthy, but we'll never reach our full potential.

And if we're not pruned properly, we'll eventually collapse beneath the weight of storms we simply can't endure.

Thankfully, Papa God is a MUCH better gardener than I, and He knows how to nurture us to our bloomingest.

Master Gardener,
Water me. Fertilize me.
Prune me. Even if the
pruning shears sting.

Got Your Goat

All of us...have strayed.... We have left God's
paths to follow our own. Yet the LORD
laid on him the sins of us all.
ISAIAH 53:6 NLT

One spring morning while I was playing doubles at a rural tennis club, a curious goat shimmied beneath the fence in the pasture adjacent to the court, entering the forbidden domain of a mean-tempered donkey.

That ornery donkey lit off after the goat like a greyhound after a rabbit. Round and round the pasture they ran. The goat skirted fallen trees to elude his pursuer, but the donkey stayed with him, curling back dark lips to a rack of large teeth aiming to nip a plug of goat hiney.

Kathy, my animal-loving tennis partner, dropped her racket, catapulted over the fence, and raced onto the field, wielding a branch overhead as she screamed, "Whoa there, you!"

A most ridiculous parade ensued—Kathy chasing the donkey, chasing the goat like a *Three Stooges* episode.

Someone finally threw open a gate, and the goat headed for the escape route. The gate was slammed behind him, leaving the donkey braying his annoyance while Kathy scrambled over the fence.

Like that foolish goat, we sometimes disregard the boundaries that have been erected for our own protection. Once we've snuck into the off-limits territory, that ole devilish donkey relentlessly pursues us until sin's consequence bites us in the behunkus.

But like today's verse reminds us, God's Son has mercifully rescued us from our just and deserved fate. Jesus accepted the penalty so we can run through the eternity gate, free at last.

Merciful Rescuer,
I see myself in that goat...
curious, mischievous, wandering. Thank You for throwing
open the gate for me.

Apples to Oranges

*Each of you should use whatever gift
you have received to serve others.*
1 PETER 4:10 NIV

Princess Buttercup jumped overboard into Shrieking Eel-infested waters in an attempt to escape the treacherous villain Vizzini but has been recaptured and deposited on the deck, drenched and shivering.

"I suppose you think you're brave, don't you?" sneers Vizzini.

"Only compared to some," she brilliantly replies. (Gotta love *The Princess Bride*!)

Comparison. It's my spiritual gift. I'm quite good at it, had lots of practice.

Actually, I jest. Comparison is *not* a spiritual gift, far from it. But you'd think it must be by the frequency with which many of us practice it.

- I'm the best cook in town.
- Her tush might be smaller, but my bust is bustier.
- I wish my husband had as good a job as hers.
- Their kid got first place in the science fair; mine only got fourth.
- She *must've* had a face-lift; why else would she look younger than me?

Sound familiar? I know, I know. I do it too. But the old saying is true: Comparison is the thief of joy. It's unfair to compare one to another when none of us is finished yet. It's like your gorgeous layer cake competing against my goopy batter. . .different stages in development.

In the comparison game, the scale is rigged by jealousy, prejudice, even runaway hormones. People are unique and incomparable: apples to oranges.

Girlfriend, we can never win when comparing ourselves to others, so please. . .*don't*. It's as suicidal as trying on bathing suits with a skinny friend.

*Generous Lord,
Help me focus on my
personal strengths and use
them to Your glory, not dwell
on my perceived shortcomings
when compared to others.*

Hats Off to Ya

I love you, GOD—you make me strong.
PSALM 18:1 MSG

As you may know, I'm crazy about hats. My closet looks like the Cat in the Hat exploded. I'm continually amazed at the smiles from perfect strangers solicited by my headwear.

Apparently I'm an oddity in American culture; I sometimes feel as if I were born in the wrong century. Or at least the wrong country.

Indeed, I felt quite at home touring the UK—every other British Tom, Dick, and Harriet sported classy head coverings. Hats are still an integral part of everyday life for them. Remember the Royal Wedding? Hey, don't giggle! I lusted after a few of those ridiculously bedecked monstrosities.

Have you ever heard about the scandalous introduction of the top hat into proper society back in 1797? English haberdasher John Hetherington donned his newly created fashion statement and strolled the streets of London, leaving chaos in his wake.

According to the daily post (newspaper, not Facebook), "Passersby panicked at the sight. Women fainted, children screamed, dogs yelped, and an errand boy's arm was broken when he was trampled by the mob."

Good. Heavens. Over a *top hat*?

John was dragged into court for flouting "a tall structure having a shining luster calculated to frighten timid people." Can't say whether he was imprisoned or not, but let's hope he was acquitted on grounds of nonsensible sensibilities.

Despite John's experience, I still say it's okay to be different. Better than okay. It's grand. Yep, it takes guts to chuck the status quo when your heart yearns for more.

So go ahead. Take the risk. Be different. Jesus was.

My hat's off to ya, sister!

Instigator of Creativity,
Help me be myself when
everyone else wants me
to be like them.

The Hard Part

But Jonah ran away from the Lord.
JONAH 1:3 NIV

In my role as the preschool Bible Story Lady at church one Sunday, I told the story of Jonah and the big fish to the four-year-olds.

The hard part wasn't bringing the bit about Jonah deliberately running away from God down to the level of little people who still get their fannies smacked when they run away from adults.

No, they got that all right.

The hard part was how to tell it so they'd understand that some grown-ups are silly enough to think they can hide from an all-knowing, all-seeing, all-powerful God.

So I asked how many of the children like to play hide-and-seek. Every hand went up.

"Have you ever picked a really bad hiding place like this one?" I put my hands over my eyes and said, "Okay, I'm hidden. I can't see you so you can't see me either."

The kids laughed hysterically.

"Or how about this one?" I tried to squeeze my jumbo adult body behind an itty-bitty kiddie chair. "Can you see me now?"

They howled.

"Or maybe you've been here." I returned to center stage, carefully unfolded a paper bag, plopped it over my head, and reached out with both hands—searching, groping, even becoming a little panicky and tearful as I fell to my knees.

Oh, man—I've run out of room and am going to have to continue this story tomorrow. Stay tuned. . .you'll be as astonished as I was at the kids' reaction.

Almighty Jehovah,
Help me always remember that
there's no place I can run where
You aren't already there.

In the Bag

Then Jonah prayed to his God from the belly of the fish.
JONAH 2:1 MSG

(Continued)

Depicting the story of Jonah to preschoolers, I was on my knees, blinded by a paper bag, groping in faux panic. "Did you leave me? Oh no! I'm all alone in this cold, dark, horrible place. And I'm *so* scared. Won't someone help me?"

No laughter this time. Something had resonated with those little people.

I hadn't expected this. Silence, so thick you could cut it with a meat cleaver. I wasn't sure what to do next.

The kids apparently identified with my aloneness, with Jonah in his disobedience. With all humankind when we choose to dig a hole of disrespect to our Creator then lie in it, isolated. . . frightened. . .confused.

Suddenly a little voice piped up. A warm voice heavy with sympathy.

"It's okay, Miss Debbie. We're still here. Don't be afraid. You're not alone."

And then I heard footsteps mounting the stage and felt a tiny hand take mine. Then dozens of hands found me, surrounding me with comfort and hope.

There I was, kneeling on a stage with a bag over my head and a huge lump in my throat, swarmed by a horde of uninhibited children who understood what it felt like to be alone in disobedience and didn't want it to happen to me.

I was incredibly moved.

It was one of those rare teachable moments that knocks your well-ordered world off its axis and cracks open the door for a glimpse into a higher spiritual realm.

Maybe I should carry a head bag around with me all the time.

*All-Knowing God,
You see me even when I can't
see You. Make me aware of
Your loving presence today.*

Feeling Your Pain

*He comforts us when we are in trouble, so that we
can share that same comfort with others in trouble.*
2 CORINTHIANS 1:4 CEV

Our Friday morning neighborhood ladies' Bible study had just begun when Lisa, an occasional attendee, appeared at my front door, visibly shaken and puffy-eyed.

"Can you pray for me?" Her voice broke midsentence. "I have to put my dog down. Pet hospice is coming at three to euthanize him."

We surrounded Lisa and prayed for Papa God to give her His supernatural comfort and peace during this difficult time.

I thought about Lisa all day. She was divorced with grown kids; Chippy was all she had. As much as I didn't want to relive the searing pain of having to put down my own sweet dog, I knew I needed to act as Jesus' ambassador. I canceled my afternoon appointments and went over to Lisa's house at two thirty.

One by one, the other Bible study girls also trickled in to add their support. When the horrible moment finally came, we were a cohesive love force.

We cried with Lisa and laughed through tears over funny Chippy stories. We were Jesus' love with skin on it for Lisa.

Jesus demonstrated the healing power of empathizing with those suffering when He mourned with Mary and Martha over their brother's death. "Jesus wept" (John 11:35 KJV). Jesus chose to enter their grief and feel their pain.

Empathy opens up a channel directly from the heart to the Holy Spirit. We can all be a love conduit if we make ourselves available.

*Compassionate Christ,
You never waste a hurt.
Use me to comfort others
as You have comforted me.*

Shackles of Eeyore

*Then his wife said to him [Job], "Do you still
hold fast your integrity? Curse God and die!"*
JOB 2:9 NASB

She was not the type to see the glass as half-full, or even half-empty. She saw it cracked and drained dry.

We don't even know her name, but Job's wife has a lot to teach us about attitude.

She'd been the unwilling corecipient of Satan's attack against her husband because of his righteous life. She was something of an innocent bystander, dragged along because she happened to be married to the target of the Evil One.

Previous to that, she'd happily shared Job's blessings of wealth, a large family, and good health. Blessings galore!

But when the going got tough, our girl lost faith in the Provider of those blessings. Hope disintegrated. Pessimism emerged. She became the distributor of gloom and doom. Like *Winnie the Pooh*'s Eeyore.

"What's the matter with you?" she likely snarked to her tormented husband as he groveled in the dust, covered in pus and sores. "You've lost everything! How can you still believe God loves you? Give it up. Here's a knife. Why don't you admit faith's a crock and end your misery?"

Job's response is the key for all of us trying to escape the shackles of Eeyore: "I *know* that my Redeemer lives." In the midst of all his suffering, he *knew*. Without a doubt.

Mrs. Job found out Hubs was right—when the Almighty restored all they'd lost and more. And we can *know* too. Redemption is just around the corner.

*Redeemer of Misery,
Please stifle my inner Eeyore.
And assure me that during my
darkest times, like Job, I can
know there's hope for my future.*

Cyber Sabbath

*"Six days you shall labor and do all your work,
but the seventh day is a sabbath to the LORD your God.
On it you shall not do any work."*
EXODUS 20:9–10 NIV

I'll never forget the day my young daughter focused her penetrating brown eyes on the back of my head as I was typing and declared, "I HATE that computer!"

Her words rocked my world.

I knew my priorities had become skewed and that I was spending far too much attention on that keyboard and not enough on my fam. I'd put her off too many times with, "Just a few more minutes." Minutes had stretched into hours.

It mattered not that writing was work, not fun time. . .it was still time away from my impressionable daughter. The daughter Papa had entrusted me to raise.

I realized that one day she would finally give up and find someone else who *would* give her attention. Before I knew it, she'd be out of the house and would have unequivocally learned the lesson I'd taught her: Mom would rather spend time with a machine than with me.

That's when I knew something had to change. I needed a Cyber Sabbath, a full day each week to unplug and focus fully on the precious faces before me. No email. No writing assignments. Not even one google. Just rest from the cyber world, in the same way Papa God took a day to rest after creating our world.

What about you, sister? As demanding as Jesus' earthly life was, He still managed to honor the Sabbath. And none of us have work that's more important than Jesus'!

*Living Lord,
When Cyber World tempts
me on my Cyber Sabbath,
remind me that unlike my kids,
it's not going anywhere.*

Whine and Cheese

*"Sin is crouching at the door; and its
desire is for you, but you must master it."*
GENESIS 4:7 NASB

Before we begin today, read Genesis 4:1–16 in your Bible. Now let's chat about some important points in this passage we can apply to our own lives.

- Verse 1: Right after Eve had her big squabble with God (chapter 3), when she'd just done the whole forbidden fruit fiasco and gotten booted out of the garden of Eden (ruining things for all mankind), she humbly recognized that her new baby was a blessing from the Lord.
- Eve knew she'd blown it. Big-time. But she didn't continue wallowing in the pigpen of guilt. She got up, squeegeed off the muck, and put her hand back in Papa God's. He wants us to learn from our mistakes then move forward with Him.
- Verses 6–7: Yahweh point-blank asks a question we all need to address: Why are we happy when we do well and angry when we don't? Without accepting Papa's forgiveness and transformation, we'll *stay* angry. Don't you hate that you yell at loved ones? Are you embarrassed by your out-of-control temper? Girlfriend, do you have anger issues? Reread today's verse.
- Verses 9–14: Cain's response to Jehovah's correction wasn't remorse. It wasn't humble repentance. It was angry defensiveness and self-pity. Woe is me. Not fair. I'm such a victim. Whine, whine, whine. Wait—am I describing. . .me?
- Verse 16: You can choose to leave the Lord's presence. Cain did. It's awfully cold and lonely away from the Son. Are you there now, sweet friend? It's never too late to come home and get warm.

....

....

....

....

....

....

....

....

*Forever Forgiver,
Like Eve, I know I've blown
it. Please forgive me. Take my
hand. Lead me forward.*

Crossing Home Plate

*Precious in the sight of the
Lord is the death of His saints.*
PSALM 116:15 NKJV

The night after my dear mother-in-law passed away, I prayed for supernatural comfort for Chuck (my husband, her only son), totally distraught. He'd lost both his parents now and felt orphaned.

I thought watching the baseball play-off game between the Boston Red Sox and Tampa Bay Rays might lift his spirits. A diehard Red Sox fan since birth, hope for a World Series pennant sprang eternal.

But not this night.

By the seventh inning, the Rays were up 7–0. I couldn't bear to witness Chuck's agony any longer and begged him to go to bed, but he refused to leave his team in the lurch.

Then a miracle occurred. Here's Chuck's account:

"With two outs, batters who had been comatose suddenly sprang to life. Four runs scored then three more in the eighth, tying the game 7–7. Then a screaming line drive to right field drove in the Sox's winning run.

"Tears streamed down my face, not because of the silly game, but because I knew God was sending me a message that Mom too had crossed home plate safely.

"Maybe, just maybe, as Mom entered God's presence with Dad's loving arm around her, God said, 'Welcome home, beloved daughter! If there's anything you need, please let me know.'

"And Mom replied, 'I need a miracle down in Fenway Park tonight. Our son misses us more than should be humanly possible, and we want to send him a special message that we're okay.'

"'As you wish,' God said. And it was so."

*Lord of Earth and Heaven,
Thank You for the assurance
that I too will cross home plate
safely one day and spend the
rest of eternity with You.*

Refreshed

Those who refresh others will themselves be refreshed.
PROVERBS 11:25 NLT

I once observed that the hardworking mother of four young sons wore the same threadbare brown sweater to church each Sunday. She and her husband both worked, but tight finances barely kept the growing boys fed and in clothes, with little left over.

As I sat in church looking at her back week after week, I prayed about how I could help this dear sister without embarrassing her. The Lord led me to send her (anonymously) a small sum earmarked for a sweater, accompanied by a note extolling her wonderful example as a Christian mother and my desire, as a sister on the same journey, to simply bless and encourage her.

My heart flooded with delight when I saw her troop her boys in the following Sunday, face glowing and shoulders a little straighter beneath a lovely new blue sweater.

We can encourage others by meeting their physical needs. Members of the early church excelled at this form of encouragement (Acts 4:32–35) and were immensely encouraged and blessed by Papa God in return. By keeping our eyes open and listening to the promptings of the Holy Spirit, we will encounter many opportunities to physically encourage others.

It doesn't have to be much. It doesn't even have to be money. . .a casserole for someone too sick to cook, an outgrown coat for a friend's growing child, a bag of BOGO groceries.

How about making it a point to look around you today? Notice—really *notice* those who might be blessed and refreshed by something you can do for them in Papa's name.

*Abba Father,
Show me someone I can
encourage this week by
meeting their physical needs.*

Whispers

*A great and strong wind tore into the mountains. . .but the LORD
was not in the wind; and after the wind an earthquake, but the LORD
was not in the earthquake; and after the earthquake a fire, but the
LORD was not in the fire; and after the fire a still small voice.*
1 KINGS 19:11–12 NKJV

I was hosting a women's Bible study in my sunroom when it first happened.

Ping. A few eyebrows elevated. I ignored the sound above our heads.

Ping. Ping. Ping. There it was again, harder to overlook as eyeballs rolled upward. I spoke louder.

PING-PING-PING-PING-PING. The noise became deafening as a stiff breeze shook the oak branches over our house and a barrage of acorns pelted the tin roof like a steroidal machine gun.

It occurred to me that hearing Papa God's still, small whispers through the overwhelming din of everyday distractions is like that. The Holy Spirit rarely screams. If we don't intentionally listen for His voice, it can get drowned out.

While searching for their first home, my daughter Cricket and her husband, Josh, found the perfect house except for one thing: it was priced well above their range. While praying about it, Cricket heard a specific offering price whispered to her heart. I told her it was too low and wasn't an option.

That night, the same figure was confirmed to her in a dream. She felt so strongly that it was from the Lord, I agreed that she and her husband should make that precise offer. To our astonishment, the offer was immediately accepted.

What a blessing! A blessing that might have been missed if Cricket hadn't been listening intently for Papa's still, small voice.

*Lord Who Whispers,
I promise to listen for
Your voice today through
the din and distractions.*

Scroogalina

"Live generously."
MATTHEW 5:42 MSG

As I walked through the upscale restaurant, I passed a slim, nervous male server-in-training being coached by a large, imposing woman whose steely countenance made even me quiver in my boots.

She was like a mean female Carson (from *Downton Abbey*).

The poor guy's hands shook as he poured freshly squeezed orange juice into sparkling stemware lined up on a tray. His face was a study in fear and concentration. Three glasses were two-thirds full and he was working on a fourth.

"You not paying," the scary supervisor commanded in a thick accent. "Feel [fill] it up." The intimidated server proceeded to overflow the glass; OJ splashed everywhere.

Generosity is a virtue many of us struggle with, especially those of us who are frugal (I hate to say *cheap*) due to a modest upbringing, skimpy nature, or Spanx-tight budget. I fit into all those categories. How 'bout you?

Women tend to be either spenders or savers. Neither is a problem in moderation, but both can grow into slobbering, devouring monsters if unmanaged.

Spenders may jump parameters and run credit card debt into the stratosphere. Trying to keep up with the Joneses, they don't recognize that the Joneses are miserably stressed and drowning in debt.

Savers risk becoming hoarders and robbing themselves (and their families) of the enjoyment of life's pleasures. Scrooge is not a role model, girlfriend. Papa God never intended us to live a miserly, stark existence. He wants us to live abundantly (within our means, of course) and enjoy the magnificent wonders He's provided on this earth.

So go ahead, Scroogalina. Loosen up. Your life's a cup—*feel* it up.

Giver of Pleasure,
Help me remember that
everything is Yours. . .
and You love to share.

Cardinal Challenge

*Our God gives you everything you need,
makes you everything you're to be.*
2 THESSALONIANS 1:2 MSG

What IS that weird flapping noise?

I slowed my power walk and looked around. My ears directed me to a parked van. I had to laugh.

A male cardinal was flitting about, tweeting and flirting with the beautiful bird in the van's large side-view mirror. He was completely engrossed, conversing with. . .himself. He'd swoop down and hover in front of his own reflection, giving himself little kisses and coos of admiration.

As I continued my exercise jaunt, I began to think that maybe we all ought to be a little more like that cardinal. Oh, I don't mean we should strive to be self-absorbed or narcissistic, but that we should have enough self-respect that we don't rue spending time in our own company.

Perhaps then we wouldn't seek escape from ourselves through drugs, alcohol, work, extra-marital affairs, shopping till we drop, overeating, or whatever our evasive tactic happens to be.

What if we begin viewing ourselves more as a Cinderella-in-progress than a done-deal-Shrek? Self-love is a good thing; it isn't bad unless taken to an extreme. Papa God fashioned us individually and takes great pride in His creation. Shouldn't we?

Beaut-i-tude is fluid, but if we try, we can tip our inner barometer toward feeling more appreciation for the beautiful women our Creator made us to be.

So how about making it your goal today to emulate my little cardinal buddy and come up with three things you love about yourself? C'mon. . .just three. Write them down; then when self-doubt begins to mock and jeer, you have proof positive that you're a pretty cool chick after all.

*Lavisher of Love,
Help me cherish myself
the way You cherish me.*

Marital Hiroshima

A gentle answer turns away wrath,
but a harsh word stirs up anger.
PROVERBS 15:1 NASB

I love my man, Chuck. I do. But sometimes he baffles me.

Like the time he noticed the philodendron in my flowerbed had grown so big it blocked the sprinkler. So Chuck, with his logical, fix-it left brain, hacked it off at its base. He'd somehow missed that the whole point of the sprinkler was to grow the plant big.

Our flowerbeds are my domain. I carefully nurture every plant, talking and sometimes even singing to them. They're my little green babies. So imagine my horror when I found my gorgeous six-foot philodendron stretched out like a dead body beside the garbage can.

I wept. Then I got mad. I was ready to blast the cold-blooded murderer.

But then I remembered the funeral I'd recently attended, when the husband of the deceased said in his eulogy, "She never looked down on me in all fifty-eight years we were married. She always looked up at me in respect. . .even when I didn't deserve it."

Whoa. Those words hit me hard. I was so convicted about criticizing my husband—often in my own mind—that I vowed to try harder to heed today's verse.

"Lord," I prayed, "help me understand, not criticize, him. I know he was only trying to help. Enable me to forgive him and appreciate all he does around the house."

So, as hard as it was, I swallowed my harsh words.

Later that day I returned to the flowerbed. Chuck, realizing he'd screwed up, had replanted the poor, droopy, dead philodendron. Awww.

> *Lord of Second Chances,*
> *Some days I need a glue*
> *stick instead of lipstick.*
> *Help me avoid marital*
> *Hiroshimas by replacing*
> *harsh words with gentleness.*

Marching

"Anyone who intends to come with me has to let me lead."
MARK 8:34 MSG

I braked my bike on the country road. Recent rains had elevated the bordering ponds so they were separated by only a narrow ribbon of asphalt.

There, between two watery worlds, marched a turtle.

She really was. . .marching. Not plodding, poking, or loitering as turtles usually do; she determinedly lifted those squat legs high and propelled herself forward at an impressive pace. For a turtle.

Where was she going in such a hurry? Running away from something? Or looking for adventure?

At that moment, a truck appeared in the distance, heading our way.

I tried to herd her off the road, but when she saw big lumbering me she instantly retreated into her shell. There she sat in the middle of the highway, thinking she was safe. Not understanding that her shell was no match for the approaching two-ton vehicle.

So I lifted her and headed toward the pond. Her head shot out, snapping at me, her feet furiously scratching my hands. She just didn't get it.

But sometimes, neither do I.

When I get brave enough to venture out of my own little world, I tend to march blindly, not knowing where I'm going but rushing like crazy to get there.

At the first hint of danger, I crawl into my shell, where I think I'm safe.

But I'm not.

That's why dependency on Papa God is so important. He has a much broader view and can see the trucks coming.

Merciful Father,
I trust You to move me where
I need to be. Forgive me for
snapping at Your fingers and
trying to scratch my way out
of Your loving hands.

Us Loves You

Guide me in your truth and teach me,
for you are God my Savior.
PSALM 25:5 NIV

I attended a Baptist church as a preteen and was quite annoyed to be stuck in Sunday night "Training Union" class. I did not wish to be either trained or unified with the other unfortunates forced to be there. So many more important things to do—bike paths to forge, *Lost in Space* to watch on TV, homework to ignore.

But no, I was held captive week after week by Mr. and Mrs. Buford, a childless, elderly couple, neither of whom had completed eighth grade in order to help their families scratch out a living on farms during the Depression. My know-it-all cronies and I scoffed at their country bumpkin speech. So totally uncool.

But there they were, faithful as the springtime rain.

"Us loves you."

It was the phrase Mrs. Buford started every class with. An occasional snicker would burst from one of us enlightened scholars, but the Bufords never seemed to notice.

Soon they'd have us racing to look up scriptures, learn the books of the Bible, and win candy for answering Bible story questions. Of course we acted as if none of this was the least bit fun. Yawn.

"Us loves you."

Mrs. Buford would close the hour with the same ridiculous phrase, a warm smile crinkling her careworn face. Somehow, I remember like it was yesterday.

Okay, hang tight for the end of this story tomorrow. (Sorry—that's what happens when your word count restrictions are tight as last year's jeans.)

Ever-Faithful God,
I'm so grateful for the faithful
teachers who have influenced
my life. I'm going to pause right
now and thank You for each
of them by name. . .

Pass It On

Teach me your ways, O Lord,
that I may live according to your truth!
PSALM 86:11 NLT

(Continued)

"Us loves you." Mrs. Buford's long-ago benediction to my class of adolescent smarty-pants echoed in my memory.

Fast-forward thirty years.

My husband, Chuck, and I are surrounded by a group of twelve-to-fourteen-year-olds, most of whom wish they were elsewhere. We are trying to teach them scriptural principles and bring God's Word to life.

But they're interested only in talking about the latest music, cool websites, and who got busted Saturday night.

Chuck asks a boy with a purple Mohawk, whose father is in prison, to read a passage of scripture aloud in answer to his question about how we know the Bible is true. The boy reads haltingly, unsure of what some of the words mean.

We explain it in terms he can understand. He's still unconvinced. Skeptical. Mistrusting. But for some reason, he keeps coming back.

I notice that he listens, *really* listens, when one of the other boys asks, "Miz Coty, why do you meet with us every week, when all we do is eat your food, wreck your house, and give you one big headache?"

The answer travels through time and explodes in my mind as if I'm hearing it for the first time.

"Us loves you."

Light of the World,
Shine Your light through me onto
others who are floundering in
darkness today. I want to spread
Your light. I want to pass it on.

Prayer Matters

The first thing I want you to do is pray.
1 TIMOTHY 2:1 MSG

My friend Cheryl works night shift at a laboratory. She also plays piano for her church. Recently, Cheryl was asked to play for the funeral of a church friend at 11:00 a.m. on a weekday. She knew it would be tough, being in the middle of her "night." But without complaint, Cheryl rushed home from work at 8:00 a.m. and set her alarm for 9:30 a.m.

She collapsed into bed and was asleep the moment her head hit the pillow.

Cheryl was so wiped, she slept right through her alarm, suddenly awakening for no apparent reason at 10:45, fully alert and ready to leap out of bed. She made it to church to play for the funeral in the nick of time.

After the funeral, an acquaintance approached Cheryl. "I just wanted to tell you," the woman said, "that when I woke up this morning, I felt strongly led to pray for you. I don't know why, but I just kept praying that God would help you in some special way today."

Cheryl realized that the prayers of this woman she hardly knew had awakened her. Her prayers had served as the catalyst for allowing Cheryl to serve Papa God and her grieving friends.

Yes, prayer *always* matters. Whether we're praying for a casual friend—for some reason we can't fully comprehend—or for someone who is hurting so badly we must allow our hearts to break alongside hers, prayer *always* matters.

King of Glory,
I love it that my prayers
matter to You.

Weenie Days

You hold me together.
PSALM 41:12 MSG

Lana's daybreak flight from Denver to Philly was late, leaving exactly ten minutes to make her connecting flight to Baltimore, where she was scheduled to give an inspirational speech that evening. Can you say *Usain Bolt* in heels?

She arrived at her gate, panting and sweaty, only to learn the flight had been canceled. The only other connecting flight would arrive too late. Lana called the event planner and was advised to rent a car.

Three hours later, when her luggage finally reached baggage claim, every car rental service was fresh out of cars. How could that happen?

Lana spent the next two hours trying to get a flight—any flight. She eventually got a boarding pass and went to recheck her bags. Wouldn't you know, the elevator got stuck between floors.

Evidently sound-activated by hysterical screaming, the elevator gasped to life and crept to the nearest floor, where Lana reported to an airport agent what had happened. Despite Lana's reluctance, the agent insisted she get back on the elevator with her to prove it was a fluke and would never happen again.

It happened again.

Then when high winds prevented the replacement flight from departing, Lana texted every friend she knew to start praying. She was NOT going to let Satan win this one. She'd had enough. Time to fight fire with fire.

Within twenty minutes, the wind died down. The plane departed. Lana gave her speech in Baltimore.

Like most of us facing terrible, rotten, annoying circumstances, Lana first nearly fell to pieces. But she didn't stay that way. Her faith kicked in and she finished strong.

Deliverer from Evil,
When I, like Lana,
face these weenie days,
help me finish as a warrior.

Barns R Us

Cultivate inner beauty, the gentle,
gracious kind that God delights in.
1 PETER 3:4 MSG

My friend Marianne has been a hunka hunka burning love all her life. A chubby child, she grew into a plump teen and then a plus-sized adult. Regardless of what she eats, she remains a large lady.

When she was seventeen, Marianne heard that wearing dark colors would slenderize a full figure, so pretty soon her entire wardrobe became navy, brown, or black.

One day when she was in her thirties, Marianne's husband, Sam, asked why she didn't wear more bright and cheerful clothing. After all, she was a bright and cheerful person.

When Marianne replied it was because dark colors made large women look smaller, he chewed on that a long moment then replied with his customary dry wit, "A barn is still a barn no matter what color you paint it."

Marianne had to laugh. Sam's unconditional love and acceptance of her size enough to joke about it was surprisingly liberating. Marianne's self-acceptance took a happy turn. She chucked her strict, self-imposed wardrobe limitations and began wearing lively, vibrant colors that reflected her Jesus-joy.

We look into a mirror and see an image, but it's not the same image God sees. Our vision, our self-perception, has been jaded by the way we've viewed ourselves since childhood: klutzy, stupid, fat, gangly, loser, damaged goods, never good enough.

But Papa sees His beautiful daughter whom He deeply loves and cherishes. I suspect it makes Him smile to see her dress in a way that reflects His radiant love that colors her life.

And as our relationship with Papa God is strengthened, so is our self-love and acceptance.

Connoisseur of Beauty,
Make me the proudest, most
joyful, reddest barn ever!

Unexpected Twists

What you hope for is kept safe for you in heaven.
COLOSSIANS 1:5 CEV

I'd just trekked down the mountain to run errands when the sky split wide open. I tucked my purse against my chest and sprinted toward the store entrance, keeping my umbrella low and angled against the blowing rain.

Time froze at the sickening screech of car tires. The front bumper of a car suddenly appeared beneath the canopy of my umbrella, skidding to a stop, actually nudging my hip.

I stared at the ashen face of the driver, his hand flying to his forehead as he exhaled a long, relieved breath.

Okay. I'm okay. I thought. *Just keep breathing. Thank You, Lord. You saved my life. Or at the very least, a long night in the ER.*

Later, the trip up the twisting, narrow mountain road took twice as long in the horrible thunderstorm with dusk closing in. Hail pounded my windshield; I slowed to 15 mph, barely able to make out the center line.

Rounding a sharp curve, a flash of lightning revealed an enormous tree falling across the road directly in front of my car. Because I was moving so slowly, I was able to brake just in time. The massive trunk leered at me from the exact spot my car would have been if I'd arrived five seconds earlier.

Five seconds. The difference between life and death. Twice in one day. Yet oddly, I wasn't afraid.

If we receive Papa God's precious gift of salvation through the sacrifice of His Son, Jesus Christ, we don't have to fear death. It's merely a door opening to the greatest adventure of all: heaven.

Lord of Eternity,
I praise You for the adventure
awaiting me on the other side.

Pigpen

"'Look, dear son, you have always stayed by me, and everything
I have is yours.... Your brother...was lost, but now he is found!'"
LUKE 15:31–32 NLT

We're all familiar with the story of the prodigal son, right? But have you ever considered the perspective of BB (Big Brother)? Yep, the sibling who resisted the call of the wild and stayed behind in the same ole faithful but boring same ole.

BB worked, toiled, and sweated, doing what he was supposed to do. He was the *good* son. The *obedient* child. To please his father, he dutifully accepted as his responsibility the un-excitement and un-adventure of staying home and working in the family business.

Unheralded. Taken for granted. Practically invisible.

Then when his rightfully-reduced-to-life-in-a-pigpen bratty little brother returned, BB was so incensed at the injustice of the hoopla that he wouldn't go near the family celebration. Through a haze of resentment, he watched his dad grill the prize T-bones and heap the family jewels on his lousy, rotten brother.

I remember when my son came home from college on weekends. His younger sister, still at home dutifully slaving away at chores, seethed that Mom and Dad bent over backward to fix her brother's favorite dessert, turned over control of the remote to his majesty, and let the bum sleep late. So unfair!

But as we reminded her, grace trumps justice (James 2:13), and for this we should be thankful, indeed. For without grace, we would all get what our sorry selves deserve, and that wouldn't bode well, even for the "good sons."

So whom do you identify most with—the prodigal or the diligent child?

Gracious Father,
Many thanks that I'll always be
on the grace side of Your pigpen.

The Real Deal

I have become all things to all people so that. . .
I might save some.
1 CORINTHIANS 9:22 NIV

Have you ever wondered, "Who am I, really?"

Like jigsaw puzzles, pieces of us are borrowed from people we admire—our heroes, teachers, and role models. Some pieces are inherited from our parents, for better or worse.

But all the pieces fit together to form the person our Creator intended us to be. Now we just have to figure out who that person is.

It's tricky, because like the apostle Paul, who wrote today's verse, we tend to be chameleons. When we're with one group of people, we act a certain way; with another group we act differently.

Now, personality morphing for the sake of the Gospel isn't a bad thing; it just makes finding the real "you" a little more challenging. And the person you think you are is not usually the person others see.

Our private selves don't always match up with our public personas.

I've come to realize it's not the public aspects of Christianity that make us who we are in Christ. Not the ability to speak eloquently, pray artfully, or sing like a nightingale. It's our roots that count, not the leaves on our branches.

Who we are in private produces who we are in public, encompassing integrity, commitment, the "realness" of our worship, and the depth of our personal relationship with Christ.

I want to be the real deal, don't you?

So the next time you look in the mirror and ask, "Who am I, really?" you'll see the reflection of Jesus.

Lord of Authenticity,
Keep me genuine, never veneer.

Investments

Don't fall in love with money.
Be satisfied with what you have.
HEBREWS 13:5 CEV

I was stunned. The restaurant menu slid right out of my hands as I stared into the face of our server. *Megan? No way. It couldn't be!*

Fifteen years earlier, Megan had been the wife of a millionaire executive in my husband's company. Megan lived a lavish lifestyle and used her wealth to encourage us lower-level wives to motivate our husbands to work harder (her husband received commission on their production).

Megan took me along on her personal shopping sprees; I watched as she casually spent thousands of dollars. Megan once insisted that I try on her full-length mink coat and matching hat. "You can have all this too," she whispered, "if you just get Chuck to devote 100 percent of his energy to creating new business."

But neither Chuck nor I were willing to pay the price of his absence from our family to attain the wealth she touted. Chuck eventually left that company for one with less income potential but that allowed him flexibility to schedule around the needs of his family. He never missed one ball game, school play, or family outing because of work.

We decided it was more important to invest in the lives of our kids than in the stock market.

And now, here we were years later being waited on by someone who'd had it all. . .and lost it when she and her husband divorced.

Yep, money can disappear in the twinkling of a bank vault key. But Papa God's enormous blessing—our families—will warm our hearts forever.

Abba Father,
Help me always remember that
the poorest people in the world
are those who only have money.

BOOP

"Are you tired? Worn out?...
I'll show you how to take a real rest."
MATTHEW 11:28 MSG

I believe women are like pots of oatmeal. At the beginning of the day, we simmer. . .little manageable bubbles of stress rise to the surface and harmlessly pop. But as the day progresses and the heat escalates, the oatmeal boils higher and wilder and meaner until it finally overflows and covers everything around it with a sticky, nasty mess.

That's you at 3:00 p.m., right?

The trick, I've learned, is knowing when to remove the pot from the burner.

My BOOP theory (Boiling Oatmeal Overflow Phenomenon—one of my Coty Near-Facts of Science) explains why I advocate stealing away for a rest break when you feel a mental break building steam. Without intervention, to quote *Star Trek*'s Scotty, "She's gonna blow, Captain!"

You know, there's a perfectly good reason why our eyelids start to droop in midafternoon. The levator muscles that constantly contract to keep our eyelids open while we're awake finally poop out and beg for relief.

Also, a chemical called adenosine collects in your brain while you're awake, piling up to make you feel drowsy. Your body yearns for sleep to allow the adenosine to disseminate. The resulting euphoric feeling is similar to the instant relief that comes from emptying your full bladder. Ahhh.

So if you need permission to rest, girlfriend, tape this reminder to your microwave:

Ode to Napping
By D. Coty, poet extraordinaire

If your afternoon bloop
is gobbledygook
from experiencing BOOP
because you're just pooped,
for the sake of the troop,
step out of the loop
until you regroup
and the fam can recoup!

Okay, Lord,
I'm ready anytime today You
want to put me in time-out.

Tow Truck

If we are faithless, he remains faithful.
2 TIMOTHY 2:13 NIV

While traveling the narrow, twisting, mountainous roads of Italy's Amalfi Coast on our anniversary trip, I drew great inspiration from four simple words someone had written on the sheer white cliffs: "You'll never walk alone."

Somehow I think I'll remember that plain but profound message long after my memories of the magnificent Sistine Chapel and statue of David fade.

Isn't that the most comforting news *ever*—to know that Papa will always be beside us, walking, running, skipping, crawling. . .regardless of the pace we set, the terrain, or how many times we plow face-first into a tree?

Hey, there are different ways the Lord goes about walking with us, especially us stubborn gals. You know Mary Stevenson's marvelous poem, "Footprints in the Sand"? Well, here's the Debora Coty version:

> *When I look back on the beach of my life, there are times I see Papa's footprints and mine side by side.*
>
> *Then there are times I see one set of prints; that, of course, was when He carried me.*
>
> *But then there are these weird trenches every few yards. That's when He dragged me by my feet.*

Do you need dragging now and then on your life journey? Thankfully, the Almighty has no qualms about being our divine tow truck when we plow into those trees.

....

....

....

....

....

....

....

....

> *Wonderful Counselor,*
> *I cherish the trenches on the*
> *beach of my life. . .tracks of*
> *Your faithfulness. They speak*
> *nothing but love to me.*

Show Dog

Everything they do is just to show off in front of others.
MATTHEW 23:5 CEV

I was surprised to see the "Best of Show" winner in real life. For dog shows he was groomed to a luster, but without the crowd, stage, and judges, he looked like any other scruffy mutt scratching fleas.

It got me thinking about how we sometimes live double lives too. All glitter, grace, and effervescent smiles in public, but turn us loose behind closed doors and watch us growl and snarl and bite.

So I asked myself, "Am I different in private than in public?" If I'm serious about emulating Christ, there should be no difference. My Christian persona should be the real deal, not just fluff for show.

It's an uncomfortable subject for many Christ followers, this double life conundrum. Why? Because we yell mercilessly at our kids and spouse at home and then appear at church like Mother Teresa on Valium. We cheat on our taxes while teaching the third-grade Sunday school class that stealing is wrong.

Jesus confronted the vileness of hypocrisy in Matthew 23. He lamented "Woe to you" no less than seven times in one chapter and associated being a show dog with the terms "blind guides," "snakes," and "brood of vipers."

Strong words. He meant business.

I believe we sometimes live double lives because we're unwilling to surrender our whole selves to Papa God; then it becomes a pride issue. Rather than choosing to change, we conceal our secret shame and go undercover as show dogs with fleas.

Never-Changing Father, I'm tired of secretly scratching. Will You please de-flea me and allow me to start over with nothing to hide?

Unforgettable

"I will not forget you!"
ISAIAH 49:15 NIV

It was a dark, somber occasion. It was, after all, a funeral.

The thing is, I don't do somber well. It's not that I don't *try* to exude dignified homage. . . . I really do. But something invariably goes amuck.

The deceased was a devoted young wife and mother of a toddler, who'd defied doctors in giving birth when a preexisting severe medical condition billowed red flags of caution. *Steel Magnolias* all over again.

The service was bittersweet; amid joyful songs of praise that our sister in Christ was now heavenly whole, tearful sniffles punctuated the quiet spaces. The minister instructed the congregation to file past the open coffin to say their good-byes.

Row after row of mourners quietly surged forward to pay their respects; organ music played softly as everyone looked on.

Then it was my turn. Rising, I felt something pop. *What was that?* I wondered, dabbing my eyes with a tissue.

Halfway up the aisle, I knew what it was: major wardrobe malfunction. My skirt began listing heavily. Groping my backside to close the gap between my busted button and gaping zipper, I made it to the casket before, in front of God and three hundred grieving souls, my skirt slid to my knees and me with it.

The lady behind me in line wrapped her XXL sweater around me and hauled me to my feet. Murmurs rose all round and. . .*seriously,* what kind of insensitive clods snicker at a funeral? I hastily apologized to the dearly departed lying there and exited stage left.

Spouse nearly busted a gut when I explained why I came home skirtless. He comforted me with today's verse, the dear man.

*Lord of the Humiliated,
Sometimes I'd rather be
forgotten, if You don't mind.*

Burning Bushes

Give all your worries and cares to God,
for he cares about you.
1 PETER 5:7 NLT

My friend Cheryl was heartbroken over having to leave her weeks-old baby to return to work. She and her husband preferred Cheryl to stay home, but bills mounted. Midmorning that first day back, she broke down, spilling her guts to a coworker.

"I miss my baby so badly I ache. I keep praying, but it would take a miracle for me to quit work. I'd need a sign from God. . . ."

That afternoon, driving home from work, Cheryl felt the blood drain from her face when she encountered a church sign proclaiming in neon letters EXPECT A MIRACLE!

Coincidence? Merely interesting timing? Karma?

Nuh-uh.

Cheryl felt that Papa God was speaking to her. Her husband agreed. It was the burning bush they'd prayed for.

So with heart in hand, Cheryl resigned, effective Friday. No plan. No job. Only faith that if God wills it, He fulfills it.

Saturday morning, Cheryl answered a knock on her door. There stood a teen neighbor who'd heard Cheryl playing the piano and wondered if she'd consider teaching her. That afternoon, another neighbor called, seeking piano lessons for her children.

One after another, unsolicited piano students appeared; calls came to play for weddings and funerals. Cheryl was able to meet her mortgage payments every month for the next four years until her kids entered preschool.

And you, my friend. . .are any bushes bursting into flame without your notice? Someone may be trying to tell you something.

Burn, baby, burn.

Yahweh Yireh
(The Lord Will Provide),
I give my worries to you today. . .
[here's where you name them].
I know You care about what
happens to me; You've demon-
strated that in so many ways.

Looking Up

You, O LORD, are...the one who holds my head high.
PSALM 3:3 NLT

Early one morning, I drove past a man walking along the side of the road carrying a black garbage bag. He was shuffling with his head down. What he didn't see, because he wasn't looking, was that he was surrounded by the most incredible, dazzling sunbeams you can imagine. He was actually bathed in light—translucent, iridescent, brilliant light.

As if a preview of heaven's luminance broke through for a moment in time.

But he missed it. He was oblivious to the awesome light show happening around him because he was looking down, collecting trash.

"Look up! Look up!" I shouted out my open window. But he only glared in my direction, shook his head at the crazy lady driving by, and dropped his gaze back to the ground.

He never knew what he was missing.

Like a sock in the gut, I knew I was seeing myself. Yep, it was me all right, trudging along so many days with my eyes cast downward, collecting my own brand of garbage. Feeling alone and forgotten when all I had to do was look up and *see* that I'm surrounded by attitude-transforming light: the presence of my Lord, Savior, and Companion through all of time.

Papa God sent me a gift that day; it came without a bow or a box. It came in a beam of light intended to lift my head so I won't miss the hope streaming from heaven all around me.

How about you? Could you be missing something incredible? Where are your eyes focused?

*Lifter of My Head,
Today, help me forget
my garbage and look
upward into Your presence.*

Booby Prize

The fruit of the womb is a reward.
PSALM 127:3 NASB

Laura, my friend who's a single mother of two teenage girls, cut a deal with her foot-dragging daughters. They'd cook while she cleaned up afterward, or vice versa. After a few *whatevers* accompanied by eyeball rolls, they chose cleanup.

Everything went fine for the first week, but then the girls developed that dreaded teenage malady, DAM: Disorder of Adolescent Memory. Amazing how stacks of dirty dishes are so easy to forget!

After encountering the third sink overflowing with crusty plates and greasy pizza pans, Laura devised an ingenious plan to solve the problem without uttering a single syllable.

That evening, she simply forgot to fix dinner. When the girls groused long and loud, Laura opened a can of Alpo, fried it up in a skillet, and served it to her astounded offspring on paper plates.

No more leaning towers of pizza. The DAM had burst.

Children. The Bible calls them our reward. Although they sometimes feel like more of a booby prize, deep in our mother-hearts, we agree: They're our first line of defense against depression, isolation, and boredom. They give us joy and purpose that no one else can.

And best of all, loving them gives us an opportunity to mirror our heavenly Father's unconditional love for us, no matter how many motherly mistakes we make.

Yep, King David, speaker of today's verse, was right—the fruit of the womb is infinitely more rewarding than a banana.

*Dearest Papa God,
Today, give me extra
appreciation for my
children. And please
remind me to tell them so.*

Wildlife Encounter

*"I will give you a new heart
and put a new spirit in you."*
EZEKIEL 36:26 NIV

One gloomy fall morning I took off work for a dental appointment, only to learn that extensive—and expensive—work was needed. How could things get worse? Spouse had been out of work with chronic illness for months, and our finances were in dire straits. My heart was a stone in my chest; my spirit was mole bait.

I decided to visit a small local zoo during my lunch hour. *Maybe the animals will cheer me up,* I thought.

But at the lion enclosure, an enormous tawny female nailed me with her steely eyes. Suddenly she lunged with a spine-tingling yowl, baring razor teeth and slashing huge claws at me between the iron bars.

Whoa. I backtracked big-time as enraged feline snarls resounded.

A half hour later, I was back. Had she really singled me out? I had to know.

Sure enough, the lioness again sprang to her feet, growling, and crouched directly in front of me. I shuddered. *So this is how a cornered antelope must feel.*

Then in one swift, calculated move, she turned and blasted urine at me with the intensity of a fire hose. I kid you not. My clothes plastered to my body. Hair dripped down over my face.

Imagine the smell of house cat urine times fifty.

Involuntary laughter bubbled up from my innards. I couldn't stop.

Papa God obviously arranged this absurd wildlife encounter to shatter my stone heart. In time, He performed a complete broken heart transplant, replacing cold hard chunks with a new warm heart and spirit.

*Almighty Creator,
Thanks for caring enough to
jolt me out of my dully-funks.
Maybe without the lion pee
technique next time?*

Quivers

*Like arrows in the hand of a warrior, so are the
children of one's youth. How blessed is the man
[or woman] whose quiver is full of them.*
PSALM 127:4–5 NASB

"Now how did he *do* that?" I asked my son's empty stroller. Twenty-two-month-old Matthew had escaped again, this time in one of the mall's posh boutiques.

A search high and low revealed no inquisitive toddler. I'd just begun to panic when I noticed a group of people laughing hysterically in front of the store's large display window.

Uh-oh. I gritted my teeth and took a look.

There, seated in the lap of an oh-so-festive mannequin, was Matthew, his chubby little arm wrapped around her neck, gleefully smashing his cookie against her painted lips, jostling her curly wig over one glassy eye.

I hurried to the back of the display, where a sliding panel locked in place left a narrow, toddler-sized opening. I tried calling Matthew over, but he was happily entertaining his adoring audience.

Realizing a toddler with groupies was not going to be reasonable, I shoved my arm through the opening and snagged his sneaker. As I reeled him in inch by inch, he dragged his new friend along, upending the entire display.

Matthew emerged clutching the mannequin's arm, a scene of utter destruction in his wake.

I hastily handed the dismembered appendage to the openmouthed manager, muttered a mortified, "I'm so sorry," and fled the crime scene with Matthew howling in his getaway stroller.

*Papa God,
I can't deny I love the arrows
of my quiver, no matter how
pointy their little heads can
be sometimes. Thank You for
the good, bad, and insane
days of motherhood.*

Serve 'Em Up

Have the same mindset as Christ Jesus. . .
taking the very nature of a servant.
PHILIPPIANS 2:5, 7 NIV

Those of us raised in the Deep South have no excuse for poor manners. "Yessir" and "No, ma'am" were drilled into us at the risk of meeting Mama's switch behind the shed.

Apologizing was considered a necessary tool for getting along with others. I think this was supposed to be "ladylike," regardless of the biting steel of the magnolia beneath.

Even today, I find myself apologizing to my steering wheel when I sneeze on it. I beg pardon when bumping an empty chair and automatically respond "Thank you" when an electronic dispenser spits out a paper towel.

Yet this mannerly attitude doesn't always carry over to flesh-and-blood humans behind checkout counters. I'll never forget the horrifying reality check when my young daughter once asked, "Mommy, why do you talk to the cash register lady so mean?"

Mean? I thought I was being *firm* and *assertive*, both completely socially acceptable. But truthfully, on the Jesus spectrum of human relations, I was demanding and unforgiving with my "I'm-the-customer-and-therefore-always-right" attitude.

I knew I could represent my Jesus better.

So I seriously considered gluing today's verse to my debit card.

Sometimes we need reminders that becoming a servant like Jesus is our life's goal. And servants actually *serve* people, considering others' needs as more important than their own. Servanthood is an attitude, not employment status.

Lord Jesus,
Help me see the harried clerks,
food servers, and employees I
encounter today as people like
me, just trying to do their jobs
and fulfill their responsibilities.
As they serve me, use me to
serve them in Your name.

Fragile Soldier

*The sufferings of this present time are not worthy to be
compared with the glory that is to be revealed to us.*
ROMANS 8:18 NASB

As I've already mentioned, one of my faith heroes is Corrie ten Boom. You likely know of Corrie's suffering in a Nazi concentration camp for harboring Jews.

But you probably don't know the suffering Corrie endured after several strokes at age eighty-six stole her speech and left her imprisoned in her own paralyzed body. For twenty-five years, she'd preached Jesus' unfailing love through books and a vibrant speaking ministry.

Then suddenly, inexplicably, everything was stripped away.

In *The Five Silent Years of Corrie ten Boom,* Corrie's faithful companion, Pamela Rosewell Moore, asked, as we often do in the face of disaster: Why? But Corrie didn't. "Her attitude was one of acceptance. God had shut her up with Himself in a kind of precious imprisonment."

Pam recounts Corrie's response of obedience, not rebellion, during the five years before her death as a "fragile soldier on her iron chariot bed."

"There had been a tremendous change in her way of life, one that could crush the spirit," Pam writes. "But that had not happened. She was living for God. I could see no difference in the attitude of this weak and silent Corrie to that of the strong speaker. She served Him then; she was serving Him now.

"Corrie had a message to proclaim. . .yet without words. . . 'When the very worst happens, the Lord Jesus remains the same.' Her life was saying that if she could be joyful and peaceful in her circumstances, other people surely could be in their easier ones, provided they too had a relationship with the Lord Jesus."

*Breath of Life,
During my times of
suffering, help me
to also become a
fragile warrior for You.*

Sitting Geese

Deliver us from evil.
MATTHEW 6:13 KJV

I'm no hunter. Nope. I'd really rather not consider where my steak comes from. I refuse to acknowledge that my bacon once had eyes and my fried chicken leg actually walked.

So when I stayed in an Alabama motel next to a Gander Mountain hunting superstore, I was a bit dismayed by the goose-in-midflight logo. *Poor little geese,* I thought. *At least they have a fighting chance to fly away.*

Then to my horror, I saw them: two long-necked geese sitting on the store lawn. A hunter would practically trip over them as he exited the doors loaded down with his brand-new ammo.

What was wrong with these dense birds? They could go anywhere, but they parked themselves smack-dab in harm's way.

So like the fix-it gal I am, I ran at them, arms flailing. "Shoo! Staying here will be the end of you!"

Did they listen? No. They stretched their wings and squawked at me. They were ready to defend their poor choice to the end and entrenched themselves deeper into enemy territory. They just couldn't see it.

Papa God spoke to me through those foolish geese. He brought to mind the times I've parked myself in harm's way yet don't recognize that my location is enemy territory. When those who see the bigger picture try to warn me, I ruffle my feathers and honk.

You know, we're all sitting geese at one time or another. Such is sinful human nature. But we *can* choose to fly to a safer place if we simply spread 'em and flap 'em.

....

....

....

....

....

....

....

....

....

....

Deliverer from Evil,
Shoo me away when I've
landed in enemy territory and
don't notice Satan raising his
shotgun to take aim at my heart.

Simple Pleasures

*How beautiful on the mountains are the feet of the messenger
who brings the good news, the good news of peace and salvation.*
Isaiah 52:7 NLT

Navigating the winding road up the mountain to our cabin, I tuned my car radio to the only station it could pick up in the twisty-turvy Smokies: country.

Country is all I heard every single morning for eighteen years growing up. Mama would have the radio blaring country music as she flapped our jacks and poached our eggs.

Themes haven't changed much. . .the gal on the radio was warbling about wanting to do something crazy. About trading her simple life for a wild night on the town drinking and carousing with her friends.

What fun, she said. Living a little, she called it.

I recalled the two invitations for nights on the town I'd received that week, both involving bars, music, and drinking.

No thanks.

I don't consider myself a prude; I love having fun. But perhaps my idea of fun is tempered because of exposure to what alcohol can do to a person and ultimately to a family. It ain't pretty. It ain't fun. And it ain't living, even a little.

I prefer simple pleasures. Walking in the early-morning woods, chasing fireflies at sundown, feeling the tickle of a pony nuzzling my palm, cuddling with someone cozy, good conversation over a dinner table, making chocolate crack and eating the whole batch (hey, this stuff's to die for; recipe's in my *Too Blessed to be Stressed Cookbook*).

My pleasures are simple but not shallow. I like to get high on joy.

What about you? Enjoyed any simple pleasures lately? You can't imagine what you're missing.

*Soul Refresher,
Help me make the time to enjoy
one simple pleasure today.*

Smiling in the Dark

Three things will last forever—faith, hope, and love.
1 CORINTHIANS 13:13 NLT

Nancy, a lovely lady I've never met, wrote me the following note:

> *I went into the grocery store and your beautiful little book,* Everyday Hope, *jumped into my cart. It must have known how many people in my life are struggling with hope. I shared it with a friend who fell two months ago, resulting in blindness.*
>
> *My friend couldn't believe the words in this book that seemed meant especially for her: "Hope isn't just an emotion; it's a perspective, a discipline, a way of life. It's a journey of choice. We must learn to override those messages of discouragement, despair, and fear that assault us in times of trouble and press toward the light.*
>
> *"Hope is smiling in the dark. It's confidence that faith in God's sovereignty amounts to something. . .something life-changing, life-saving, and eternal."*

After reading Nancy's email, I dropped to my knees right there in front of my computer and prayed for her friend. My heart went out to her. How devastating it is to face sudden drastic changes that deal a serious blow to our underlying hope. Yet we all do at some point in our lives.

Hope is vital to a dynamic, thriving faith. . .according to today's scripture, one of the big three that will remain to the end of time. It's our lifeline to eternity.

Hope is the buttercup lifting its delicate head from a charred field.

Hope is the reason we persevere when all seems lost.

Hope, dear sisters, is simply Jesus.

> *Hope of the Hopeless,*
> *I place my complete trust in*
> *You when light cannot be found.*
> *Then I can smile in the dark.*

Think Fast

*"When you fast, don't make it obvious....
And your Father, who sees everything, will reward you."*
MATTHEW 6:16, 18 NLT

The news was devastating. My friends Rachel and Kim both received diagnoses, within weeks of each other, of terminal cancer (Rachel stage 4 breast cancer, Kim stage 4 uterine). Each was told they had one year to live.

What could I do to help my dear friends? I couldn't just sit around feeling depressed and helpless; I had to do *something*.

I embraced two truths that have been proven repeatedly in my walk with the Lord: 1) Prayer is the least and the most we can do, and 2) Prayer innervates the muscles in the hand of God.

Someone suggested biblical prayer and fasting. I really didn't know much about it, so I did a Bible study. I learned that prayer and fasting (P & F) go hand in hand; dozens of scriptures encourage believers to perform this act of personal deprivation for various reasons:

- As an act of intimate personal worship (Luke 2:37).
- As an outward sign that we dedicate our hearts and bodies to God (Joel 2:12).
- To discern God's will when we're making important decisions (Acts 14:23).
- As our sincerest demonstration of caring and intercession for the ill (Psalm 35:13).
- P & F should be performed secretly before God, not to impress others (Matthew 6:16–18).

I discovered that P & F is not only encouraged but *expected* of believers who want to take their relationship with Papa God to a higher level.

More tomorrow. . .

*Living Lord,
The idea of giving up food
for even an hour scares me.
Open my spiritual eyes
to new possibilities.*

Bare Bones

She. . .stayed there day and night,
worshiping God with fasting and prayer.
LUKE 2:37 NLT

(Continued)

Yep, there's something mysteriously profound about the self-deprivation aspect of fasting that opens a virgin section of your heart to deeper communion with Papa God. It's difficult to explain. Hunger strips away the fluff of life like nothing else and brings you down to the bare bones of what's really important.

And you won't know what that is until you're there. . .spirit naked, yearning, and raw, seeing truths you never saw before with eyes alive with sudden clarity.

But I didn't know any of that at the beginning.

So with great trepidation, I decided to dedicate every Tuesday to P & F (prayer and fasting) for my dying friends, Rachel and Kim (who, incidentally, didn't know each other). Now, this decision didn't come lightly—it was a drastic, frightening new dimension to my faith life that I wasn't at all crazy about. In fact, I dreaded it with every fiber in me.

But I did it anyway. And the rewards were life-altering.

My reasons for choosing Tuesdays were not terribly spiritual—Tuesdays were super busy at work, and I thought maybe I could tolerate hunger better by keeping occupied. I somehow missed the point that hunger is the reason for fasting. Every time you feel a hunger pang, you stop to focus intense prayer on the object(s) of your fast instead of your gnawing desire for food.

I later changed my work schedule to afford me more freedom for focused prayer. At home, I took lots of prayer walks to remove the temptation of that oh-so-convenient fridge that constantly called my name.

More tomorrow. . .

Jesus Who Knew Hunger,
Teach me to listen to You,
not my growling stomach.

P & F

David prayed desperately to God for [his] little boy.
He fasted, wouldn't go out, and slept on the floor.
2 SAMUEL 12:16 MSG

(Continued)

There are all kinds of fasts, including forty-eight or twenty-four hours, partial days, no food or drink, liquids only. . .no "right" or "wrong"—whatever you and Papa agree upon. I first opted for an eighteen-hour food fast (clear liquids only) from 7:00 p.m. Monday until 1:00 p.m. Tuesday. I skipped breakfast and took a late lunch so there was no need to explain myself to anyone. It was a good starting place. Later, although it was never easy, as I got more acclimated to fasting, I increased to twenty-four hours.

After three months, I felt led to tell Rachel and Kim about P & F Tuesdays on their behalf; they were both intensely moved and grateful.

Okay, I know you're wondering about the results of all this sacrificial suffering—was it worth it? Did the Almighty hear our pleas for mercy? Did my friends live?

In a word, yes.

Yes, it was more than worth it—I've *never* felt closer to Papa God, nor experienced the incredible combination of His power and tenderness so personally.

Yes, the Lord heard our pleas and deluged us with mercies, new every morning.

And yes, my friends lived, really *lived,* both admitting they experienced life more fully during those days of dedicated prayer than ever before.

Rachel (age thirty-five) ran into the waiting arms of Jesus eighteen months after her diagnosis. Kim (fifty-six) astounded doctors by surpassing the year she was given and is still with us three years later.

Would I recommend P & F during your time of crisis?

Absolutely. Unequivocally.

Merciful Father,
In desperate times,
help me remember there
is something I can do.

Lord of the Towel

"If I then, the Lord. . .washed your feet,
you also ought to wash one another's feet."
JOHN 13:14 NASB

Readers often share with me personal concerns and request prayer; it's surprising how often it's about forgiveness. I guess we're all lousy at this forgiveness thing, but thankfully, it's a skill that improves with practice.

I love the lesson on forgiveness Jesus imparted at the Last Supper. Take a moment and read John 13:1–15. Even with death looming, Jesus demonstrated firsthand how to humble oneself and forgive the unforgivable.

He washed filthy feet.

Yuck. Doesn't sound very appealing, does it? Isn't there a, well, *nicer* way?

Peter sure hoped so when he jerked his dirt-encrusted toes away and shouted at the Savior of the world, "Never shall You wash my feet!"

When Jesus replied, "If I do not wash you, you have no part with Me," Peter overreacted with something like, "Well then strip me down to my skivvies and scrub me raw!" (My paraphrase.)

Ya gotta love ol' Pete—what a drama king!

But as well intentioned as he was, Peter wasn't getting it. Jesus washed the feet of *everyone* present. . .even Judas, who led His lynch mob. Jesus was showing us that there's no limit on humility. No shelf life on forgiveness. No restrictions on whom we serve.

As much as Jesus loved Peter, He knew His friend was about to stab Him in the back. Peter would run away and even deny their relationship. Yet Jeshua grabbed a towel, knelt down, and tenderly washed away the dirt.

Forgiveness.

Lord of the Towel,
Today I'd like to wash away
the dirt and start afresh with
_____, who hurt me
deeply. Humble me. Strengthen
me. And hand me a foot.

Diana's Lamp

*"Sin is crouching at your door; it desires
to have you, but you must rule over it."*
GENESIS 4:7 NIV

I was six years old and in big trouble. I'd done something horrible.

It happened at the house of Diana, my nine-year-old neighbor, a tall, gentle girl who was kinder to me than all the other big kids.

A bunch of us were playing in Diana's room when gravel crunching in the driveway announced the arrival of Diana's father, a grizzly bear of a man—towering and burly, with a deep military voice. He was very strict and often barked orders to Diana and her little brothers, who obeyed immediately.

When he drove up that day, everyone suddenly remembered a reason to go home.

I saw the sad look on Diana's face as the other kids fled, so I stayed and played.

After tiring of board games, Diana picked up her baton and suggested we go outside to twirl; a hard-and-fast rule allowed no batons or balls inside the house. I grabbed my baton and couldn't resist trying to impress Diana by whirling it around my neck right then and there.

The sound of shattering glass stilled my heart as Diana's bedside lamp crashed to the floor. The huge shadow of Diana's father filled the doorway.

Diana intentionally stepped between her father and me as his face turned crimson and the large vein on his forehead began to pulsate. "Who's responsible for this?" his voice boomed as he eyed the shards of ruined lamp on the floor. Immobilized by fear, I stared mutely at the mess, unable to breathe.

Continued tomorrow. . .

*Purveyor of Justice,
When I do wrong things,
give me strength to admit it.*

Sacrifice

He was beaten that we might have peace;
he was lashed—and we were healed!
ISAIAH 53:5 TLB

(Continued)

Diana held up her baton and answered, "It's my fault, Daddy." She gently pushed me into the hallway and closed the door behind me.

I listened outside the door, quivering, as Diana's dad shouted about rules, learning responsibility, and paying for a new lamp with her own money.

When I heard the stinging lashes of his leather belt, I couldn't take any more. I ran and didn't stop until I was in my own room, sobbing on the bed. I knew Diana was at that moment receiving the worst kind of punishment in my place. I deserved that belt, but she willingly took the pain for me.

I had to do *something*. I shook my piggy bank and gathered the handful of coins that fell out.

Diana answered my knock with red, puffy eyes. I held out my pitiful offering, knowing it wouldn't be nearly enough to pay for the lamp, but she shook her head.

"No," she said softly. "It was an accident. It's all over now, so let's not talk about it anymore." And we didn't.

But I've never forgotten. Even now, a tear escapes when I think about what Diana did for me. She sacrificed herself on my behalf through every lash of that belt.

So reminiscent of what Jesus did for me—and for you. He sacrificed Himself in our place, accepting our rightful punishment and loving us through every lash of the whip and pounding of nails into His flesh.

Even unto death.

....

....

....

....

....

....

....

....

Sacrificial Lamb,
How can I not be moved when I
consider what You did for me?
I love You with all my heart.

Those Days

Clothe yourselves with humility.
1 PETER 5:5 NIV

One morning I swept into the rehab center where I worked as a hand therapist, adorned in my new black pants. I admit I might have started styling a smidge when I noticed a few patients staring at my chic outfit.

Then I heard a horrified gasp and the receptionist grabbed my arm.

"Debbie, *what* is on your rear end?" she whispered hoarsely.

"Uh, I don't know," I replied, turning circles like a mutt chasing its tail, unable to catch a glimpse of my dry-clean-only derriere. "Is it cat hair? I noticed my cat snuck into my car last night and slept in the driver's seat."

"Nooo." She looked a little seasick. "It's definitely *not* cat hair. Globs of something gooey and disgusting are stuck to your backside and dripping down your pants."

I loped into the bathroom to get a better view in the mirror. Apparently my ornery calico had upchucked her freshly digested breakfast all over my driver's seat before I unknowingly wallowed in it.

So there I stood in my Fruit of the Looms, scrubbing my dry-clean-only pants in the sink while the receptionist flitted about trying to help. I was glad at least my panties were fashionable. The only thing worse than wearing regurgitated Friskies in front of an audience is high-top cotton grannies.

Unexpected crises happen to all of us. It behooves us to expect the unexpected so we're not blindsided. Keeping our senses about us—especially our sense of humor—is crucial to surviving life's faux pas.

Have you experienced any cat puke days lately?

....

....

....

....

Creator of Laughter,
Please send me a few
extra laughs to keep in
reserve for those days.

Rip-Off

Thou shalt not steal.
EXODUS 20:15 KJV

Today's scripture took on new meaning for me when my brand-new website was kidnapped and held for ransom.

No kidding.

I never knew such a thing was possible until my long-suffering spouse/webmaster logged on at 7:00 a.m. to add finishing touches the day my new website was scheduled to be unveiled. He'd been up working on it until 2:30 a.m.

But instead of his wife's wonderful new cyber home that he'd spent countless hours building, he found a blank screen. Then, letter by eerie letter, a profanity-laced message appeared, stating that this site has been heisted by "Hacker Ali." To get it back, payment must be arranged through the [French] e-dress provided.

We were shocked. We were furious. We were one of many.

Maybe you're one too.

Intellectual Property Theft: A shattered sense of security. Being forced to forfeit precious time and money to regain what was rightfully yours in the first place.

Papa God takes stealing seriously. And so should we. Even seemingly innocuous, every-one-does-it transgressions like pocketing the extra dollar the clerk mistakenly gave in change, taking office supplies home from work, or fudging on income tax.

Why is it a big deal? Because stealing dishonors our Savior. Not only is He watching, but often little eyes are soaking up our example of living *real* Christianity, regardless of social mores that dismiss integrity and idolize pirates, cool criminals, and all things "gangsta."

If we don't live our faith out loud, they won't.

And that would be the most tragic rip-off of all.

Lord of Integrity,
To You, mini-stealing is the
same as mega-stealing. Help me
remember if I ignore this short
but powerful commandment,
I'm no better than Hacker Ali.

More to Love

An honest answer is like a kiss of friendship.
PROVERBS 24:26 NLT

We'd just begun refreshments at the baby shower I was hosting when Sandi rushed past me toward the bathroom, white-faced, her hand covering her mouth.

Emerging a few minutes later, Sandi admonished me, "Deb, you said, 'Make your own parfait,' so I did. Then I spooned on dark chocolate from that teensy Crock-Pot beside the table and took a bite. But it wasn't chocolate. It was potpourri."

Just gotta love our BFFs (Blessed Friends Forever)! Here's more to love:

- Girlfriends see us through touches and crushes (what touches our hearts and crushes our souls).
- True girlfriends rue comparisons. One unique being cannot be compared to another unique being.
- A bestie tattoos herself on your soul.
- "Girlfriends are blessings at every age." (My friend Pat commenting on her elderly mother and her octogenarian friends giggling like teenagers.)
- A genuine girlfriend listens patiently while you tell a story that leads you to another. . . and another. . .and another, without ever finishing any.
- "May your crown in heaven be so heavily jeweled that you can't hold your head up and have to wear it as a belt." (My benediction to a BFF bringing me dinner.)

It's said, "We'll eventually forget what others say or do, but we'll never forget how they make us feel." Girlfriends make us feel alive. And treasured. Even when honesty pinches. We can trust them to tell us when the quiche is dry, our earrings are tacky, or that we put the potpourri in a stupid place.

We are loved regardless. Even if we accidentally poison them.

....

....

....

Love Divine,
I treasure my girlfriends. Help
me show them so today.

Sweet Touch

"He will not fail you nor forsake you."
1 CHRONICLES 28:20 NASB

Just before dawn I crossed the campground where I was later speaking at a women's retreat. A rustic dock on the lake beckoned to a sunrise front-row seat.

My soul was weighed down with baggage I couldn't jettison. I'd just finished praying for help when I spotted the dock.

As I crossed the creaky, worn planks, suddenly an enormous flock of birds swooped in, covering every square inch of wood. They landed all around me, as if I weren't there. I stopped in my tracks so as not to startle them, but even in the predawn twilight I could tell they weren't afraid.

Wait, I thought. *Don't wild birds fly AWAY from people, not TOWARD them?*

At that moment, the glowing sun peeked above the horizon and painted the lake the color of creamsicles. We all turned as one to drink in the beautiful sight. . .a bird battalion and me, witnessing the dawn of a glorious new day together like dear old friends.

The warm light seeped into my heart and then my very soul as my winged friends and I worshipped our Creator together. I can't explain how I knew they were worshipping. I just *knew.*

The weight of my inner luggage disappeared. My heart took flight. I felt free and unburdened and loved. Sort of how a bird must feel as she soars above the lake on a summer breeze.

It was a lovely grace note—a sweet touch from Papa to remind me how much He cares about me. Regardless of how high I allow the baggage to pile.

Master Designer,
Assure me today, by Your
sweet touch, that You're
sensitive to my feelings.

Beauty IS the Beast

The fear of human opinion disables;
trusting in GOD protects you from that.
PROVERBS 29:25 MSG

While riding my bike through a nearby subdivision, I noticed a very attractive teenager walking up her driveway. At least that's what I thought. Then she turned around.

It wasn't a teenager, or even a twenty-ager. The strikingly beautiful woman with long shiny blond hair, stylish size 4 skinny jeans, and awesome boots was fifty. I'd met her and her young daughter years ago.

Ah, her daughter. Keri, as I'll call her, was chubby, nondescript, and shy from the day she was born. Now nearing twenty, she's still, well. . .chubby, nondescript, and shy.

How must it feel to grow up with a drop-dead gorgeous mother? I thought, pedaling by. Gotta be rough to be the plain vanilla daughter of a Cookies & Cream Deluxe who turns heads wherever she goes.

Don't we all live on a comparison hamster wheel? There's always someone prettier to compare ourselves to and make us feel that we don't measure up—a friend, sister, cousin, coworker, celebrity.

So what?

Papa God created us—each and every one of us—a masterpiece. In our natural state, rough-hewn and raw. And He loves us lavishly, just the way we are. It's taken years to accept my perceived flaws, flab, and funky features, but I can now celebrate myself—a happy little Chunky Monkey.

Not one of us needs to settle for plain vanilla. Our flavor is custom churned through the creative passion of our Master Designer, not the sprinkles we add.

I hope dear Keri realizes she can be mocha mint chocolate chip if she wants. Because her unique flavor comes from the inside out.

Beautiful Savior,
Today I celebrate the
you-nique, marvelous
flavor that You've
hand-mixed just for me.

Trash Girl

"Love your neighbor as yourself."
MATTHEW 22:39 NIV

Unbelievable! There it is again—my neighbor's trash, blowing onto my lawn for the umpteenth time.

This problem has long been a bee at my picnic. I constantly find bits and pieces of THEIR refuse in MY yard.

C'mon, these people *must* see what's happening. One night, after a greasy pizza box languished in the gutter all day, I shoved it back into their yard with my foot so there would be no doubt who "owned" the trash. Next morning, their newly delivered newspaper lay within two feet of the pizza box. Three hours later, the newspaper had disappeared and the box was back in my yard.

Okay. I realize gnashing my teeth and muttering under my breath is not the best way to witness to these people. It doesn't really speak well of Christ's love in your heart when you're tossing rotten apple cores over their fence.

So how do I go about loving my neighbors on a day-to-day, trash-in-my-driveway basis?

Hmm. Changing my *her*spective seems to be first in line. If I can see them through Papa God's eyes—through His filter of compassion—maybe love will eventually follow.

My heart did soften when I learned the husband's in chronic pain due to multiple back surgeries and the wife works two jobs to make ends meet. Maybe that's why picking up garbage isn't a priority for her and impossible for him.

The picture's becoming clearer. Jehovah gave me a strong back and agile fingers so I can serve these needy people in a unique ministry—as their trash girl.

And maybe tonight, instead of tossing apple cores, I'll bake them an apple pie.

Limitless Lord,
Teach me to love as You do.

Crumbs

I don't understand why I act the way I do.
I don't do what I know is right. I do the things I hate.
ROMANS 7:15 CEV

I was only gone for ten seconds. When I returned from the kitchen, the last half of my sandwich had disappeared from my plate. A telltale trail of crumbs led behind the couch.

"FENWAY! You thief! What have you done with my lunch?"

A wagging stubby tail betrayed my wicked pooch busily working on his forbidden bounty. He must have realized I was *really* angry because two chocolate brown eyes peered at me around the side of the couch as he assumed his "Aren't-I-adorable?" pose. A crumb of onion bread clung to his furry chin.

Into the brig he went. Social butterfly that he is, solitary confinement is the only punishment that speaks to him, so his sentence was fifteen minutes locked in the bathroom.

By the wailing that ensued, you'd have thought I beat him with a crowbar.

Awww. I started feeling bad for the poor puppy. He certainly sounded repentant. He was sorry he'd sinned. Maybe he couldn't help himself. I shouldn't punish a dog for being a dog, should I?

I opened the bathroom door and knelt with my arms stretched wide to receive my contrite canine. He burst out of prison and ran right by me, through the kitchen, across the living room, and behind the couch to finish his sandwich.

He was sorry, all right. Sorry he'd been caught.

It got me thinking about my own repentance sincerity and what the Bible has to say about being truly sorry. More tomorrow. . .

Merciful Father,
Thank You for so often
overlooking that crumb of
onion bread on my own chin.

Living Proof

"Stop sinning and turn to God!
Then prove what you have done by the way you live."
ACTS 26:20 CEV

(Continued)

Like Fenway, I sometimes find myself in the paradox of insincere repentance. My head knows it was wrong to speak critically of that annoying person and my heart asks my heavenly Father for forgiveness, but my mouth turns around and does it again at the next opportunity.

I may wail and yip and howl about being repentant, but if I repeat the offense, it was all just noise. The "sorry" didn't take.

Yahweh speaks of second chances in the parable of the barren fig tree in Luke 13:6–9 (please look it up). When the landowner wants to destroy the figless fig tree, the caretaker steps in and promises to personally nurture the little tree toward change if it's given just one more chance.

In the same way, Papa God generously gives us second chances to sincerely repent when we sin. And sincere repentance means an attitude alteration. . .a change of *her*spective *and* behavior. Are we truly willing to allow Him to change our hearts? We'll know because true repentance will be evidenced by our actions.

As animal trainers have shown us, even self-centered, tummy-driven canines like Fenway can alter their behavior if they're motivated enough.

How much more can we, children of the King, choose to reflect genuine repentance by changing our actions to reflect our Father's heart?

> *Adonai Echad (The*
> *Lord Is Our God),*
> *I know what I did made*
> *You sad. Please forgive me.*
> *And enable me to become living*
> *proof that I'm truly sorry.*

Hidden

*"There is nothing hidden that will not be
disclosed, and nothing concealed that will
not be known or brought out into the open."*
LUKE 8:17 NIV

Rachelle ran to find her husband, Scott. "It's gone!" she screeched. "My wedding ring—it's gone!"

"Now don't panic," Scott said in his steady, logical voice. "It's got to be here somewhere." So they searched. Then searched some more. No pillow, couch cushion, or throw rug remained unturned. But the $4,500 diamond ring would not be found.

"I just don't understand what could have happened to it," said Rachelle tearfully. "I'm sure I left it on my nightstand, and no one has been in our bedroom but us." Her woeful eyes once again scanned the room. . .and landed on the couple's ten-month-old basset hound staring back at her.

[Gasp!] "Us and Coraline."

As if on cue, Coraline's head dropped and her tail tucked beneath her.

"Guilty as charged," said the veterinarian as he scanned X-rays of Coraline's stomach. "You know, basset hounds are known for eating rocks."

Who'd a thunk it?

You and I don't generally eat rocks, but we sure do swallow some hard realities we'd like to keep hidden. Bad habits, secret vices, questionable forms of entertainment. . .even thoughts that rank high on the nasty scale.

We think nobody knows. But Somebody does.

In today's scripture, Jesus Himself assures us that nothing will remain hidden; everything will be uncovered at the proper time. *Everything.*

That certainly motivates me to clean out my deepest, darkest inner closet. How about you?

*All-Knowing God,
X-ray my soul and show me the
rocks that need to be removed.*

Ob-sicles

GOD rewrote the text of my life when I
opened the book of my heart to his eyes.
2 SAMUEL 22:25 MSG

My four-year-old grandbuddy just discovered what obstacles are. He calls them ob-sicles (like Popsicles) and he actually thinks they're fun. At least jumping over, under, and around them in our homemade obstacle course is.

We grown-ups don't find much enjoyment in obstacles, though, do we?

My friend Ron sure doesn't. He feels that his happiness is blocked by seemingly insurmountable obstacles—incessant physical pain, the threat of job loss, relationship struggles. Day after day, his obstacles evoke anxiety, bitterness, and pain.

Ron said he just can't picture what a life of trust should look like when he feels so horribly overwhelmed.

And then one morning he woke up and decided this day would be different. He wanted joy and satisfaction to permeate his soul. He knew it wouldn't come from his circumstances, so it would have to be a choice that he made. . .not just once, but many, many times each day. A choice to trust that God's Word is true, a choice to rely on Papa's strength when he had none, a choice whom he would serve this day.

Ron made his choice. And he said it aloud: "Today I choose God. And tomorrow I will make that choice again."

You know, it's tempting to pray for the elimination of obstacles in our lives, but the creek would never dance if Papa God removed the boulders.

Ron learned that big changes come one step at a time. And the first step over any ob-sicle is the most difficult.

....

....

....

....

....

....

....

> *Unwavering Lord,*
> *Today I choose happiness, not*
> *in the circumstances in which*
> *I find myself, but in whom I*
> *find in my circumstances.*

Radical Grace

God's grace has set us free.
ROMANS 6:15 NLT

"Good match."

"Nice slice."

"I hate your stinkin' guts."

Which of these would you *not* expect to hear while shaking hands across the tennis net at the end of a match?

Well, I've heard them all. Although the last was supposed to be tongue-in-cheek, I suspect there was a hidden truth there. Sometimes losing clogs our spirits with nastiness. Whatever graciousness might usually reside there is thrown under the bus of frustration.

So imagine my surprise when, at the end of a grueling match a few weeks ago, my opponent (who lost) did something completely unexpected. I can still hardly believe it. Are you ready? . . .

She gave me her shoes. *Her shoes.* Yep. She shook my hand, asked my shoe size, then handed me the eighty-dollar Nikes she'd worn only once. "Try them on," she said, wiping her sweaty face. "They don't fit me right. If you like them, they're yours."

Boy did I backpedal, big-time. She'd been a tough, no-nonsense competitor, and I was ready to dislike her. Then she sucked the wind right out of my sails. Radical grace totally derailed me. I couldn't put a cohesive sentence together. Sputtering nonsense, I plunked down, tried on the perfectly fitting shoes, and watched her walk away barefoot.

Why would someone be that nice? Why is extending radical grace to someone you don't know or even like so shocking? . . . Especially for emulators of Jesus. He was the epitome of grace in forgiving His own executioners. Aren't we supposed to be becoming more like Him?

" 'Love your enemies. . . . If someone slaps you on one cheek, offer the other cheek also. If someone demands your coat, offer your shirt also' " (Luke 6:27, 29 NLT).

I love my new tennies. I think about that incredibly gracious gal every time I wear them. And they remind me to be radical.

Creator of Radical Grace,
Teach me to think more like
You, react more like You,
treat others more like You.

Whatever

*Whatever your hand finds to do,
do it with all your might.*
ECCLESIASTES 9:10 NASB

As I entered the restroom in the bowels of the county fair, I noticed right away it was different. Unlike the grody, grimy, get-your-business-over-quickly-and-flee-this-nasty-place fare we've come to expect from public restrooms, this one actually gleamed.

No icky grime in the corners, no misplaced sprinkles or puddles on the floor, no graffiti on the stall doors. The tiles gleamed. A faint whiff of gardenias scented the air. And someone with a very pleasant voice was cheerfully humming a hymn.

It was. . .well, *lovely.*

Upon exiting my stall, I noticed a white-uniformed attendant busily polishing counters and sinks. I couldn't help but comment on the surprising cleanliness of the bathroom. She smiled from ear to ear. "There's not a speck of dirt beneath, behind, or across these seats," she said. "You can go to any other bathroom in the whole park, and trust me, you'll come back here. It's the best!"

I left that bathroom uplifted by the obvious pride this woman took in her work and thinking of today's scripture. *Whatever,* it says. Regardless of the lowliness of the job before you. . . scrubbing floors, changing diapers, chopping onions, cleaning up doggy poo, digging ditches.

Whatever it is. . .do it with all your might. And be proud of the fruit of your labor. You will not only please your heavenly Father, but you'll be infused with a strengthening dose of self-worth and purpose.

*Lover of Diligence,
Help me find joy in doing even
the most menial tasks well
and to Your glory. Now please
excuse me, I'm suddenly in the
mood to scrub my potty.*

Unplanned

And because the L<small>ORD</small> loved him,
he sent word. . .to name him Jedidiah.
2 S<small>AMUEL</small> 12:25 NIV

Did you hear about the general who had an affair with a married army wife while her husband was deployed? Then when the general found out the woman was pregnant, he sent her husband to his death on the front lines.

Adultery, deceit, murder. . .what kind of man would do this?

The story doesn't end there. The baby died, but the couple went on to have another child. A child who should have borne the shame of his parents on his shoulders, right?

Nope. That didn't happen at all. The child was Solomon, the eventual king of Israel and wisest man who ever lived. At birth, he was given the spiritual name Jedidiah, which means "Beloved of the Lord."

And the general was David, the one God called "a man after my own heart" (Acts 13:22).

So why was there no shame involved here? One word: *redemption.* The sins of Solomon's parents were not only forgiven by Papa God; they were redeemed. . .because every child is known—even before his or her conception—and "Beloved of the Lord."

Unplanned pregnancy is a shock, even today, but redemption is waiting in the wings, along with Papa's anointed purpose for this dear little life.

Each time I cradle my sweet adopted grandbaby in my arms, I thank God with all my heart that her mother chose to give her unplanned child life. And I pray that like Solomon, she—and her courageous mother—will always feel beloved of the Lord.

Creator of Life,
Please show Your love to young
women struggling with
unplanned pregnancies.
And redeem all lives involved
for Your higher purposes.

Payday

"Go into all the world and preach
the gospel to all creation."
MARK 16:15 NIV

During a dinner discussion, my ten-year-old daughter mentioned that her Sunday school class was studying the Great Commission, and how, just before ascending to heaven, Jesus had given His disciples—including us today—the assignment to share the good news (Gospel) of salvation with all the world.

My salesman husband, who had long worked on straight commission, asked if she knew what "commission" meant.

"Sure," she replied, pausing to pull her thoughts together. "It's what you get paid at the end for what you did in the beginning."

Isn't that a refreshing way to look at the commission—the *reward*—we'll receive when we get to heaven one day and stand in the presence of almighty God?

What indescribable joy awaits us when we're surrounded by not only dear friends and family with whom we shared our faith during our dirt (earth) phase but also the souls reached by worldwide missions we supported with our time, money, and energies.

It's easy to get so wrapped up in our own little world of schedules, meal-planning, family responsibilities, keeping our eyebrows semi-regularly plucked and legs shaved, and completing our myriad of church and work duties that we forget there's a BIG world out there, hungry for the good news of Jesus.

The only way for most of us to "go into all the world" (except perhaps by internet) is to support worthy missions. I'll share more about one in particular tomorrow.

So how 'bout it? Isn't it time you invest in your own Great Commission by supporting (every smidge counts) the well-researched mission of your choice?

Everlasting God,
Lead me to the best
investment today for my
heavenly payday tomorrow.

She-Goats

*"Go and make disciples of all nations, baptizing them in
the name of the Father and of the Son and of the Holy Spirit."*
MATTHEW 28:19 NIV

Tears sting my eyes as I read the letter from the Kenyan child our family sponsors through Compassion International. Now in grade four, Yvonne has begun writing in English.

> *Dear Coty Family,*
>
> *Greetings in Jesus' name. I am thanking you for the Christmas shillings. I bought a she-goat for milking and maize for my family.*
>
> *Thank you for your hug to me through letters. I would like to hug you, too. I love you very much. I am praying for you. Are you praying for me? When I grow up I would like to be a doctor.*
>
> *It is hot and sunny. We dig our shamba [garden] for planting. I like to swim in river Kanyambori. Do you like swimming?*
>
> *In Chronicle, I learnt how King Solomon prayed for wisdom and was given it. I believe there is nothing impossible to God. Even me.*
>
> *Thank you for all support you give. I wish you a nice life.*
>
> *God bless you,*
> *Your child Yvonne.*

Thirty years ago, our own children chose a child to sponsor as a birthday gift from us. We continue the tradition today with our grandbuddies, who are delighted with a friend from another culture to correspond with for life.

The sponsored child not only gains a faithful pen pal but education for a better future, medical care, clothing, and the good news about Christ. CI's motto: "Releasing children from poverty in Jesus' name."

There are many worthy ways to "make disciples of all nations." Dear sister, won't you pray about which is right for you?

*Merciful Father,
Please give me more
mercy so I can minister
to others in Your name.*

Flawed Heroes

Humility leads to honor.
PROVERBS 29:23 CEV

Like everyone else in the stands, I shouted encouragement to the struggling runners who'd been passed in the race. Two twelve-year-old athletes at the Junior Paralympics track meet strained toward the finish line on stiff legs encased in metal braces.

One was my niece, Andie. Despite severe vision deficits and cerebral palsy, she'd wanted to compete. Within centimeters of the red flag, her opponent edged ahead and Andie staggered across the finish line in last place. But instead of being heartbroken, she was exuberant to have finished the race!

Andie is one of my heroes. She never lets her imperfections stop her from trying.

Thankfully, heroes aren't perfect. Three of the biggest Old Testament heroes were Abraham, Isaac, and Jacob. But they each had some major flaws.

To prevent a lusty Egyptian king from murdering him to seize his gorgeous wife, Abraham lied that she was merely his sister and then stood there mute as a corncob while the king added her to his harem.

Isaac showed blatant partiality to one of his sons over the other.

Jacob plotted to deceive his blind father and steal his brother's birthright.

Yet these flawed fellows are the pillars of the Judeo-Christian faith.

I find that reassuring, don't you? It allows you and me to become heroes ourselves. We, driven mothers who bark, bite, and devour at the worst of times, also affirm, comfort, and inspire the rest of the time.

These are the qualities our children will remember.

These are the qualities that make us heroes.

*Jehovah Nissi
(My Victorious Banner),
Make me humble in my
imperfections and a deserving
hero to my children.*

Waisting Away

"Everything that lives and moves about will be food for you."
GENESIS 9:3 NIV

In my fiftieth year, I finally got serious about my health and lost forty pounds. But I got less than I bargained for.

My heaping C cups became scant teaspoons. Freddie and Flopsie, my faithful Bobbing Twins for decades, were reduced to identical ant bites. I felt like a giant Gumby. I'd never worn padded bras in my life, but suddenly I had to buy bras that looked like cereal bowls lined with Kotex.

Why is it that in the battle of the bulge, unwanted baggage like flesh fanny packs and thigh saddlebags fight to the bitter end, but our few assets are the first evacuees?

I shouldn't complain. A friend who lost eighty-five pounds commented about her deflated bosoms: "They always used to bounce into a room ahead of me; now they drag in behind."

People react differently when you lose weight. Some applaud. Others bring you mounds of cheesecake. A few avoid you. One kind soul concluded that I could no longer afford food and slipped me a twenty.

A positive side effect of my Debbie do-over year was finding that by resolving a source of acute self-consciousness (my weight), I was able to take my eyes off myself and focus more on Papa God. Sure, I lost a few inches, but I gained insight that our outsides are not always reflections of our insides.

You can look great but feel wretched. Botoxed on the outside but crinkle-fried on the inside. It doesn't matter that your teeth are straight if your attitude is warped.

Breath of Life,
Help me remember that if
Your peace isn't in my heart
when I'm heavy, it won't be
there when I'm thin, either.

Oasis

You are my hiding place.
PSALM 32:7 NIV

The spotted calf in the field caught my eye as I drove to work one morning. A mere toddler in bovine society, he romped, cavorted, nose-butted the larger calves and nipped at the tails of mama cows who stomped him away in annoyance.

So full of life. So full of joy. He made me smile. A seed of longing sprouted in my chest to do something for the sheer joy of it. Unhurried, unstructured, unrequired. Simply because I wanted to.

I remember feeling that way a long, long time ago, don't you? That sunny-June-morning feeling when the entire day was filled with endless possibilities to fill any way you pleased.

So how do we get that back in the midst of our ever-busy, urgent-paced, production-oriented adult existence?

During a break at a writer's conference recently, I stole away to a sun-dappled park bench. Surrounded by the serene sounds of fountain spray and chirping birds, I soon found myself sprawled across the bench on my back.

A breeze ruffled my hair as I watched white puffy clouds meander overhead. A lazy hawk would occasionally bank left and glide through my field of vision.

And there it was. An unexpected slice of heaven. The quenching answer to my thirst for that long-lost moment of childhood freedom. Rest. Respite. A spiritual oasis of freedom for the weary and burdened.

But oases don't just magically appear. We have to look for them. And choose to embrace them while we have the chance. Because oases can vanish before we know it in the hot, dry desert of endless responsibility.

Lord Who Values Rest,
Help me recognize and enjoy
the refreshing oasis You
graciously provide for me today.

Not a Suggestion

"Remember the Sabbath day by keeping it holy."
EXODUS 20:8 NIV

I'll never forget how difficult it was for my eight-year-old daughter to remember the five classifications of vertebrates. As part of her second-grade homework, she'd been trying to memorize those pesky classifications for a solid hour: Birds, Amphibians, Fish, Reptiles, Mammals. But Cricket had formed a block in her saturated little mind and simply couldn't retain them.

Suddenly, I had an idea: Acronym! "BAFRM" (pronounced "baf-room") employed the first letter of each word. Worked great until she reached R; groping in thin air, she stuttered "rrrroom" . . ."rrrotten". . ."rrrrectangle."

Exasperated, I bellowed, "NO! *Reptiles!* Rep-tiles! Say it one hundred times until you get it!" (Not one of my proudest parenting moments.)

So off she went. . .rep-tiles, rep-tiles, rep-tiles. . .one hundred times.

When she finally finished, I droned, "Now. . .what are the five classifications of vertebrates?"

"BAFRM. . ." Her tiny forehead furrowed in concentration. "Birds, Amphibians, Fish. . .[long pause] Tiles-Rep."

"Whaaaaaaattt????"

"But I said it one hundred times," she cried. "Tiles-rep, tiles-rep, tiles-rep. . ."

Sigh.

Some things are just plain hard to remember. Take the fourth commandment, today's scripture. In our week's bustling busyness, the Sabbath often becomes another get-it-all-done day. One last chance to tie up flailing ends before the next workweek slams us.

But Jehovah made this commandment (not a suggestion!) one of the top ten for good reason: we *need* physical rest, emotional restoration, and spiritual restitution (returning to our rightful owner, Papa God, which is by my definition, holiness).

Girlfriend, if we can't devote *one* day to Papa, we might as well lock ourselves in the BAFRM.

El Roi (God Who Sees),
Help me do whatever it
takes to remember to
keep the Sabbath holy.

Combat

"Be strong and courageous, and act; do not fear nor be dismayed, for the LORD God, my God, is with you."
1 CHRONICLES 28:20 NASB

I climbed the stage steps, trembling as I reached for the handrail. I was about to speak to four hundred hot-tea-and-scone-satiated women who'd paid real money to be there. They expected something worthwhile in return.

Gulp.

Who do you think you are, speaking to these women? They need someone with real wisdom like Beth Moore or Joyce Meyer. You're not a speaker. You're gonna FAIL! And your hair looks like porcupine roadkill.

Satan's bombardment was relentless. The Father of Lies was clever, for there was a sliver of truth in his accusations, enough to rifle me with doubt. A partial lie is harder to combat than a blatant lie.

I hadn't wanted to be a speaker. When I answered Papa's call to write, I never imagined it would come to this. A speech therapist had actually diagnosed me with *anomia*. Words just wouldn't come when I needed them most.

After my first few books came out, one thing led to another. . .and here I was—ironically—mounting a stage, praying desperately. Today's verse blazed across my mind in neon; I recited it again and again until the Evil One fled. Calming warmth like Holy Spirit honey poured over my skittish heart, replacing fear with the confidence of Papa God's presence.

I suddenly realized it didn't matter how poorly or wonderfully I spoke. Those listening would hear only what He wanted them to hear, the Holy Spirit speaking directly to their hearts.

And hey, any porcupine would be proud to wear my hair. Take *that*, Devil.

Lord of Truth,
When the Father of Lies attacks
today, give me Your strength
and courage for combat.

Haves vs. Have-Nots

All you haves and have-nots, all together now: listen.
PSALM 49:1 MSG

My face prickled with heat, but this time it wasn't a hot flash. It was the humiliating realization that I was a Have-not and powerless to fix it.

We all know they exist: the Haves and the Have-nots. Even today's scripture recognizes the distinction.

First the Haves, those accepted in a specific environment. . .the got-it-on girls, the movers and shakers, the cool chicks. The respected, natural leaders others seem to automatically fall in line behind. They're not necessarily boastful or cocky; some are actually quite humble. But they definitely *belong* and everyone knows it.

Then there are the Have-nots. Those who are *with* the group but never really *in* the group. They're on a different level—a slightly lower level—and although the Haves may be friendly enough and include them as a part of the whole, there's an invisible barrier separating them.

You get it. Because you've been there.

We've all been in situations when we're Haves and others when we're Have-nots. Naturally we gravitate toward the former and avoid the latter if at all possible. Nobody wants to feel like a Kmart purse in a rack full of Pradas.

But sometimes those Have-not situations are unavoidable. You may be in one right now—at work, in your neighborhood, at church, or even among extended family.

So how do we cope as Have-nots? How can we keep our self-esteem from tanking and leaving us feeling like scabs on a mangy dog?

Stay tuned tomorrow for more on this subject.

Knower of All Things,
Nothing hurtful gets by You. . .
hostility, prejudice, malice.
Give me Your perspective
of grace when I'm on the
receiving end of injustice.

Kickball Captain

"His mighty arm has done tremendous things! He has scattered the proud and the haughty ones. He has brought down princes from their thrones and exalted the humble."
LUKE 1:51–52 NLT

Go where you're celebrated, not where you're tolerated.

Great advice, right? But not always possible. Sometimes life's circumstances toss us into situations where we may be unappreciated, disrespected, and dreadfully uncomfortable.

I was in one of those groups recently—people who made it crystal clear they were my superiors. I skulked home feeling wretched from being repeatedly stuffed onto the bottom shelf, or worse, ignored completely. And the situation would be ongoing for many months. Ugh.

Like being chosen last for the eighth-grade kickball team every single week for the entire school year.

So I prayed. *Lord, throw me a life preserver—one that will hold my head up and shoulders back when I'm with these people. I know my best will never be good enough from their viewpoint, so please help me endure. No, not just endure, but enjoy myself. . .if that's even possible.*

And you know what? He sent me today's verse. An important message that helped me blossom in my smallness—a special reminder that Papa God delights in making small people, well. . .bigger.

So I returned to them a bigger woman. Internalizing this Life Saver verse gave me a new attitude. I smiled. I was gracious and felt confident. Because I knew something they didn't. It's okay if I'm on the bench today, because one day all we lowlies will be called into the game.

And who knows? I may even get to be the kickball captain!

....

....

....

....

....

....

....

....

*Exalter of the Lowly,
Help me remember that
Jesus, born in a barn, rose
from lowliest of the lowly to
become Savior of the world.*

Duct Tape

"God, be gracious! Put me together again—
my sins have torn me to pieces."
PSALM 41:4 MSG

I rushed home from my tennis match (I lost. . .*grrrr!*), late for my neighborhood Bible study. With no time to shower, I spritzed fruity body spray over my sweaty tennis clothes and threw my purse and Bible into my bicycle basket (yes, yes—I have a basket like the Wicked Witch of the West).

Careening down the driveway, my front tire whacked the mailbox, popping the basket off and flinging my Bible and purse contents across the cul-de-sac.

Double *grrrr!*

I heaved that aggravating basket into the bushes and left the stupid flat-tired bike lying in the gutter. I might have even kicked it. *I hope somebody steals it,* I thought, angrily gathering my broken stuff. I stomped to my car and tore off, a living testimonial to Christianity at its finest.

The next day, having forgotten all about my little confrontation, I was already astraddle my metallic offender before I realized it was no longer in the gutter. The basket was back on, and the tires had been reinflated.

How on earth. . . ?

Glancing down, I had to grin at the black duct tape securing the basket in place. *Awww.* It wasn't pretty, but it sure spoke love. Apparently Spouse had witnessed my wipeout and, without saying a word, had gathered up my Humpty Dumpty and put all the pieces back together again.

You know, Papa God does the same for us. He graciously gathers the pieces of our brokenness and puts us back together. Our duct tape scars may not be pretty, but they sure speak love.

Mender of Broken People,
I cherish Your duct tape in my
life; love does indeed cover a
multitude of sins (1 Peter 4:8).

Fading Unfazed

Your beauty should not come from outward adornment....
It should be that of your inner self, the unfading beauty of a
gentle and quiet spirit, which is of great worth in God's sight.
1 PETER 3:3–4 NIV

As an over-fifty woman, I get the gist of this scripture, but the kicker is the *unfading* part. My inner self might exude vibrant beauty, but what am I supposed to do with the exterior, which is fading like a crimson sofa in the Sahara?

Oh, I've tried to rejuvenate myself. My first attempt at highlighting produced skunk stripes like Cruella de Vil. Curls don't work for me either. After my fifth failed perm, my exasperated hairstylist concluded I have "glass hair."

Swell. I'm an inverted Cinderella.

My specialty seems to be branding myself with my curling iron for momentous occasions. The morning of my most important meeting with book publishers *ever,* I seared the shape of Florida into my forehead. The eve before a family portrait, I imprinted a skull-shaped tattoo on my neck to be forever pondered by future generations.

Lovely.

Then, after starving myself for months to lose weight, my grumplitude spiked off the charts and my fam tried to convince me they liked me better fat.

Sigh. Beauty just ain't fair.

But Papa God knew that. That's why He tried to save me—and you—from all the fretting, expense, and frustration of adorning ourselves in the name of faux beauty. He wants us to aspire to true beauty...the kind that radiates from within.

Beautiful Savior,
Forgive me when I lose sight
that nurturing a gentle and
quiet spirit is infinitely more
important than matching
accessories.

Generating Mercy

*"God blesses those who are merciful,
for they will be shown mercy."*
MATTHEW 5:7 NLT

I watched my tennis partner grimace. I'd been paired with a gal who was playing for the first time in four months because of a neck injury. She could barely turn her head; her movement was significantly impaired, but she wanted to try.

So it wasn't surprising that we lost, but *how* we lost was eye-opening.

Once our opponents realized that my partner wasn't up to par, they repeatedly forced her toward her bad side, causing intentional pain and risking reinjury.

I was taken aback at this blatant display of what life would be like without compassion. Without mercy.

Ugly. So ugly.

The next day I watched my preschool grandbuddy Blaine wrestling on the floor with his two-hundred-pound daddy. When Blaine was gently pinned, he cried, "Mercy!" and his daddy released him. The two laughed together and started again.

Blaine willingly entered into the struggle knowing that if he got into trouble and needed mercy, he would receive it. Because love was present.

What a difference love makes in our behavior. . .our relationships. . .our compassion. It's the underlying reason we Christ followers should treat others with respect, courtesy, and yes, mercy. We receive mercy from Papa God. We, in turn, extend it to others.

To *all* others. Including the guilty who don't deserve it.

Because even if they're not yelling, "Mercy!" on the outside, if we listen hard enough with our spiritual ears, we can hear the cry from a deeper place.

*God of Mercy,
Make a difference in my behavior
today with Your overpowering
love. Help me show mercy to my
offenders—the gal who insults me,
that perpetually cranky neighbor,
the man who cuts me off in traffic.*

Mellow Yellow

For You, O Lord, have made me glad by what You have done,
I will sing for joy at the works of Your hands.
PSALM 92:4 NASB

Autumn. The word itself is enough to make you wax poetic. Especially on my mountain.

Well, it's not really *my* mountain, but I've considered it so since my in-laws built the tiny cabin nestled deep in the Smokies at about 4,200 feet of elevation. When my kids were small, we trekked to the cabin every fall, and now that my kids are having kids, we still trek to the mountains every fall.

Tradition's like a warm, snuggly blanket.

An autumn walk in the woods is simply magical. The green foliage has melted into thirty shades of yellow. . .like an explosion of butter. You can almost taste the deliciousness of it. A twinge of russet here and a spackling of crimson there are the perfect accents to the profusion of amber.

A crisp breeze ruffles the leaves of the treetops and you're sure Papa God is leaning down from heaven, whispering something very, very important meant for your ears only.

I can't help but pull an Anne of Green Gables and rename "the woods" its rightful title: the Forest of Golden Whispers. I get the feeling that this has been its real name for untold centuries, and I'm the slowpoke just now catching on.

So I take it all in. Ahh. I feel peace whispered into my soul by the Creator of all this mellow beauty. And I'm so glad I came.

Where is your own Forest of Golden Whispers, my friend?

Bountiful Creator,
The stunning work of Your
hand both calms and ignites
my heart. Help me drink it in
and truly enjoy the beauty
of the season.

Respect

Whatever you have learned or received or
heard from me, or seen in me—put it into practice.
And the God of peace will be with you.
PHILIPPIANS 4:9 NIV

Technology has now provided yet another way to make people feel insignificant. It's being perfected by those who, under the guise of friendship, use online social media for commercial gain.

I suppose they've always existed—those who join churches or clubs to have access to a larger clientele pool for which to promote their cause/book/business/whatever. But it's extra annoying when they invade the cyberspace in our own homes.

It's bad enough when their eyes flit around while they're talking to you at a social gathering, checking out who's more important so they don't have to waste any more time on you than absolutely necessary. We've all had our share of those.

But it's just as obvious online when they never ask one personal question, ignore your comments, and ramrod their own agenda into every correspondence you receive from them. Which are, of course, almost all mass emails or forwards to reach the widest audience possible.

It's unthinkable that Jesus, if He still wore an earth suit today, would ever trample an individual's worth to use her for His own benefit. No, Jesus did just the opposite—He sacrificed Himself for those who tried to use Him for their own agenda.

So do me a favor, will ya? If I ever bore you to tears droning on about my life, books, children, grandbuddies, granddog, or the wart on my big toe and neglect to make you feel like a person of interest, respect, and dignity, *please* tell me. Or whack me with a brick.

Creator of Human Dignity,
Help me treat each person I
encounter today with respect.

Stuck in Crete

The reason I left you in Crete was that you
might put in order what was left unfinished.
TITUS 1:5 NIV

Like Titus, all of us have been stuck in Crete at one time or another. Some of us are there now.

In New Testament times, the remote island of Crete wasn't a great place to be. The apostle Paul lamented that "the people of Crete are all liars; [they are] cruel animals, and lazy gluttons" (Titus 1:12 NLT). Yet Paul left his beloved assistant, Titus, there to sort out the fledgling church's mess.

Not likely a mission Titus volunteered for, but Paul chose him intentionally. He knew Titus needed time in Crete for his own good.

The Crete you and I get stuck in today isn't geographical.

No, our Crete is a mind-set—a place that may involve isolation, stress, or even suffering. A place we don't necessarily want to be, but our assignment is to stay until Papa God sends us elsewhere.

During our time in Crete, He may want us to clean up unfinished business or accomplish specific tasks before we move on. Or Papa may be developing within us the patience and trust necessary to wait for His will in His timing.

Titus was a wonderful role model of how not only to tolerate Crete but to prosper there. According to 2 Corinthians 7–8, Titus didn't pout about his "unfair" situation. He realized that his temporary discomfort was allowed by Yahweh to stretch his personal parameters. Titus knew he was where he was supposed to be and found joy in submission to God's plan.

Master of Perseverance,
I recognize that I'm stuck
in my own personal Crete
for a reason. Please give me
patience. And a rowboat.

Nudges

"When He, the Spirit of truth, comes,
He will guide you into all the truth."
JOHN 16:13 NASB

While pushing my cart through the grocery store paper goods aisle, I was struck by the nagging notion that I should buy extra toilet paper. *Whatever for?*

And then the face of someone going through financial struggles popped into my head. As I stared at the Quilted Northern, I couldn't banish Julie's face from my thoughts. *Buy toilet paper.* Sigh. So much to do today, but. . .oh, okay.

I worried about my presumption of Julie's need as I approached her front door with several bags of groceries. What if she was embarrassed by my act of unsolicited "charity"?

But Julie looked pleasantly surprised as I toted the bags in and began to unload on her kitchen table. Then when I pulled out the eight-pack of Charmin, she burst into tears.

Between sobs, she explained that her family had just finished their last roll of toilet paper; paper products had become a luxury item for their severely strained budget. She'd been collecting newspapers to stack in the bathroom when I arrived. To her, that toilet paper was proof positive that God heard her prayers and that He cared.

Newspapers.

I wept in my car all the way home. What if I hadn't heeded that holy nudge in the grocery store? I would've missed the blessing of meeting someone's rudimentary needs and acting as the hands of Jesus. Julie would have lost out, but I would've lost out too, because I wasn't sensitive to the Holy Spirit's promptings.

Have you met Him? The Holy Spirit, I mean. If not, please allow me to introduce you. More tomorrow. . .

Master of Mysteries,
Make me ever more aware
of Your holy nudges.

Triplets

The Spirit who lives in you is greater than the spirit who lives in the world.
1 JOHN 4:4 NLT

(Continued)

The Holy Spirit is the communicator of the Father, Son, and Holy Spirit trinity. A friend once mislabeled the trinity as "The Triplets," which I think actually helps clarify the three-persons-in-one nature of God.

The Holy Spirit wears many hats; His day is packed. (You and I thought *we* were busy!) The Holy Spirit's duties include:

- Guiding believers (Acts 13:2)
- Being our constant companion (John 14:16–17)
- Warning of danger (Acts 20:23)
- Counseling and teaching us (John 14:26)
- Comforting us (John 14:16)
- Giving us specific instructions (Acts 1:2, 8:29)
- Making us bold (Acts 4:31)
- Helping us discern truth (John 14:17)
- Helping us fight the Enemy (1 John 4:4)
- Developing our miracle memory (John 14:26)

That last one—miracle memory—is like muscle memory. My piano teacher always said, "Practice makes perfect," and it's true with faith too. Repetition of specific movement creates muscle memory. That's how pitchers learn to hit the inside corner and gymnasts land a back tuck on a skinny beam.

Faith works the same way. By practicing our faith every day, we'll automatically default to trust instead of fear when trials come.

And fighting the Enemy? Read today's verse aloud. That's spiritual warfare, girlfriend. We engage in it daily whether we realize it or not. Satan and his demonic spirits never take vacations. But the Holy Spirit is constantly on guard duty and ready to intercede at our first yelp.

More tomorrow. . .

....

....

....

....

....

Spiritual General,
I get the difference between an
unholy spirit and the Holy Spirit.
The first has a BB gun and the
second an AK-47. I'm immensely
grateful He's on my side.

Tune In

*"The Holy Spirit. . .will teach you all things and will
remind you of everything I have said to you."*
JOHN 14:26 NIV

(Continued)

So how does the Holy Spirit work?

I believe the Holy Spirit speaks to believers like radio waves broadcasting invisibly through the atmosphere. If your spiritual antenna isn't tuned in, the message will sound garbled, like a radio station off by a millimeter.

Or you may miss it altogether.

To receive messages, you must make the effort to tune your receiver to His frequency and LISTEN for His still, small voice. And. . .you must choose to *obey* His guidance—even when it's inconvenient or costly. Don't cast it off as your vivid imagination, or because you're crazy busy, or the idea is too far-fetched to believe.

Like a gift of toilet paper.

You know, Yahweh has a history of sending directives that don't make sense to their recipients:

- Noah was asked to build a boat in a desert.
- Joshua was instructed to conquer impenetrable Jericho by yelling at a wall.
- Simon Peter was told he'd catch fish if he lowered his nets on the OTHER side of the boat (wait, don't fish swim on *both* sides of boats?).
- Mary and Martha were assured their brother was only sleeping when he'd been deader than a fence post for four days.

Whether the Holy Spirit speaks through inner urgings, persistent thoughts, sermons, friends, or scripture sharper than a two-edged sword, He's trying to get through to us. He wants more than anything to be our Helper in living a victorious Christian life.

Even if He has to whisper behind the squeezable Charmin.

*Dearest Holy Spirit,
Speak to me today. I'm listening.
I'm tuning my spiritual antenna
to Your frequency.*

Hidden Labels

"You're the God who sees me!"
GENESIS 16:13 MSG

I often get frustrated when my daughter is trying to teach me some new technological gizmo that I can't seem to grasp. I find myself pulling out the *dumb* label I keep tucked inside my shirt and plastering it across my chest in neon letters.

Wearing this label, I feel justified that I can't learn anything new; it's just who I am—"the way God made me."

But Cricket doesn't buy it. "Mom," she says in an unsympathetic tone, "quit playing dumb. I know you're not. You *can* get this. Now stop hiding behind the 'old dog' mask and concentrate on this 'new trick.'"

We often rely on labels to clarify our identity. If we're not sure who we really are—or maybe don't *like* who we really are—perhaps we can hide behind a label that reflects who we wish we were.

Or, as in my case, we use labels as an excuse. Destructive labels like *dumb* or *fat, loser* or *helpless.* Possibly *worthless* or *damaged goods.* These types of labels may relieve stress by temporarily lessening others' expectations of us, but they erode our confidence. If we wear them long enough, we eventually forget about their presence. Or power.

These labels shape our thinking, which subconsciously modifies our behavior to fit the label.

So, what secret labels do you have tucked inside your shirt? Do you hide them so well that nobody knows they're there but you? I've got news for you, sister: Someone knows, and He ain't buying it either.

> *God Who Deplores Excuses,*
> *I'm so glad You don't believe*
> *in labels. When You look at me,*
> *please look past the labels I've*
> *plastered on myself and see*
> *the me You created.*

Hangin' Tough

*We get knocked down, but we
get up again and keep going.*
2 Corinthians 4:9 TLB

OCTOBER
18

The man we hired to trim the bushes didn't see the bird's nest until it was too late. Without its leafy covering, the nest was now completely exposed to the blazing sun, and the poor mama bird sitting on four eggs looked completely done in. I'd never seen a bird with its beak open and tongue hanging out like a panting dog.

My heart went out to this courageous little mama who'd been thrust into an unexpected crisis. All afternoon she stayed, her head drooping lower each passing hour in the punishing Florida heat.

When she finally left the nest, I moved it to a more protective location nearby. It looked like the perfect solution, except for one thing. The bird didn't return.

I'll never know if she was unable to find the relocated nest or if she gave up when the going got too tough. But it broke my heart.

Motherhood does that to all of us, sometimes. Chronic fatigue, disappointment, and never-ending pressure make our heads droop lower each passing hour. The heat is too intense. We seriously consider leaving our nest, never to return.

Watching that little bird made me think: How do I respond when the going gets tough? Do I hang in there for a while but then give up just before the perfect solution presents itself? Or do I persevere like our biblical role model of endurance?

Jesus endured despite ridicule, beatings, imprisonment, deception, and desertion. People failed Him time after time, but He rose above disappointment and kept going. His strength came from keeping His eyes on His Father, not on Himself.

*Precious Savior,
Teach me perseverance
by keeping my eyes on
You when things get tough.*

Boogie Down

Praise his name with dancing.
PSALM 149:3 NIV

I've finally accepted my dark little secret. I'm a boogieholic. I've tried to stop, but I just can't help myself. That's why I serve in children's church—I can let loose with the kiddies and nobody stares.

But hey, I'm not alone. You know who you are.

Yes, the Lord God gave some of us the boogie gene. We wriggle warriors cannot squelch the uncontrollable urge to physically respond to music, regardless of circumstantial inappropriateness. . .juking with the grocery cart down the cookie aisle, bopping to blaring CDs at red lights, waltzing like Cinderella to elevator Muzak.

Containing it is like trying to hide freckles.

You know what? There's unique exultation in the gut-level release of unfettered praise dancing. The Hebrew word for dance, *mahol*, also means "whirl; leap for joy." The unique purity and beauty of self-expression through spontaneous joyful movement has been found in countless cultures since the dawn of creation.

I definitely think spirit-inspired dancing can draw us closer to Papa God, whether in humble worship or in jubilation over His merciful blessings.

King David certainly thought so when he danced before the Lord with all his might in celebration of the arrival of the ark of God in Jerusalem (2 Samuel 6:14). Miriam, Moses' sister, was sure of it when she led the women in jubilant dancing after Jehovah's deliverance from the Egyptians after the parting of the Red Sea (Exodus 15:20).

And I believe Papa thinks so too. After all, the boogie gene was His idea.

My Strength and
My Song (Isaiah 12:2),
Thanks for the freedom of
praise and joyful dancing You
bring to my spirit. Help me
hear Your music in my soul.

Love Languages

"Love one another."
JOHN 13:34 NIV

I pulled into our driveway and dragged my carcass through the door after a nine-hour, scarf-a-crate-of-cookies-to-stay-awake marathon drive. I was whipped.

I just wanted to throw my luggage in a heap on the floor and myself in a heap on the bed.

Then I saw it.

There on the kitchen table, stacked as high as a cereal box, were comics painstakingly saved from every newspaper during the twenty-five days I'd been gone. That's a *lot* of comics.

It took me an hour to sit down and read them all, but read them I did. Why? Because I heard, touched, and felt love in every word.

Spouse knew my love language is "Acts of Service," meaning that the way to speak love to me so I actually hear it is to perform small services for me. He knew the funnies are the only reason I subscribe to newspapers. He also knew that regardless of how many times he said "I miss you" while I was away, I would *really* feel it by this simple deed that proved he cares about the little insignificant things I care about.

Because I matter. To him.

And he was absolutely right.

What a guy.

According to Dr. Gary Chapman's *5 Love Languages*, we don't all speak the same love language. When you think you're expressing love to someone, they might not hear the message you intend because they no-speaka-dat-language.

Your personal language might be Words of Affirmation, Quality Time, Gifts, Acts of Service, or Physical Touch, but theirs may not. To truly communicate love, we must be fluent in the receiver's language.

Prince of Peace,
Help me identify and become
fluent in love languages so
that nothing gets lost in
the translation.

Sweetly Ripened

God has made everything beautiful for its own time.
ECCLESIASTES 3:11 NLT

I have a theory about aging.

I call it the Increasing Gravity Phenomenon. The IPG postulates that the earth's magnetic pull increases annually. Yep—the magnetic core of the earth is sucking everything loose toward it more and more each year.

Like one of those vacuum tubes at the dentist's office that, when you close your lips around it, pops your eyeballs out of their sockets and would suck down your tongue if it wasn't attached back there by your hangy-ball.

I'm a believer in the Increasing Gravity Phenomenon. The evidence is right there on the back of my arms and dangling off my chin.

Speaking of loose skin, if you ask me, the reason so many of us mature, sweetly ripened women develop kyphosis (hunchback) is because we're subconsciously trying to hide the majority of our chins by rounding our shoulders and protruding our heads forward. (Now don't you dare tell me you've never done this for a picture!)

I call it the chicken-neck maneuver. Disguises jowls and wattles too.

Then there's the Clark Gable phenomenon that appears on the upper lip when estrogen disappears. At least we don't have to worry about spiderweb lines around our lips—the mustache covers them right up.

No, seriously, aging is good. For cheese. And remember—the best meats marinate for a looong time. Ever been compared to a rump roast?

The good news is that middle age has its benefits. You make lots of new friends. . .people you meet for the first time whom you've met a half-dozen times before.

*Creator of Aging,
I'm just glad to be here.
Help me focus on what's
remaining instead of
lamenting what's lost.*

Dearest Treasures

"Store up for yourselves treasures in heaven....
For where your treasure is, there your heart will be also."
MATTHEW 6:20–21 NIV

I'll never forget Thelma and Louise, the field mice who moved into our mountain cabin the winter I left the full bird feeder propped against the living room wall.

While we were gone, our furry guests busily deposited birdseed in every possible nook and cranny. I picture them stuffing their bulging cheeks and making trip after trip to store their treasure for future feasts, thinking they'd soon be kicking their little mice feet up on a matchbox and enjoying the good life.

Come spring, we found piles of birdseed sequestered in hidden cubbies; plentiful pawfuls were spread throughout every cabinet, closet, and drawer, even between the bedsheets.

Sadly, we also found the spent bodies of Thelma and Louise keeled over from sheer exhaustion beside the empty bird feeder. They'd worked themselves to death in their futile attempt to store up treasure.

You know, treasure comes in all shapes and sizes; one's birdseed may be another's money, trendy clothes, big house, newest iPhone, or flashy car. It may even be developing a superkid. Or abs of steel. Or a workhorse reputation.

Treasure is anything that we deem important enough to strive for…to yearn for…to sacrifice for.

But earthly treasures—however permanent they may seem as we struggle to acquire them—may fade, corrode, or be stripped away. The only lasting treasures are those we store in heaven; the souls we introduce to Jesus.

Our dearest treasures are the things we spend most of our time and energy on. Tell me, sister, what are yours?

Everlasting Lord,
Help me define and refocus on
my dearest treasures today.

Mighty Mites

"More blessings come from giving than from receiving."
ACTS 20:35 CEV

"Swell," I monotoned. "I can almost buy lunch." I held up my whopping $20.15 paycheck for an article I'd written.

"As long as we skip dessert," Spouse cheerfully agreed. "And just think how delighted God will be with your two-dollar tithe!"

My tithe? Why, I hadn't even considered offering Papa such a pittance. . .a raindrop in the sea.

Then I remembered the story of the widow's mite in Mark 12:41–44 (look it up). She probably wondered if contributing her two pennies was worth walking to the temple for, but Jesus sure thought so. He called her our model for giving.

Okay, I resolved, *if Jesus thinks my mites are valuable, my mites He'll have.*

My tithe (10 percent of my income as described in Deuteronomy 14:22) that year for ten published articles totaled $230. I asked Papa where He wanted to use it.

A teacher friend told me about a deaf teenager who'd overcome innumerable obstacles to become the first in his poor immigrant family to ever graduate high school. Pedro, a senior, worked in a restaurant after school to afford basics his parents couldn't provide for his younger siblings.

I asked my friend to deliver my mites to Pedro with an anonymous note praising his diligence in obtaining an education and asking the Lord to bless his efforts. Pedro was astounded that a total stranger would give him what he perceived as a fortune. Moved to tears, he sent a heartfelt thank-you note back that began, "Dear angel from God. . ."

Giver of All Blessings,
I realize that my mites are
indeed raindrops. . .small indi-
vidually, but together they flow
as a mighty outpouring of Your
grace. And they're all Yours.

Masquerade

"The truth will set you free."
JOHN 8:32 CEV

An ear-piercing scream came from the bedroom. I was helping my daughter Cricket and her husband move into their new home. But obviously something was wrong.

As I dashed into the clothes-strewn room, I found Cricket and her friend Stephanie climbing each other like human ladders, squealing like demonized pigs, and pointing toward the corner.

There quivered a wee baby squirrel, his terrified eyes round as quarters.

His mama must have hidden him away in what she thought was a safe, cushy nest of clothes while the moving van doors stood open. Didn't turn out as safe as she thought.

Hiding places are often ineffective, aren't they? Seems like we're always found out sooner or later.

Like Jonah, who ended up human sushi until he realized he could run but he couldn't hide from the Almighty.

Or Esther, a Jewess living incognito in Persia until "such a time as this" when she blew her cover to save her people from annihilation.

And of course, Joseph, the Egyptian ruler who finally popped his cork at the appearance of his turncoat brothers and admitted he was an undercover Hebrew slave.

So why do you and I continue to hide? Why do we conceal parts of ourselves. . .cloak our true motives. . .wear masks?

The Lord sees through our disguises and knows all our hiding places. And that's a good thing. Because like today's verse reminds us, there's freedom in truth.

Freedom. It's worth the risk of unveiling our masquerade.

*Abba Father,
I know I can trust You.
Give me courage to
remove my mask today.*

Heave Those Sheaves

Come before his presence with singing.
PSALM 100:2 KJV

One cold October morning in the Smokies, my family headed to church, a forty-minute trek over the river and through the woods. But whoops! The bridge was closed for repairs, so we followed weathered signs nearly hidden by weeds to a steeple-topped country church with a cemetery on one side and outhouse on the other.

Climbing the plank steps, we were greeted by surprised smiles and heartfelt handshakes as if we were the only visitors this little church had seen in a long time.

We sat on a wooden pew as the entire congregation (all fifteen of them) gathered around an old upright piano in the corner. I mean to tell you, the Holy Spirit filled that place as the off-key choir joyfully and robustly brought in the sheaves, leaned on the everlasting arms, and claimed their place in line when the roll is called up yonder.

One grinning, white-whiskered fella belted out, "When the rolls is served up yonder, I'll be there!"

For me, it was a nostalgic, sweet, worshipful journey back to my grandmother's Georgia kitchen when her ancient radio would serenade us with glorious old hymns on Sunday mornings before church. I loved them as a child, and I love them now.

I doubt many of the modern-day worshippers in my urbanized mega-church have ever heard those beloved hymns, much less felt their heart transported to the Almighty's throne by a foot-stomping group of mountain folk in their best frocks and overalls.

More's the pity. Sometimes we really oughta heave a few sheaves of our own.

Lover of Heart-Songs,
I lift up my voice to You today.
Please accept my song offering
as sweet music to Your ears.

Muffin Top Grannies

"You will have plenty to eat, until you are full."
JOEL 2:26 NIV

After a hard day, there's just no better comfort food than a chocolate chip cookie warm from the oven. Or two. Or ten.

Slice-and-bake was a wicked enough temptation, but now Satan himself has created those giant tubs of premixed cookie dough. They're straight from the Fire and Brimstone Bakery. I'll never admit to being one of those pathetic women who sneaks spoonfuls of raw cookie dough. Uh-uh. Not me.

Just don't give me a Breathalyzer test.

Still, there's something creatively satisfying in mixing your own cookie dough, don't you think? I found myself in the dubiously delightful position of testing dozens of cookie recipes when I was writing my Too Blessed to be Stressed Cookbook. It was pure ecstasy.

Like my longtime dream of my doctor saying I need to gain a little weight had come true. Test. . .tweak. . .test. . .tweak. . .eat, eat, eat. Yep. Pure ecstasy. For the moment.

Ten pounds later, I couldn't fasten my bra. Those humpback whales on my outer thighs were looking preggers, and my cotton grannies sprouted muffin tops.

Isn't it Newton's third law of physics that states for every action there is an equal and opposite reaction? Well, Deb's third law of munching states that cookie consumption is inversely proportionate to cookie application, meaning one-fourth pound of consumed batter equals four pounds of thigh-u-lite.

Bottom line? There are consequences for overeating. There are consequences for sin. Whether it's binging food, money, sex, alcohol, drugs, attention. . .you do the vice, you pay the price.

Purveyor of Justice,
Help me consider the
consequences before I
overindulge today.

Developing Camel Knees

For this reason I kneel before the Father.
EPHESIANS 3:14 NIV

James, author of the epistle and half brother of Jesus (James's parents were Mary and Joseph), was nicknamed "Old Camel Knees" because of calluses he developed while kneeling in prayer.* Kneeling is out of vogue in many modern-day Christian circles, but I find it's the best position to get my heart in the right attitude for prayer.

But what exactly is the function of prayer? How does it work? Can we really influence the Creator of all things by our simple petition?

For centuries, religious scholars have pondered these questions and still don't understand. All we know for sure is that throughout His Word, Papa God repeatedly tells us to pray.

My favorite analogy of prayer is a magnifying lens. Picture a child in a sunny field holding a magnifying glass over a blade of grass. A wisp of smoke ascends from the spot where a super-heated sunbeam is trained. Soon a flame erupts. The lens serves as a focal point for the broad rays of the sun to exponentially increase their potency into a powerful beam.

The way I see it, prayer similarly reins in the broad attention of Jehovah to focus His supernatural power on a specific area.

We must, however, resist the temptation to view prayer as a free pass to success. The Almighty does not provide "Golden Midas Touch" tickets or "Skip to the Head of the Line" coupons because we follow a magical formula or develop three new knee calluses.

But He does promise to hear every prayer. Even if we speak in camel.

....

....

....

....

....

....

....

....

....

....

....

> *Emmanuel (God with Us),
> I view my camel knees as a
> badge of honor. The thicker
> they are, the more heart time
> I'm spending with You.*
>
> *Recorded in AD 325 by
> Eusebius of Caeserea in an
> account of church history.

Dousing Fires

*If we could control our tongues, we. . .could
also control ourselves in every other way.*
JAMES 3:2 NLT

I watched my friend Donna's face crumble. Guilt surged through my innards like molten lava. She was disappointed. *In me.* And she had every right to be.

I'd blown it, all right. Donna had confided to me that her young son had recently been experiencing seizures and she was terrified. Without thinking, I casually mentioned this to a group of mutual friends. . .not as an urgent prayer request, or in order to help Donna's family (potentially redeeming reasons), but simply as a matter of human interest.

The same way you'd discuss a three-legged dog.

A week later, several of the girls brought it up to Donna. "How did you know?" she asked, concern etching her face. "We were trying to keep it private for now."

"Deb told us," they replied. All eyes turned to me.

Oh, man.

It was at that moment I realized I'd breached her confidence. Betrayed her faith in me. Let her down. Shame seared my conscience.

Many of us don't let thoughts marinate nearly long enough before we spew them out of our mouths. We have blabber control issues.

Raise your hand if this is you. It's okay. 'Fess up. My hand's up; is yours?

As Christ followers, we want to honor Him with our speech. Instead we spend an awful lot of time dousing forest fires sparked by our blazing tongues.

Don't despair, dear friend. There's hope for our loose lips! The Creator of self-control is happy to loan us a muzzle if we sincerely want to change (Psalm 39:1).

*Master of Discretion,
Shut my mouth, Lord.
That's all. Just shut my mouth.*

Goading

Let my words and my thoughts be pleasing to you, Lord.
PSALM 19:14 CEV

When I was nine, my sister was two years older and light-years girlier. She wore wraparound skirts, hair bows, and shiny pink nail polish.

I lived barefoot, wore ratty cut-off jeans, and spent my time riding bikes, climbing trees, or playing baseball.

Hence my big problem.

Since it was just the two of us, during long summer days when I wanted to go outside and snag a few grounders, there was no one but Cindy to play with. And she never wanted to face the heat, dirt, and bugs of a scorching Florida afternoon.

When begging didn't work, I resorted to goading her with the big ammo:

"Fatty, fatty, two by four, can't get through the bathroom door. . ."

The fact that Cindy was about as big around as a licorice stick never seemed to matter, for she was at the age that every girl thinks she's fat. And I quickly learned that the surefire way to get something I wanted was to goad her into it.

A goad, by definition, is a pointed rod used to urge animals forward. To prod. To prompt. To guide a big hairy beast from one place to another (no offense, Cindy!).

Verbal goads can serve to prod, prompt, or guide humans from one place to another too. . . as in moving people from non-belief to belief, from agnosticism to theism, from an egocentric worldview to a Christ-centered perspective.

Bet you're wondering where all this is going, right? Tune in tomorrow to find out!

Teller of Truths,
Am I guilty of selfishly goading
to get my way? I hate to think
I'm a manipulator, but the shoe
seems to fit. Almost. Ouch.

From Nonsense to God-Sense

The words of the wise are like goads.
ECCLESIASTES 12:11 NIV

(Continued)

The concept of goads weighed heavily on me during the week after a dear Christian friend passed away. The heaviness in my spirit was not for my friend—although I missed her dreadfully, I had no doubt she was joyfully dancing an Irish jig in heaven's hoppingest dance hall.

No, it was about her brother, an intellectual know-it-all who views Christianity with disdain. He'd spent the last evening of his sister's life on earth denouncing to me the "blatant weaknesses" and "contradictions" of the Bible as she lay there on her deathbed, painfully taking it all in.

My friend had confided in me many times her yearning for the light of Jesus to break through her brother's darkness. The Almighty is, after all, in the mind-changing business.

I keenly felt the weight of her unfulfilled burden, asking myself: Do my words goad people in a Jesus-ward direction? Do I actively seek to move people from one spiritual place to another? Am I a godly goader?

As author Jill Briscoe puts it, "Do our words. . .prick their consciences? Move them from meaninglessness to meaningfulness? From nothingness to something-ness? From nonsense to God-sense?"

So I prayed for Papa to give me wise goading words for this man. Not academically impressive words, but words brimming with Jesus-joy that will break through his intellectual defenses to prepare the way for the Holy Spirit to penetrate his heart darkness with a shaft of blinding light.

Not unlike what happened to another know-it-all named Saul on a road to Damascus.

Saver of Souls,
Burden my heart with souls
desperately needing to move
from nonsense to God-sense.

Spooky

" 'Those who honor me I will honor.' "
1 SAMUEL 2:30 NIV

This is the night you don't want to leave your black cat outside.

Did you know that Halloween originated with the ancient pagan Celtic festival of Samhain, celebrated on November 1? The night before Samhain, the dead were believed to return as ghosts roaming the countryside. People left food and wine on their doorsteps to appease these wandering souls and wore masks to hobnob with the ghouls.

In the eighth century, the Christian church tried to reclaim this unholy holiday, proclaiming November 1 "All Saints' Day" or "All Hallows' Day." But many were reluctant to let go of what they perceived as innocent spooky fun, dubbing the preceding night "Hallows' Eve," which became "Halloween," and eventually introduced trick-or-treating.

Halloween caught on and is now the second most commercialized holiday after Christmas, with six billion dollars spent each year on costumes and candy.

Some Christ followers choose not to acknowledge this dark celebration of superstition; some see no harm in it.

When my children were young, our church hosted an annual "All Saints' Eve Party," a Halloween alternative that included games, candy, Bible stories, and costumes commemorating Bible characters or pretty much anything except witches, goblins, or devils. The idea was to keep the focus on holy rather than horror.

Each believer must make her own decision about how to handle Halloween; it's my prayer that we will not criticize or condemn the choices of others who come to different conclusions than we do.

It's really between you and Papa. Nobody else.

If we allow something like this to divide us, Satan truly will have the last laugh.

*Father of Light,
Show me how to honor
You in everything I do.*

Marchin' In

Let the saints be joyful.
PSALM 149:5 KJV

"Oh when the saints. . .go marchin' in. Oh when the saints go marchin' in. Oh Lord, I want to be in that number. . .when the saints go marchin' in."

I'll bet you, like me, have sung that song scads of times without really thinking about the meaning, am I right?

So today, on All Saints' Day, let's chew on it a smidge.

- Who exactly are the saints?
- In the song, where are the saints marching into?
- Why would I want to be there?

The answer to the first question is a bit controversial. Roman Catholics have traditionally celebrated a form of All Saints' Day (as I mentioned yesterday) for centuries. On November 1, they commemorate those who have attained the "beautific vision in Heaven," a specific status of sainthood (like Saint Augustine and Saint Francis of Assisi; I understand Mother Teresa is currently in the process).

Many Protestants consider all Christ followers as saints and honor believers past and present on All Saints' Day. So according to the song, the saints are marching into heaven; dollars to donuts you and I surely want to be in their number when our day comes.

So let me hear you humming, girlfriend!

I mean, really, why *not* celebrate our salvation on a special day? I can imagine a huge smile on Papa God's face as He taps His foot and nods in time to a New Orleans jazz band rendition honoring His beloved children marching into their forever home.

Hey, I'll gladly take any reason to be joyful, won't you?

*Great Band Leader,
I celebrate my salvation
today. I can't thank You
enough for the joyous
promise of heaven. Woo-hoo!*

Blinders

Help everyone who is weak.
ACTS 20:35 CEV

Nothing is more decom-stressing than kicking back at a restaurant to enjoy food someone else has prepared in pans you don't have to scrub, served on plates you don't have to wash, right?

Well, except for the time my friend Laura attended a church-affiliated planning meeting at a local pancake house.

The speaker stood at one end of the clustered tables and spoke while the food was being served. Laura had only taken a couple of bites when she suddenly began choking. She struggled for the next ten minutes, in turn gasping for air, turning purple, and coughing up food and water.

Her husband, also the group's trained CPR person, was seated directly across from Laura and never saw or heard a thing. As Laura choked, the speaker, standing directly behind her, kept on talking as if nothing was wrong. For inexplicable reasons, the people present were somehow blinded to Laura's attack.

Everyone was stunned when they learned of her horrible experience right under their noses. How could this near-tragedy have happened?

It's a mystery.

But perhaps it's a lesson to all of us about the danger of being so absorbed in the task at hand that we inadvertently don blinders to the needs of flesh-and-blood people in our midst. People just like us at some point in our lives.

People suffering in plain sight.

*Compassionate Judge,
Please forgive me when I'm so engrossed in my own agenda that I don't see the needs of someone right under my nose. Clear my vision when Satan does his durndest to blind me.*

Rocky Road

*"You know me, Master God, just as I am. You've done
all this not because of who I am but because of
who you are—out of your very heart!"*
2 Samuel 7:20–21 MSG

I dunno. Maybe it's a common tiny dog thing. Our five-pound granddog (who lives with us) shivers nonstop from October until March. If the temp dips below sixty-five, Rocky quivers like a tower of Jell-O.

I sometimes slip a heated beanbag in his doggy bed. If I forget, he turns his well-practiced pathetic puppy-dog eyes on me, shaking like his paw is stuck in an electrical outlet.

One chilly day I got home early and walked into our bedroom. I noticed the light beaming from the electric blanket control, so I went over to turn it off. Spouse, who isn't exactly known for his benevolent canine affinities, popped up behind me saying, "What are you doing?"

"I must've left the electric blanket on this morning," I replied. "I'm just turning it off."

"No," he said, looking suspiciously sheepish. "Don't."

It was then I noticed a lump beneath the bedcovers. The lump moved. For heaven's sake—the man who frequently threatened to "nuke that yappy mutt in the microwave" had tenderly put the shivering dog in our bed and turned on the electric blanket.

Makes me consider the way Papa God treats me. Like Rocky, I'm needy and dependent on my Master's care to get by day to day. He feeds me, cleans up my mistakes, tolerates my yapping, and when I turn my poor puppy-dog eyes upward and beg for mercy, He's more than happy to take me into His bed and turn up the heat.

It's a common tiny person thing.

*Generous God of Comfort,
I'm humbled and grateful
for Your traveling mercies
on my own Rocky Road.*

Let's Party!

*Then Moses. . .and the seventy elders of Israel climbed
up the mountain. There they saw the God of Israel.*
EXODUS 24:9–10 NLT

After forty years of reading the Bible, I discovered something new. I hope I'm not the only clueless wonder here.

Were you aware that Moses wasn't the only person (besides Adam and Eve) to see God and live to tell about it? According to today's scripture, there were dozens. Apparently the Almighty threw a party for a handpicked bunch in His mountain hideaway.

Exodus 24 records that after the children of Israel had departed Egypt and were just beginning their wilderness trek, seventy-four Hebrew leaders were invited up to Mt. Sinai where they shared a meal together in God's presence (verse 11).

How incredibly cool is that?

Can you imagine munching manna appetizers with the King of the universe? My imagination runs wild just considering what the party chatter must have been like:

"So, Lord, what does Your agenda look like for the next, say, forty years?"

"Hey Moses, did you try the quail wings? Secret's in the sauce!"

"I saw you double dipping, Aaron. Gross. Were you raised in a barn?"

"Should we stay and wash dishes, Yahweh? Good help is so hard to find these days."

Isn't it incredible that God loves His children so much, He intentionally seeks our company? He *wants* to spend time with us. He desires to hear our thoughts and share His with us.

Do we give Him the same consideration?

How many times have I closed my Bible after four verses because I'm sleepy? Or left a prayer unfinished because I got sidetracked?

*Great "I Am,"
If I rethink my priorities,
could I possibly make the
A-list for Your next shindig?*

Healed

"Your faith has made you well."
LUKE 18:42 NASB

I adore studying scripture in various translations and commentaries, unearthing every smidgen of application to my own life. Won't you open your Bible to Luke 18:35–43 and join me as Jesus heals a blind man?

- This story is recorded in three of the four Gospels: Matthew, Mark, and Luke.
- Jesus was likely quite emotional on this trip to Jerusalem, knowing He was about to die. He'd just tried enlightening His twelve disciples (verses 31–34)—His closest friends—but they didn't get it. The heartache must have been staggering.
- The blind man was a professional beggar, accustomed to being ignored.
- He'd already heard about this mysterious healer, so when Jesus passed by, he hollered his brains out, refusing to remain invisible.
- The broken man first asked for **mercy** then healing. He knew which was most important.
- Jesus' own peeps told the guy to shut his face (verse 39). Why would anyone *not* want Jesus to show mercy to someone? Were they jealous? Compassionless? Or like me, squeezed dry by a too-tight schedule?
- "Jesus stopped" (verse 40). I LOVE this. Jesus allowed Himself to be interrupted. He wasn't too busy, stressed, or preoccupied to meet someone's needs. *Hmm.* Then why am I?
- When Jesus' true power was revealed, the man made an instant decision to follow Him, glorifying God and sharing the incredible news with everyone he saw.

The blind man not only saw the light; he saw the Christ. Whereas he had once believed *about* Jesus, now he believed *in* Jesus. And he told everyone.

Oh, sister, that you and I might be so bold.

*Eye-Opening Lord,
I too once was blind. But
now I see. Help me act like it.*

Power in That Name

Then everyone will be praising the name of the
Lord Jesus Christ because of the results they see in you.
2 THESSALONIANS 1:12 TLB

Names are important, aren't they?

I realized this truth when I visited my parents' church and my eighty-eight-year-old father introduced me to his friends by my sister's name. No doubt it wouldn't have mattered to them, but I was surprised how much it mattered to me.

"Daddy, you only have two daughters and I'm not that one," I gently rebuked him. "I'm Debbie, the youngest."

"Well, you sure are, aren't you?" he replied, squinting to get a better look at me. I'd been sitting beside him for the past hour.

"He's never known how old I am either," I said with a grin to Daddy's octogenarian friends.

"How could I?" Daddy quipped back. "It changes every year."

I recently did a personal Bible study on the name of Jesus and was struck anew by just how important His name is to those of us who call Him Lord. Here's why:

- Jesus' name was foretold by an angel before He was conceived (Luke 2:21).
- We're gifted with eternal life by believing in the name of Jesus (John 20:31).
- There's healing power in the name of Jesus (Acts 3:6, 4:10, and 16:18).
- We find courage and boldness by using the name of Jesus (Acts 9:29).
- We're forgiven and remade by the name of Jesus (1 Corinthians 6:11).
- We're able to love the unlovable through the name of Jesus (1 John 3:23).

Yes, there's power in a name. Especially *that* name.

Name Above All Names,
Help me keep Your name holy
and precious, and to never,
ever use it disrespectfully.

Mirrors Are Stupid, Stupid, Stupid

*Like a gold ring in a pig's snout is a
beautiful face on an empty head.*
PROVERBS 11:22 MSG

That dreadful summer day, I stood cowering on the high-dive platform at the public pool. As a chubby twelve-year-old, I was self-conscious about my changing body and felt shamefully exposed to the world in my bathing suit.

We were visiting my grandmother in north Georgia, and she'd insisted that I spend the afternoon at the community pool "making friends." Well, I was far too shy to speak to anyone I didn't know (hard to believe, I know), so I ended up splashing around the shallow end by myself.

After watching happily screaming kids leap from the highest platform for an hour, I'd finally gotten up the nerve to ascend the ladder to heaven. It was sure high enough to reach the pearly gates but felt more like hell when I got there.

One peek over the edge and I was paralyzed with fear. I couldn't go forward or back. I just stood there. Terrified.

An older girl behind me urged, "Go on, jump!"

Nuh-uh.

"Jump, will ya?" she snapped. "You're holding up the line."

I. Could. Not. Move.

She shook her head with contempt. "You shouldn't have come up here. You're chicken. You're fat. And you're *ugly.*"

I jumped. It was the only way to hide the tears.

*Altogether Lovely Savior,
Because You made me in
Your image, I know that viewing
myself as ugly is a slap in Your
face. You didn't make me ugly;
I made me ugly. Help me always
remember that in Your eyes,
I'm beautiful.*

Low Boil

*Fix your thoughts on what is true,
and honorable, and right.*
PHILIPPIANS 4:8 NLT

On her way to Bible study one morning, my friend Mary was stuck at an infinity light—you know, the interminably long traffic light at which you sprout a cauliflower bum before it finally lets three cars through.

Mary was on low boil by the time she reached first car position. To unzip the pants on her rotten attitude, she grabbed her Bible on the seat beside her and flipped it open.

Her teeth had just begun to ungnash when a car horn blared behind her. Oh, yikes—the light was green! As Mary shifted her foot to the accelerator, the intersection in front of her exploded in an ear-splitting collision of metal on metal.

A speeding truck had run the red light, T-boning the oncoming car that was precisely where Mary would have been if she hadn't been reading her Bible.

Near misses. Averted disasters. Life-altering circumstances that almost happened but didn't. Gifts of grace, they are directly from the hand of a loving, present Father.

Grace is abundant in our everyday lives, whether we're aware of it or not. The fact that we roll out of bed in the morning is the result of grace. That we keep breathing in and out all day. That we're able to buy milk and eggs for our families.

Each of those things is a gift we didn't earn and don't deserve. Grace and more grace. Abundant grace. Amazing grace.

Mary says it's easier now to endure infinity lights—she invests the time marveling at Papa's everyday grace.

*Emmanuel (God with Us),
You truly are. With us.
Wow. BIG wow. Help me
see Your marvelous grace
today in every breath I take.*

Becoming a Barnabas

Encourage one another and build each other up.
1 THESSALONIANS 5:11 NIV

As you may know, Barnabas was one of the first converts to Christianity at Pentecost. He was known for his selfless generosity and ability to settle disputes among believers. He earned the nickname "Son of Encouragement" (Acts 4:36).

Paul chose Barnabas as his trusted companion. I imagine that he greatly enjoyed the company of his upbeat friend and *needed* the countenance boost that an encourager brings.

Suzanne is my Barnabas.

Yep, she's my encourager. We were both Christian magazine writers who felt the Lord's leading to dive into the intimidating sea of book publication at the same time. We met as random (now really, is anything random with Papa God?) roommates at a California writer's conference and have lit up the cross-country cyber-highway ever since.

Suzanne and I jive like peanut butter and jelly. Peas and carrots. Forrest and Jen-nay. We edited each other's first few books and even cowrote a devotional for aspiring writers together: *Grit for the Oyster.*

Our personalities complement each other in all the right places. We're like two pieces of a bigger, God-ordained puzzle. We don't always agree, but since our relationship is based on trust and truth, we agree to disagree, and the respect we have for each other remains intact.

So who is your Barnabas? Which friend makes a smile tug at your lips and lightness spring to your heart when they come to mind? Perhaps today is a good time to thank your encourager for being your advocate and sustainer, the one you depend on to haul you out of the potholes in your life journey.

*One Who Knows,
I am so grateful for my friend
and encourager, _____.
So now I ponder: Whose
Barnabas am I?*

Devil's Last Laugh

*Be on your guard.... Your enemy, the devil, is like a roaring lion,
sneaking around to find someone to attack.*
1 PETER 5:8 CEV

The wall jumps out and whacks my shoulder as I stagger down the hallway. The sidewalk swerves while I'm walking my dog and I land on all fours in my neighbor's shrubbery.

Drives me batty, this Tilt-a-Whirl from Hades. The hangover that isn't. The devil's last laugh. Vertigo.

The world spins out of control with every head movement. It's like you just rolled off a merry-go-round that was shoved by a 250-pound linebacker. Only it doesn't stop after you get off.

I've actually played tennis in the throes of vertigo. The risks include falling flat on your face while serving and impaling yourself on the back fence chasing a lob. I know, I know—only a tennis junkie would subject themselves to playing like a marionette being operated by a giant invisible hand with a nasty twitch hovering over the court.

But you can't just stop living when things aren't perfect, right?

We all have our devil's last laugh. That plague you can't shake. The thing that makes you miserable and just won't stop. Yours may be a medical condition like mine, or it might be something subtle like guilt or shyness or defeat.

Regardless, it's the devil's devious way of staying under your skin. Of making you feel weak and powerless and impotent as a child of God.

So how do we take back the last laugh? Keep going. Despite the annoying hindrances designed to sideline us. Don't let Satan win. Resolve to stay in the race even with a pebble in your shoe.

*Omnipotent Coach,
Send me in. I want to win.
I will have the last laugh.*

Keeping It Real

"I tell you the truth."
MATTHEW 5:18 NLT

I sat mesmerized on the rough wooden pew as the young backwoods mountain preacher who doubled as a farmer during the week and preacher on Sundays strode purposely to the rickety wooden pulpit. He preached a rousing sermon encouraging his flock to "Walk Close to the Lord," complete with an unforgettable illustration that went something like this:

"When I was a boy, my daddy used to take me coon huntin' after dark. Some nights, the woods were pitch black and Daddy would walk in front of me to blaze a trail.

"As long as I was right behind him, followin' in his footsteps, I was protected. But the minute I started daydreaming and straying from the path he'd prepared for me... *WHACK!* A low branch he'd pushed aside would pop back in my face and knock the snot outta me.

"Followin' our heavenly Father is like that. If we don't stay close and follow directly in His footsteps, we're gonna get the snot knocked outta us by the devilish tree limbs of life."

Whoa. By his simple but explicit analogy, that earnest young preacher translated a profound spiritual truth into terms everyone could grasp and would likely always remember.

In our effort to modernize, sterilize, homogenize, and appeal to the cultured masses, our churches may have lost something precious—that element of "real" often deemed too simplistic and unsophisticated for today's worship services.

Maybe we just need to have the snot knocked outta us once in a while to reconnect with the raw, first-love joy of followin' Jesus.

*Lion of Judah,
I promise that today, You lead,
I'll follow. Real close. And maybe
the snot will stay in my head.*

Compassion

Even in darkness light dawns. . .
for those who are gracious and compassionate.
PSALM 112:4 NIV

Dorsey, a young man in his twenties, was always the first to arrive in our church kitchen and the last to leave after everything was spick-and-span. His gift was service, and he joyfully gave his time, energy, and organizational expertise to provide years of delightful meals for his church family.

One dark day, the horrific news spread that Dorsey had been diagnosed as HIV positive. He was strongly advised by church leadership not to return to the kitchen. No alternative role of service was discussed, no counseling offered, no. . .nothing.

Dorsey eventually faded from view with few calls or visits from his previous church friends. My family was privileged to pray for Dorsey and maintain contact with him and his parents as they struggled through full-blown AIDS.

I vividly recall the night Chuck and I were returning from a dinner engagement when I suddenly felt a strong urge to visit Dorsey. Not tomorrow. . .*now*. He was bed-bound in his parents' home and unable to speak, but his eyes lit in recognition when we held his hands.

It crushed my heart to sit there, brushing the sweaty hair from his forehead, remembering the countless times he had selflessly served me. Now it was my turn to serve him. I sang his favorite praise song and whispered how much Papa God loved him.

He nodded.

Three hours later Dorsey was in heaven.

It took me a long time to heal. Judging from the tears on my cheeks right now, perhaps I still haven't.

But this I know: Compassion is always the right thing. Always.

Dryer of Tears,
Please let me see those going
through dark times through
Your compassionate eyes.

Rubbish

*"There is much rubbish. . .we ourselves
are unable to rebuild the wall."*
NEHEMIAH 4:10 NASB

Nehemiah was frustrated. He had taken time off work to tackle a project, but everything was going wrong. It was a much bigger task than he'd anticipated: mounds of rubbish were in the way, progress was slower than an earthworm race, and nobody would help until he squawked like a chicken.

Sound like the last major project you attempted?

While studying the book of Nehemiah (grab your Bible and join me!), I totally related to these contributions to the poor guy's discouragement in trying to rebuild the great wall around Jerusalem:

- **Fatigue.** Makes it way too easy to quit.
- **Frustration.** Rises exponentially with the amount of rubbish I'm dealing with.
- **Failure.** Feelings that cause me to lose hope and want to walk away.
- **Negativity.** To counteract feelings of failure, I must change my *her*spective by upgrading the way I see, think, and speak to a more positive tone.
- **Fear.** Spreads quickly and sucks the power right out of my faith.
- **Feeling overwhelmed.** I must ask for help; don't try to do it all myself.
- **Clutter.** I can reorganize my life to declutter and get rid of the rubbish.
- **Isolation.** Remember what the Lord has done for me and draw strength from other believers.

Yep, the walls you and I must build may not be stones and mortar like Nehemiah's, but just like he did, we must clear away the rubbish to begin.

*Sovereign God,
Clearly show me the rubbish in
my life causing discouragement.
And please provide a BIG
wheelbarrow to haul it away.*

Keep On Keeping On

God blesses those who patiently endure.
JAMES 1:12 NLT

Whatever our foe—unemployment, rejection, divorce, abuse, personal loss, illness, fatigue—we may feel beaten down and don't see how we can possibly endure.

But sweet friend, there's hope. Others have done it.

Let's look at three biblical role models of perseverance.

Ruth tragically lost her husband, friends, and home but chose to follow God's guidance to accompany her mother-in-law to a foreign country, where Ruth was *different*.

Rather like you moving to a remote Kenyan village. Hard. Lonely.

Because Ruth persevered, she was blessed with new love and new life, completing the lineage that produced King David, and later, Jesus Christ.

Hannah not only had to share her husband with another woman; she was barren—a public disgrace in her day. For years she endured cruel taunting from "the other woman." Hannah was greatly distressed and wept bitterly.

But here's our takeaway: she kept on praying.

The Lord mercifully blessed Hannah with her heart's desire, and Hannah's child grew to become the mighty prophet Samuel.

Jesus, of course, was our gold standard example of endurance through hardship. He persevered through ridicule, beatings, imprisonment, deception, and desertion by His closest friends. People failed Jesus again and again. But He rose above disappointment and hurt. He kept His eyes on His deeper purpose—saving the very ones who had wounded Him most.

So what about you—are you feeling beaten down? Struggling daily to endure? Can't seem to rise above it?

Well, what you can't rise above you must pass through.

Jesus will help you do it. Take His hand.

*Lord Jesus,
I'm in a hard place right
now. I know You've been
there too. I'm leaning on
You to get me through this.*

Monsoon

*If you help the poor, you are lending to the Lord—
and he will repay you!*
PROVERBS 19:17 NLT

I noticed the dark clouds when I started my prayer walk, but in Florida, you can't tell when they're gonna just lie around threatening or actually produce. I was thirty minutes from home when the first fat drops fell. Within seconds it monsooned.

I trudged down the road like a drowned rat and stuck my cell phone in my underwear to keep it dry. Yep. A drowned rat with a rectangular rump.

Turning a corner, I came upon a car, engine running, parked at the curb in front of a house. Hooray! A woman was in the driver's seat. Double hooray!

At first I thought my chances of getting offered a ride home were good. Then I saw the driver eyeing me warily. She turned away, looking everywhere but at me. Like I didn't even exist.

Her body language was clear: *Go away. You'll find no help here.*

I walked up to her window, pulled the dripping hair from my face, and stared imploringly at her, but she focused straight ahead at the rain pounding her windshield, refusing to acknowledge my presence or my plight.

Hope drained away like water in a bathtub.

Swimming home, I thought about the homeless woman I drove past yesterday. Her sign said NEED FOOD FOR FAMILY. ANYTHING WILL HELP.

Did I stop? No. Did I help? I didn't.

She's drowning in the downpour every single day. Yet I keep sitting in my nice, dry car staring straight ahead, my body language clear: *Go away. You'll find no help here.*

I can change that. Yes. But will I?

*Deliverer of the Downtrodden,
Help me really see the monsooned people You send my way.*

Metamorphosis

Bless the LORD. . .who pardons all your iniquities.
PSALM 103:2–3 NASB

A new friend confided her homosexuality to me. She wondered if she could keep attending our church; she wanted to know more about God but had been told in the past that her lifestyle merited a one-way ticket to hell.

I assured her that she was welcome and that Papa God meant for church to be a hospital for sinners—which includes *all* of us—not a sanctuary for saints.

She asked where to start reading the Bible I'd given her. I suggested Romans 3:23: "For *all* have sinned and fall short of the glory of God" (NASB, emphasis mine).

The next week, she eyed me coldly. "Are you messing with my head, or what?" she asked, opening her Bible to a Romans passage condemning, among other sins, homosexuality (1:24–32). "If you don't want me in your church, just say so." The pain of rejection radiated from her eyes.

"I *do* want you here, but I won't apologize for God's Word. He does hate sin and considers homosexuality a sin. . .but He *loves* you. I'm a sinner too. We all are. The sins in my life—and some are listed right here in this very passage—are just as grievous to God as yours."

I paused. She sniffed.

"Papa God loves us and wants us to seek Him regardless of our behavior. He's concerned with our hearts above all."

Our friendship deepened over the following months, and I was blessed to see her accept Christ as her Savior, emerging like a beautiful butterfly from a stagnant cocoon.

There's no heart He can't change. Not mine. Not yours.

*Master of Metamorphosis,
Thank You for pardoning
my sins and enabling me to
spread my new butterfly
wings through Your love.*

Sam Creed

"There is no other god who can rescue like this!"
DANIEL 3:29 NLT

Vain Babylonian King Nebuchadnezzar built a giant gold statue of himself and ordered everyone in the kingdom to bow and pay homage. . .or die.

He may have thought he was all that, but three young Hebrew slaves didn't. Shadrach, Meshach, and Abednego worshipped the one true God and flat refused to kneel to a hunk of metal, knowing the alternative was death in the bowels of King N's fiery furnace.

That was gutsy all right, but not as gutsy as what they did next.

The three boys answered King N's snide question, "What god will be able to rescue you from my power?" with what I call the SAM Creed (an acronym of their names): "If we are thrown into the blazing furnace, the God whom we serve is able to save us. He will rescue us. . . . But even if he doesn't, we want to make it clear to you, Your Majesty, that we will NEVER serve your gods or worship the gold statue" (Daniel 3:17–18 NLT, emphasis mine).

But even if he doesn't. . . Five powerful words of life or death trust.

In a nutshell, the SAM Creed states "I believe the God I serve is able to save me from this disaster. But even if He chooses not to, I will still serve Him."

Will you repeat it with me now, sister?

In the Bible story, Yahweh did indeed work an incredible walk-with-me-through-the-fire miracle and King N declared today's verse.

In your life story, are you ready to claim the SAM Creed as your own? Even as you face that horrible diagnosis, devastating loss, or financial ruin?

*All-Powerful God,
I believe You are able.
Always. I choose to trust
You no matter what.*

Bouncing Babies

"Be fruitful and multiply."
GENESIS 9:7 NASB

I've learned a few things while obeying today's verse. . .

- **Pregnancy brings you closer to your honey.** After I jumped out of the car in our driveway to toss my cookies in the grass, Spouse tried to comfort me. Soon we were throwing up side by side. It was the most romantic thing ever. Those two brown spots on our lawn were the envy of all my friends.
- **Make new friends.** Average-size breasts become huge globes that take on their own personalities. It's like having two bouncing buddies go everywhere with you. I called mine the Bobbing Twins, Freddie and Flopsie. I addressed them directly: "Freddie, please stop knocking everything off the counter," or "Flopsie, you're gonna have to squeeze into this DDD cup."
- **Expectant daddies happily share TMI.** On the first day of our childbirth class, a young farmer admitted, "We ain't never had any babies, but we've birthed lots of cows." Another fellow exclaimed, "My wife's having them Briggs and Stratton thangs."
- **Your body refuses to listen.** A month after giving birth, I played tennis with my friend Julia (also a nursing mother). Suddenly, a wailing infant in a passing stroller triggered that mysterious internal milk breaker. Julia and I simultaneously clutched our chests like gunshot victims. "Stop it, Freddie! Not now, Flopsie!" I pleaded with the Twins as two dark, wet spots appeared in strategic locations on my white tennis shirt. Julia and I mopped ourselves between points with a soggy sweatband, bringing strange new meaning to the term "Bosom Buddies."

*Master of Miracles,
Many, many thanks for
the blessing of babies.
Make me more like You because
they may end up being like me.*

Cheek Tweak

He puts a smile on my face. He's my God.
PSALM 42:5 MSG

I walked toward the convention center, quivering in my new boots. I was headed to a cavernous hall stuffed with publishers, bookstore owners, literary agents, publicists. . .the gatekeepers of Christian publishing.

I was majorly intimidated. This was the big time. All the players were here. I felt like a pet rock at a Barbie Doll convention. So out of place. Confidence subzero.

Then it happened: a cheek tweak from Papa God. Just like you might do to a scared little kid you wanted to love on.

As I entered through the enormous doors, I became aware that the two smiling young male staffers manning the entrance had apparently just said something to me.

"Uh, excuse me?" I stammered, unable to resist smiling back at their engaging expressions. Wait. Could that be. . .admiration? Nah. . .probably just indigestion.

"You're rockin' that hat, girl," said the cutie about one-third my age.

"Oooh, yeah," agreed the cool dude whose diapers I might have once changed. "Rockin' it gooood. Smokin'!"

Rockin'. . .stylin'. . .smokin'. . .these are not terms usually applied to me. But I could tell they weren't making fun. They really meant it: Go, girl.

The absurdity of it all brought instant anxiety-reducing laughter to my stressed-out spirit. "You made my day, guys. Thanks!" I called, facing the lion's den with my chin higher and shoulders straighter.

Papa God knew I needed something outside the box to give me that little zing of confidence I was missing. Hey, I'm no pet rock. I'm Seffner Barbie!

*Lord of the Unexpected,
I love Your cheek tweaks! Keep
on using laughter to release
Jesus-joy in my soul and remind me
of Your never-ending affection.*

I Once Was Blind...

*"This happened so that the works of
God might be displayed in him."*
JOHN 9:3 NIV

I still choke up when I recall the day my then five-year-old niece Andie, born 80 percent blind, came home from Sunday school after hearing the story of Jesus healing the blind man.

Her mother (my sister) noticed Andie eating her lunch extra slowly that day, obviously contemplating something very seriously. Sweet, earnest little Andie, who had struggled her whole short life to function in a visual world, said, "Jesus made the blind man see. When will Jesus heal me?"

When, indeed.

Jesus did heal some and still does today. Why not everybody?

That's a question every Christ follower asks at some point. I believe He does offer healing to everybody, although not always in the way we expect. Grab your Bible and let's look for clues in the ninth chapter of John:

- Jesus approached the blind man, not vise versa (verse 1).
- The man's handicap wasn't anyone's fault (verse 3).
- Jesus offered healing in order to show His Father's light to the dark world (verse 4).
- If Jesus' saliva was the catalyst for healing, why not simply apply straight spit instead of making mud to smear on his eyes (verse 6)?
- Why did Jesus instruct him to travel to a distant pool to wash off the mud (verse 7)?
- Jesus intentionally healed on the Sabbath, knowing the religious leaders would pitch a hissy fit (verse 14).
- When our guy got in deep trouble, Jesus came searching for him (verse 35).

So, girlfriend, think over these points the remainder of today and we'll discuss them again tomorrow.

....

....

....

....

....

....

*Almighty God,
I love studying Your Word.
Thanks for inviting me
to ask hard questions; I trust
You with the answers.*

But Now I See

*Jesus then said, "I came into the world to
bring everything into the clear light of day."*
JOHN 9:39 MSG

Okay, let's discuss the points raised **yesterday**:

- Although the sick often approached Jesus, this time it was all Him. Jesus initiated contact. Isn't it comforting to know it goes both ways? Not only can we approach Him about our needs, He's often a step ahead and two to the right.
- We like to cast blame when something goes wrong, don't we? Jesus didn't.
- Jesus cares about our suffering and also about those silently suffering in faithlessness. His fingerprints on our lives **are** meant to be light in their darkness.
- Holy spit! Jesus intentionally added dirt to create conspicuous mud, rather than applying a coat of transparent saliva. Why do you suppose that is?
- Yep. Visibility. Jesus instructed our guy to bypass the nearby Jordan River (where nobody would've spazzed out like if he'd entered a *pool* filthy) and travel all the way to a pool in the distant Tyropoeon Valley. Jesus apparently wanted all who saw him en route asking, "What's with the mud shades, dude?"
- Jesus was sticking it to the uptight, rules-obsessed Pharisees who just couldn't grasp that law-obedience without heart-relationship is useless. Putting the healed man on trial created an even greater platform for people to hear about Jesus.
- After the Pharisees booted the healed man, Jesus wouldn't leave him floundering. He dropped everything, searched for him, and sealed the deal on his faith.

So what's the deal with your faith? We all sprout cracks in the seal now and then. It's okay. Jesus will mud it up with some holy spit.

*Great Healer,
Patch the cracks in my
faith seal and keep me whole.*

Hoppin' Mad

With the LORD is unfailing love.
PSALM 130:7 NIV

When I was eight, a head cold prevented me from going to school, so Daddy took me to work with him. He was a laboratory technician in a small hospital.

I loved watching the centrifuge spin vials of blood or looking through the microscope at "squigglers" on glass slides. Even more fun was poking my finger through the holes of the large metal container in the refrigerator. It held several dozen toads used for medical tests.

Midmorning, while Daddy was out delivering lab reports, I started wondering what it would feel like to actually hold one of those squishy amphibians. I slid the heavy container out of the refrigerator, onto the floor. As I lifted the lid, every last one of those fat toads leapt from their prison and liberated themselves down the hallway and throughout the hospital. I stood by helplessly as patients screamed and staff scrambled.

Lorda mercy, what had I done? I steeled myself for the volcanic blast sure to come.

But while the other hospital personnel grumbled under their breath and glared at me in exasperation, Daddy quietly shook his head and turned away with a smile tugging at the corners of his mouth. Then he bought me lunch.

Nothing more was said.

I knew I'd committed a terrible, horrible sin. I deserved to be punished. But Daddy forgave me. And then he kept on loving me anyway.

Just like the way our heavenly Father treats us when we blow it.

Papa God,
It's incredibly comforting to
know that even when I make
You hoppin' mad I will always
be forgiven and loved no less.

Torn

You know me inside and out.
PSALM 41:12 MSG

My friend Ruthanne was a piano teacher and songwriter who frequently performed her original music. She was often asked to sing at church services and special events and was frequently told what a blessing her musical gifts brought others.

Then one day, Ruthanne and her family moved to a new city and a new church. Ruthanne was thrilled—at first—to see that the new church was brimming with excellent musicians. They'd played together for years at a very high skill level and attracted many other community musicians to the praise band.

A bit intimidated, Ruthanne waited two years before gathering enough courage to offer to share a song she'd written for Mother's Day. It was a delightful, toe-tapping, joyful song about the funny side of motherhood. I loved it and encouraged her to share it with the congregation.

We were both floored when she was turned down cold by the church leadership with no audition and no explanation.

It appeared that politics and other invisible underlying currents were at work. But that didn't make Ruthanne any less hurt. Her self-worth was severely wounded. She was torn about whether to continue pursuing her music at all.

But thankfully, Ruthanne was grounded enough in belief that her heavenly Father wouldn't have given her musical talent if He didn't want her to use it. So she kept at it, eventually incorporating her unique music in a national ministry, bringing encouragement to thousands.

*Great Physician,
I know You never intended
for Your beloved church to kill
its own wounded. Please help
me encourage—not discourage—
someone today. And when
I'm inadvertently wounded,
heal me with the salve of
Your faith in me.*

Escaping the Pit

Share with the Lord's people who are in need.
ROMANS 12:13 NIV

I was sinking deeper in the pit. You know that pit well. . .the one dug by exhaustion, discouragement, and near-despair.

I'd fallen in headfirst a week earlier when my beloved daughter Cricket was rushed to the ER with a raging fever and convulsions. Five months pregnant and desperately ill with Hyperemesis gravidarum, a virulent infection had attacked her weakened body.

Saving her life became top priority.

I sat helplessly in the ICU day after day, worrying about everything. . .my best friend fighting for her life, the strong drugs they usually didn't give pregnant women and couldn't predict how the unborn baby would be affected, a confused three-year-old at home feeling lost without Mommy.

Nurse Godzilla guarded Cricket like a bulldog during the day shift. No one was allowed in except Cricket's parents and husband, and not simultaneously. It was a lonely vigil. Growing despondent due to prolonged uncertainty and isolation, I prayed that Papa God would find a way to send flesh-and-blood encouragement.

One afternoon I was sitting beside Cricket's bed, deep in the pit, when the curtains parted and in walked Lilli, Rene, and Michelle, dear friends from another state who'd heard about Cricket's hospitalization. They'd come on faith that they would be able to pray for Cricket in person, and when they arrived, lo and behold, Nurse Godzilla herself miraculously admitted them without hesitation.

I fell into their loving arms, feeling Papa God's warm, enveloping love with skin on it. He was right there in that room with us, reaching out through the presence of friends to haul us out of the pit.

> *Living God,*
> *Make me the You with skin on it*
> *to someone in the pit today.*

Giving Thanks

What a beautiful thing, GOD, to give thanks.
PSALM 92:1 MSG

With our crazy-busy schedules, it's easy to let our stressings outweigh our blessings, isn't it?

So during this season of Thanksgiving, let's spend a little time intentionally expressing gratitude to the Creator of all good things. Here are a few suggestions for which to give thanks (feel free to add to the list):

- Papa God (who loves and cherishes me more than any earthly father ever could).
- Jesus (I can never be thankful enough for what He did on the cross for me).
- Family (even the nuts in my batter).
- Health (focusing on what works instead of what doesn't).
- Food on my table (maybe even a little too much, according to my scale).
- My church (what would I do without my fellowship of believers?).
- Friends (my life preservers in the stress-pool of life).
- Fun (sooo grateful for the zest in life that makes me happy!).
- My country (sweet land of liberty, of thee I sing!).
- Political leaders (the people who shape our nation's culture).
- Church leaders (for strength, wisdom, and the Holy Spirit's guidance).
- My bed (no bedbugs).
- Clothes (a size smaller would be good too!).
- Papa's beautiful world (mountains, woods, lakes, seashores, plains, deserts. . .all incredible!).

Hey, did I mention that I'm uber thankful for YOU, my BFF: Blessed Friend Forever? I hope these suggestions kick-start you toward an attitude of gratitude this Thanksgiving.

Giblets (who thought of chopping up bird guts into perfectly good gravy anyway?) slide down a lot better when we're thankful to eat at all.

Dearest Papa,
Thank You. For everything.
You make my heart sing.

Thimblefuls

Come before him with joyful songs.
PSALM 100:2 NIV

Remember the opening scene in the classic 1989 Christmas movie *Prancer,* when the teacher circles her class, trying to pinpoint the overly enthusiastic, off-key singer cluelessly ruining the Christmas carol?

Well, that child was me. I've always loved to belt out songs despite my thimbleful of talent. "Make a joyful noise unto the LORD" (Psalm 100:1 KJV). Yep, I'm a joyful noiser. And curiously unashamed. Rather than singing blessings, my bless sings!

Mostly because of a wonderful man named Bill George, our minister of music. Big G, as I affectionately called him, herded me through church choirs for decades. Mama would drop ADD me off at choir practice and Big G would do his best to rein me in.

But in my *her*spective, I was Gladys Knight and everyone else was a Pip.

Big G always dealt graciously with my limited talent. I recall volunteering once to lead the teens in a cappella songs around a campfire. When I inadvertently changed keys four times within two minutes, I found myself croaking solo as everyone gawked at me openmouthed.

Big G simply smiled and gently guided us back to one followable melody.

In retrospect, I see that Papa God used Big G to prepare me for my ministry today. I belt out a humorous song at the end of each speaking engagement, never self-conscious or embarrassed to slide off-key; it's just part of the funny. The ladies always leave with a smile on their faces and a new song in their hearts.

Especially my sister joyful noisers.

So tell me, girlfriend, what thimbleful of talent might Papa God want you to use for His glory?

*Elohim (Mighty Creator),
I'm grateful that You gave me
talents—some in buckets, some in
thimbles. Help me use them all.*

Standing Ovation

He has caused his wonders to be remembered.
PSALM 111:4 NIV

Some juicy tidbits to chew on today about getting older:

- **Age is the great equalizer.** Outer beauty doesn't count for much anymore; inner beauty is what shines bright.
- **Ruff it.** I've decided to handle stressful situations like my dog would; if I can't eat it or play with it, I'll just pee on it and walk away.
- **We can work for Jesus at any age.** Frail, eighty-year-old Mary Ann leads Bible studies in jail. She prays in the courtroom whenever one of "her girls" appears in court. "I go in weak, but I go out strong; God provides the strength I need."
- **Feistiness sharpens like aged cheese.** When the male physical therapist at the rehab clinic where I worked kept correcting the way an eighty-four-year-old woman was doing her exercises, she responded, "Why does every man in my life think he should tell me what to do?" She received a standing ovation from every woman in the clinic.
- **Chocolate is the secret to longevity.** One-hundred-year-old Peggy Griffith of Abbotsham, UK, consumed thirty chocolate bars per week—per WEEK—for ninety years. That's 14,000 pounds of chocolate, people!
- **Adjust your focus.** The key to assuaging anxiety about aging is to focus more on what we have left than on what we've lost.
- **Things could always be worse.** You could be a female kangaroo, pregnant for her entire adult life. When the joey in her pouch graduates, the embryo in her womb climbs into the pouch and a new embryo fills the vacated womb. And the beat goes on. . . .
- **Muzzle it.** Success is making it through menopause with your husband and one friend left.

*Mighty Jehovah,
Today I'm thankful for life.
If only my body were as
forgiving as You are.*

Mundane Blessings

*No matter what happens, always be thankful,
for this is God's will for you who belong to Christ Jesus.*
1 Thessalonians 5:18 tlb

One day I realized my faith had caught the sniffles. A little snot here, a hacking cough there. . . nothing huge, but something that required attention. You never know when neglected spiritual viruses might escalate into consumption of the soul.

Checking my spiritual temperature, I found that a crucial element of my faith was missing: thankfulness. I was cruising along, performing all my faith duties, but something was lacking. There was no gratitude in my spirit for the mundane blessings of every day.

Seriously, isn't life really made up of 90 percent routine, so easy to overlook as Papa's intentional blessing?

Thankfulness is a power-packed element of spiritual health that keeps our Creator-creation perspective intact. It's the acute awareness that the source of our usually unconsidered everyday blessings—such as a warm breeze, lungs to draw it in, senses to feel its pleasure—is the Master Designer.

Looking at it this way, the mundane becomes downright thrilling! We see annoyingly noisy kids as happy, carefree children; work duties become a privilege many are without; household chores wouldn't take so long if we lived in a grass hut swarmed by flies.

As we cultivate everyday gratitude, worship for our Provider boosts our spiritual health better even than Grandma's chicken soup.

So what do you think? Is it time to slap the spiritual thermometer under your tongue too? Maybe an injection of thankfulness is just what the Great Physician ordered.

*Holy One Worthy
of My Gratitude,
I refuse to let thankfulness be
a casualty of my overstressed
schedule. Make me feel blessed,
rather than entitled, in my
marvelous everyday mundane.*

Anytime, Anywhere

But he [Jesus] said, "If they kept quiet, the stones
would do it for them, shouting praise."
LUKE 19:40 MSG

It was a little confusing, I'll admit, but it was a hoot watching the interpreters at the international women's church conference, each simultaneously speaking in different languages during my speech.

One group had headsets, with a male translator in the back of the room doing his durndest to translate bizarre Debora Coty terms sprinkled throughout my presentation, like "joy-sucking dully-funks." He kept shooting me bug-eyes. I apologized afterward for making him blush when I mentioned that when girls get together, they talk about the three B's: Boys, Boobs, and Babies. (Tee-hee!)

Another translator standing about ten feet from me spoke aloud to her group, which created an interesting echo whenever I paused for breath. I kept finding myself mesmerized by her flying lips instead of focusing on what I was about to say next.

I like to close my talks with an original funny sing-along song, and it got funnier and funnier because half the audience couldn't understand the English lyrics and had no idea what the hand gestures meant. The Haitian ladies were amazing, making up their own motions and ad-libbing a sort of cool, smooth calypso rhythm that wasn't even in the song. We ended up forsaking the "right way," following them around the room in an impromptu praise conga line.

Isn't it awesome how there's no *right way* to praise and worship? Culture is no barrier; language doesn't really matter; and location is irrelevant. An attitude of gratitude is all you need. Anytime. Anywhere.

My Sweet Savior,
Help me seize the moment
sometime today to have my
own little praise and worship
time. Just You and me.

Betrayed

As for my companion, he betrayed his friends...
PSALM 55:20 NLT

Ever suffered a friendship gone sour? Of course you have. We all have. Perhaps your friend betrayed your trust after you'd deemed her safe and let her into your heart. That's what happened to David.

Take a few minutes and read 2 Samuel 15–18. King David's son Absalom plotted to steal his father's throne and recruited David's close friend and trusted advisor, Ahithophel, to help him. Ahithophel spied on David while pretending to be his friend and secretly fed Absalom information to stoke the rebellion.

Ouch.

It became a full-blown conspiracy of multilayered deceit before the plot culminated in David fleeing the palace for his life, weeping over the betrayal of these two he'd loved. It's believed that David wrote Psalm 55 during this time of grief.

Yep. Sure sounds the way I've felt upon a friend's betrayal, haven't you?

"I am overwhelmed by my troubles" (verse 2).

"Oh, that I had wings like a dove. . .I would fly away and rest" (verse 6).

"It is not an enemy who taunts me—I could bear that. . . . Instead, it is you—my equal, my companion and close friend. What good fellowship we once enjoyed as we walked together" (verses 12–14).

Betrayal leaves raw wounds that take time to heal. The hurt is so heavy, it feels like it'll crush us. My friend Lali once said, "The worst breakup I ever had was with a girl."

Have you been devastated by the festering, lingering wounds of a friend's betrayal? Are you ready to ask Papa for help?

Great Healer,
You alone can replace my anger,
bitterness, and regret with
forgiveness, redemption, and
hope. Please begin the miracle
of forgiveness in me today.

Shots in the Dark

*Jesus answered, "I am the way
and the truth and the life."*
JOHN 14:6 NIV

The day Spouse and I arrived in Spain with our traveling companions, we were hungry and exhausted after our ten-hour plane ride. So after checking into our hotel, we snoozed a few hours then hit the sun-drenched street in search of sustenance.

We came upon a lovely little bistro exuding mouthwatering aromas, so we gathered around a marker board at the entrance that listed a dozen lunch items.

They were all in Spanish. Go figure.

Our Spanish was pretty much limited to "Yo quiero Taco Bell."

We drifted inside, where random food pictures decorated the walls. Perusing a menu, we remained clueless, although I did recognize the word *pollo* (chicken) from my ancient high school Spanish class.

Fun-loving souls that we are, we decided to risk a shot in the dark and point to an item on the menu containing the most words we couldn't pronounce, pledging a solemn vow to eat it, whatever it was.

Fortunately, mine turned out to be a delicious pizza-like thingie. Not everyone fared as well. Three words: Slimy. Nasty. Shudder.

You know, some people shoot in the dark with faith too. After taking a cursory glance at different religious beliefs, they deem them undecipherable. So they close their eyes and point to the menu.

But Jesus wants us to come to Him with eyes wide open. To learn, ask hard questions, and search for answers. Only then will we find the Truth.

*Master of All Truth,
Make me a diligent seeker of
You. No more shots in the dark.*

Hard Doesn't Mean Impossible

Jesus looked at him and loved him.
MARK 10:21 NIV

While reading the Gospel of Mark, I noticed something eye-opening in the account of the rich young man who did all the right things—kept the Ten Commandments, loved his neighbors, probably even flossed daily.

When this "good" fella (by the world's standards) asked Jesus what he should do to earn eternal life, Jesus shocked the Armani sandals right off his feet: "Sell everything you have and give to the poor. . . . Then come, follow me" (Mark 10:21).

WHAT? Nuh-uh.

No doubt his face fell. He was expecting to hear something like, "Go to church six times a day to show your incredible devotion to Me." Or maybe the ultimate in self-sacrifice, "Take over permanent two-year-old nursery duty at the temple."

But wait. Read today's scripture.

Wow. Jesus LOVED this dude but still asked him to do something hard. Really hard. Something that, in the guy's way of thinking, was downright impossible. He was majorly attached to that red convertible.

The litmus test for loyalty often starts with our wallets.

Sadly, he failed the test. When it came to all or nothing, he took all.

Hey, could it be that Jesus does the same for us—loves us to pieces but still asks us to do something really, really hard?

I think Mother Teresa, serving in the festering, disease-ridden slums of India, knew the answer to that.

As did Katie Davis Majors, the American teen who moved to the wilds of Uganda and adopted thirteen daughters to share Papa God's love firsthand (katiedavis.amazima.org).

So. Who are we missing?

Ah, yes. You. And me.

What hard thing might our loving Savior ask of us today?

*Living God,
When You ask me to
do something, I will.
No matter how hard.*

Zombie Mode

*When I was in trouble, Lord,
I prayed to you, and you listened to me.*
JONAH 2:2 CEV

Chuck and I were up to our eyeballs in baby drool and diapers one weekend as we volunteered to stay with our twin six-month-old grandbabies and four-year-old grandbuddy while their bedraggled parents attended a marriage retreat.

I understood "bedraggled" intimately after trying to convince the twins that a bottle was oh-so-yummy when they were accustomed to snuggling Mommy's much cushier feeding apparatus.

So after NO sleep the first night, fun, smiley Mimi morphed into Zombie Mimi. Preschooler Blaine amused himself while the adults focused on keeping the babies alive despite the wee boy's propensity for stuffing his sock down his throat and the girl's cliff-diving hobby.

Blaine wondered if he could watch a Larry Boy DVD. Now, lest you're out of the preschool loop, Larry Boy is the VeggieTales superhero whose exciting adventures teach little people biblical principles in a most entertaining way.

"Great idea!" we responded. But alas, the DVD player was deader than a cue stick. I could almost hear Satan's wicked snicker.

I seriously considered a karate kick to the devilish machine; Chuck suggested heaving it out the window. Our patience had trotted down the road with the milk cow.

"Let's pray about it," Blaine innocently suggested. He bowed his head, closed his eyes, and mouthed a heartfelt request to the Almighty as we stared at our little spiritual leader. He'd no sooner finished and turned expectantly toward the TV than POOF! On it flickered.

"God must want me to see Larry Boy," Blaine concluded with a happy grin.

"And a little child shall lead them" (Isaiah 11:6 KJV).

*Infinitely Patient Father,
When I'm mired in zombie mode,
help me remember You're not.*

Queen of Diamonds

Whatever your hand finds to do, do it with all your might.
ECCLESIASTES 9:10 NASB

Multitasking is a way of life for most women. Too many things to do, not enough time. To survive, we become multifaceted, like a diamond reflecting shafts of light a dozen places at once.

But being the Queen of Diamonds can be hazardous.

One Sunday morning, I was riding to church with my family, cutting off my daughter's too-long jeans to hem while simultaneously reviewing my Sunday school lesson (I taught third graders) and scarfing my breakfast muffin. When I held up the newly shortened pants, a piece of coral fabric fluttered to the floorboard. Oops! I'd cut a chunk out of my dress beneath the pants on my lap. I had no choice but to wear my holey dress to the holy service patched with duct tape.

Not the fashion statement I'd hoped for.

Still, multitasking has its rewards.

I once overheard a kid say to another kid, "That lady has muscley arms and moves real fast . . .you know, like a mom."

But we diamond girls can burn out if we're not careful. Remember the multitaskers in the Bible who learned the importance of taking a break: Martha, whom Jesus personally rebuked for prioritizing tasks before relationships; Eve, who was trying to start a world and keep it clean; Mrs. Noah, who must've worn out a dozen shovels and mop buckets on an ark full of animals.

(Hey, next time you're complaining about cleaning your bathroom, think about Mrs. Noah's—it was the whole ship!)

The point is, there are times to let your diamond shine and times to put it back in the velvet box.

Emmanuel (God with Us),
Help me discern when it's
time to rest and refresh.
Um. . .maybe today?

Delegate

*"This is not good. . . . You're going to wear yourself out. . . .
This job is too heavy a burden for you to handle all by yourself."*
EXODUS 18:17–18 NLT

Read today's scripture aloud. Now, tell me. . .is Papa God trying to tell you something?

Moses was the original recipient of this message. It actually came from his father-in-law, Jethro, who was acting as God's bullhorn. Moses had been crazy-busy, the nation's sole supreme court judge, trying to be all things to all people.

When Jethro came to visit, he was appalled that "the people stood about Moses from the morning until the evening" day after day (Exodus 18:13 NASB). Moses was stressed out big-time. No chance to exercise, gather his thoughts, chill to his music, watch his kid's soccer match, even take a decent potty break.

So Jethro made a suggestion. A GREAT suggestion: *Delegate.* Choose trustworthy people to help you, teach them how to do their part, and then back off and let them have at it.

Moses wisely listened. He delegated his responsibilities and lightened his load. And I suspect he suddenly began enjoying beautiful sunsets again.

How about you? Are you overextending yourself? Spreading your time or energies too thin? Regardless of how well-intentioned we are, we're only human, and the Master Designer, who created us and *knows* our limitations, wants us to set parameters, to pick and choose the way we spend our finite energies.

Overdoing not only robs our joy and ability to live in the moment, but it steals fulfillment and effectiveness from the priorities Papa has appointed as our primary focus for this particular season of life.

*Breath of Life,
I know You never intended
me to do this all alone.
Help me learn to delegate
my responsibilities.*

Shaken

" 'Because he is at my right hand,
I will not be shaken.' "
ACTS 2:25 NIV

"Fire!"

I startled awake from a dead sleep, the dreaded word vibrating through my every molecule.

"Fire!" I heard it again, this time recognizing my husband's voice.

Sitting up and staring dumbly at my surroundings, I groggily realized I was in bed. Oh, yeah—I had been taking a much-needed afternoon nap. But now I smelled smoke.

I jumped up and ran into the smoke-hazy den, where through the back porch window I saw Chuck throwing a bucket of water. The smoke alarm started screeching. I raced over to open the metal porch door, but it was superheated. *Oww!*

Peering through the window, I saw glowing embers surrounding a blacked lump that used to be a large potted silk fern. Black soot shot up the plank walls and darkened the white metal ceiling. The floorboards were charred and chunks of smoldering fiberglass from the four-foot fountain in the corner—the one now sporting a gaping hole in its side—were scattered to the far end of the porch.

To say we were shaken is an understatement.

Chuck had doused the fire with water from the fountain, but our panic blazed on. What if we hadn't been home when the electrical short somehow caused the potted fern to explode, turning pieces of the fountain into flaming projectiles? The entire wooden porch would have quickly become an inferno, eventually engulfing the house as well.

But we *were* home, and by the grace of God, Chuck heard the explosion and was able to respond quickly.

Be still my heart.

....

....

....

....

....

....

....

....

....

> *Elohim (Mighty Creator),*
> *Thanks for always being at my right*
> *hand. Please remind me of that next*
> *time I'm shaken and stirred.*

Road Rage

Don't use foul or abusive language.
Let everything you say be good and helpful.
EPHESIANS 4:29 NLT

I slammed on my brakes, shouting, "What's the matter with you, moron?" as the bald man in the red convertible cut me off in traffic.

A little voice from the backseat piped up: "What's a moron?"

Another voice answered. "Someone evil like a Klingon, only stupider."

Uh-oh. What was I teaching my children? At that moment I felt like the moron.

Road rage is becoming an expected—albeit still frowned upon—part of the driving experience. I find it frightening to witness the dark side of those I love (including myself) come bursting forth when hunched behind a wheel. Spewing venom, muttering threats, wishing evil on other drivers—what would Jesus think of us if He were in the passenger seat?

We should be praying, not cursing, as we jockey for position in the fast lane.

But how do we accomplish this?

I recommend carrying a prayer pad in your purse and/or in your car (I do both)—somewhere you can easily reach it. When you're sitting at long red lights or stuck in traffic, pull it out and jot down your prayer requests. Don't wait—start praying for them right then. Lift your heart concerns to the Lord and don't forget to document His answers.

I've been using this technique for the past five years and can testify that it's a *her*spective changer. A surefire way to replace road rage with prayer and praise.

Holy Spirit,
Quench my rage and redirect
my passion toward the
One who can create poppies
from poopies.

Expecting

*I will not fear though tens of
thousands assail me on every side.*
PSALM 3:6 NIV

When my pregnant daughter Cricket invited me to her twelve-week sonogram, my first impulse was to shout "NO!" and run the other way. A decade peeled away and I was suddenly transported back to a tiny sterile cubicle in another OB office.

It was my own twelve-week sonogram visit, and I was thrilled to be expecting our third child at age forty-two after five devastating miscarriages. This time, everything seemed fine. I was already in maternity clothes and feeling appropriately nauseated. My two teenagers were supportive. Since Chuck had to work, I'd asked my mother to come for my appointment; we giggled like school girls in anticipation.

Then I watched the technician's friendly smile fade as she searched with the probe. She abruptly turned off the screen and left the room. Dark, hollow dread snaked from the pit of my stomach and filled my chest. My mother's face melted. The doctor came in to explain my lifeless womb.

Would I now have to relive that nightmare with my daughter?

But I saw the excitement and joy radiating from her eyes. This was her first baby, and I knew it was a precious honor she offered me. How could I not accept?

As history seemed to be repeating itself, I nervously crowded with Cricket and her husband into the tiny examining room. My heart was in my throat as the technician prepared the ultrasound probe.

At the risk of making you throw this book across the room, I'm going to have to continue my story tomorrow. Please forgive me. And stay tuned. . .

*Almighty God,
Thank You for always
being there. . .even in
my darkest moments.*

Trapping the Weasel

For God has not given us a spirit of fear,
but of power and of love and of a sound mind.
2 TIMOTHY 1:7 NKJV

(Continued)

I'd prayed incessantly for Cricket's unborn baby and had given my fear repeatedly to Papa God, but somehow the paws of that wretched, weaselly creature slithered in and wrapped themselves around the soft vulnerability of my mother-love, attempting to squeeze my breath away.

Please, Father. Please let this baby be okay. Please.

At that moment, a tiny beating heart filled the screen and teensy arms flailed around a safe, warm womb protecting a living, thriving, miraculous baby.

Tears flooded my eyes—as they do even now as I tell the story—in grateful relief and joy for Jehovah's amazing grace.

Yes, fear is a covert weasel that can sneak under the fence and wreak havoc without us even being aware of the wily beast. Did you know weasels are fearless and aggressive hunters that attack much larger animals? Weasels stalk their prey, waving their heads side to side, picking up the scent. Then they kill with a lethal bite to the neck with their razor-sharp teeth and lap the lifeblood of their victims. Ick.

Sounds a lot like fear to me.

So I'm investing in weasel traps; I'm increasing my trust in Papa God every day by ingesting His Word, spending time in His presence, and choosing to believe that He can track, outsmart, and cage any ole fear weasel stalking my heart.

Jehovah Nissi (Our
Victorious Banner),
Thank You for offering me
victory over my fear weasel.
That shrewd beastie will
never spring Your trap.

DECEMBER 10

Moses Mantra

"Who am I to go?... Please send someone else."
EXODUS 3:11, 4:13 CEV

After 430 long years of captivity, God chose Moses, a fumble-tongued, murderer turned nomad, to lead the Israelites from bondage. What was Moses' reaction?

"Say WHAT? No way! You've gotta find somebody else, Lord; I'm the wrong person for this job!" (My paraphrase.)

There it is—the Moses Mantra: I am SO not qualified!

I too claimed the Moses Mantra when Papa God first called me to write. I'll bet three nickels you've done the same when Papa's holy elbow nudged you to attempt something out of your comfort zone, right?

The Bible is full of people who, by outward appearances, weren't qualified for the work to which Yahweh called them:

- Saul, a donkey herder, was chosen by God to be the first king of Israel.
- David, a musical shepherd, was called to be the next warrior king.
- Paul, a dreaded vigilante against Christians, was appointed to become the greatest evangelist of all time.
- Rahab, the Gentile prostitute, was handpicked by Jehovah to become an ancestor of Jesus, a Jew.
- Mary was just a teenager when she was chosen as the nurturer of God's own Son.

I suspect each of them hollered the Moses Mantra at the top of their lungs. Yet God provided them with specific skill sets for the work He had designated for them. Just like He does for you and me today.

Our calling might be a surprise to us, but not to Him. We've already been chosen.

....

....

....

....

....

....

....

....

> *Jehovah Shammah*
> *(The Lord Is There),*
> *It scares the bejebees out of*
> *me when You ask me to do*
> *something new. Help me get*
> *past the Moses Mantra and*
> *trust that You've got this.*

Ain't Dead Yet

Even when I am old and gray, do not forsake me, my God.
PSALM 71:18 NIV

My fortieth birthday dawned cold and bleak. Work was passé. Nobody remembered my birthday. I was embedded in the armpit of gloom as I drove home. I felt *old*.

Suddenly, calling my name from a stranger's front yard was a red Honda four-wheeler bearing a FOR SALE sign. My car turned in by itself. Although I'd never ridden an ATV, I was all atwitter when a droopy-mustached fellow sauntered over dangling the key.

"Howdy, ma'am. Guess you'll be a-wantin' to take 'er for a test drive," he drawled, tipping his cowboy hat.

"Uh. . .yep. That's what I'm a-wantin' to do," I said. "Now, how do I start?"

The Marlboro Man's cheek twitched. "Well, first ya gotta get on." He stared at my skirt, black hose, and pumps.

"No problem!" I hitched up my skirt to throw an elegant leg over the saddle, er, vinyl seat. "So where does the key go?"

He cringed.

Following an elementary operational course, the tombstone cowboy retreated to his front porch, head in hands, while I cut donuts into his front yard. *Yee haw!* I felt young again!

Sometimes, ya gotta confirm you're still alive, you know? We can feel as old at twenty-seven as we do at seventy-two.

Trigger, as I dubbed my mechanical steed, quickened my pulse as we later careened down mountain creek beds and ripped around ledges, echos of hysterical laughter in our wake.

My kids rolled their eyes. My husband hid his face. But by dingies, I never felt old again.

The Marlboro Man would be proud.

So what's your Trigger?

God of All Ages,
Thanks for triggering
fresh joy in me during
every season of my life.

Shaft

"I will not abandon you as orphans—I will come to you."
JOHN 14:18 NLT

As Chuck and I toured the Holy Land in 2000, Golgotha's craggy skull-like cliff reflected my own spiritual barrenness after multiple heart-wrenching miscarriages. For two long years, my wounded faith lay dormant in the infertile soil of pain.

Had God deserted me? It sure felt that way.

Chuck took my hand as we turned away from the harsh death mask of Calvary to the lush beauty of the Garden Tomb. Gorgeous flowering plants stirred hope in me. And. . .could it be . . .a seed of joy?

As we approached Jesus' empty tomb, Chuck stepped back to take pictures and motioned for me to enter without him. As I stood beside the large round stone carved to seal the small cave, my eyes burned with emotion.

I felt vulnerable. So vulnerable.

I knelt and laid my hand on the crudely chiseled stone cavity that once held the body of my Savior during His most vulnerable time on earth. Suddenly, I was infused with a renewed sense of God's sovereignty. No power was strong enough to keep God's Son in the grave! Surely He could be trusted to take care of little me.

Comforting peace enveloped me.

A photo Chuck snapped of me entering Jesus' tomb later revealed an amazing sight: a shaft of sunlight broke through the surrounding rock walls and rested on my shoulder like a blazing sword. . .as if the Almighty Himself were reaching down from heaven to comfort and anoint me.

I believe He was reminding me that His loving touch will always be on my shoulder. And yours too. *Always.*

Emmanuel (God with Us),
Thank You for never leaving
me. Even when I feel alone,
You are here.

Squashed

"Do not judge, or you too will be judged."
MATTHEW 7:1 NIV

Riding my bike out in the country, I came upon a colorful little snake coiled in a patch of sunshine in the road. Of course I had to stop.

Now, bear in mind I was raised near a swamp. Never held much fear of snakes and have, in fact, been known to tuck one away in a pocket or two.

But this little guy wasn't a pocket dweller. He was a poisonous coral. They don't strike like rattlers and aren't really aggressive. They only bite in self-defense, and then they have to sorta chew on you to do any damage.

From a safe distance, I admired the crystalline pattern of the vivid red, black, and yellow stripes, a masterpiece of design. I have no idea why the Master Creator felt we needed poisonous snakes (or mosquitoes or head lice!) but He did, and this one was a beauty.

A shiny silver pickup approached, driven by a young dude in a cowboy hat. He slowed down a mite to see what was so interesting to the gal on the bike and then swerved way over to intentionally run over the little snake with his oversized tires, squashing reptile innards everywhere.

The smirking, self-appointed judge drove away. I was incensed.

That snake wasn't bothering anyone, just enjoying sunbathing on a warm road. My eyes teared up at the unjustness of destroying a creature whose only offense was being what God made him.

I suddenly felt the sting of prejudice. The unfairness, the disrespect of judging something—or someone—simply by their appearance. Or their tribe. Or their ancestry.

God Who Knows,
I leave the judging to You. I
refuse to squash anyone.

Nuggets

*Go after a life of love as if your
life depended on it—because it does.*
1 CORINTHIANS 14:1 MSG

A few nuggets of wisdom I've mined from four decades of marriage:

- Women are more complicated than men. Probably because it was harder to create us out of a rib; men were just a ball of dirt.
- Problems that arise need to be placed in one of three categories, *not* ignored:
    1. Intentionally overlook/wait
    2. Compromise
    3. Deal with head-on
  (My advice to my daughter-in-love on the day of her wedding to my son.)
- It's possible to be jealous of inanimate objects. My girlfriend insisted, "My husband's having an affair with his iPad."
- TIVI (pronounced, ironically, "TV") = Testosterone Induced Vision Impairment (another Coty Near-Fact of Science). The unexplained phenomenon that renders males selectively blind to spills, stains, crumbs, or dirty clothes on the floor.
- Husbands tend to follow the letter of the law. My friend Lali received a box of expensive chocolates before leaving on a trip. She instructed her fella, "Don't eat all the chocolate while I'm gone." She returned home to find three crumbs left in each wrapper.
- "A happy marriage is the union of two good forgivers." (Ruth Bell Graham)
- In Genesis 2:20–21, God made Eve as a helper to Adam. That's because God took one look at Adam and said, "This guy needs help!"
- Weird is good. Weird is why we fall in love over and over again—with the same person. Over the years, you and your husband grow weird in the same way. . .a way nobody else understands. It's that weirdness that binds you together.

*Love Divine,
Thank You for his weirdness;
help me see him today
through Your loving eyes.*

Back to the Beginning

He helps me, and my heart is filled with joy.
PSALM 28:7 NLT

Remember the scene in *The Princess Bride* when the Brute Squad empties the Thieves Forest and a very stubborn Spaniard refuses to leave? Inigo Montoya has lost his way. His one friend (Fezzik) has disappeared, and his quest to kidnap Princess Buttercup fizzled.

So he follows instructions from his boss, Vizzini: "When somezing goes wrong. . .go back to the beginning."

Reminds me of the days after Jesus' resurrection.

The disciples fled like field mice in a snake pit during Jesus' trial and crucifixion but regrouped for His appearance in the upper room (John 20:26). After Jesus proved He was indeed the living, breathing Messiah, He vanished.

"What do we do now?" they must've cried. "How do we find Him again?"

The faithful ladies who'd encountered the empty tomb and then its newly evacuated occupant related Jesus' instructions: "He is going ahead of you to Galilee; there you will see Him" (Mark 16:7 NASB).

So back to the beginning they went. . .to the very place Jesus called them to Himself three years earlier. The place they'd first encountered the One who changed *everything*—the place where joy, excitement, and wonder blew their sandals off.

And Jesus met them there. Being in His presence fired them up enough to change their world.

The beginning's a *great* place to return to when we've gotten lost and off-track. When our friends and goals have disappeared, when our vision for the future is gone.

His presence will surely fire us up enough to change our world too.

....

....

....

....

....

*Risen Lord,
When I feel lost, please
show me the way back
to my first love. . .You.*

Hoofprints

The Lord will keep you from all harm—
he will watch over your life.
PSALM 121:7 NIV

As Chuck and I drove along the winding, twisty road to a church on the other side of our mountain, we tapped our toes and sang along to '70s music. Elton John, the Beatles, Norman Greenbaum . . .so easy to lose yourself in their groovy, far-out beats.

Just as we rounded a curve, a large deer bounded out of the woods directly in front of our car. Unable to stop, Chuck's only option was to swerve into the other lane. We hadn't seen another vehicle all morning, but suddenly one was speeding right toward us.

The animal turned his head first toward us then at the approaching car. As if making a calculated decision, he spun around and fled from whence he came, his white-tailed haunches disappearing into the dense forest.

Whew! Felt like hoofprints across my heart.

The pinched, white face of the passing driver confirmed what we already knew: any alternative move on the part of the deer would have likely sent one or both of our cars careening down the side of the cliff yawning rail-less on the side of the road.

Gulp. Good-bye, Yellow Brick Road. Hello, Spirit in the Sky.

We continued on to church, a little more trembly and a lot more aware of the fragility of life. It could be all over in the flash of an antler.

We thanked Papa for another everyday miracle proving that He's got our backs. And if He's on our side, honestly—who can be against us? Not even Bambi.

My Protector,
Thank You for watching
over my life. It's such a relief
to know I'm in Your hands.

Mr. Carbunkle

The way you treat others is the way you will be treated.
LUKE 6:38 CEV

In my dream, I was playing Clue (remember that childhood board game?). Three strangers and I were moving our game pieces through the mysterious mansion trying to figure out who-done-it. Definitely not Miss Scarlet in the parlor with a candlestick.

Suddenly a player exclaimed, "Why, it's Mr. Carbunkle!"

The other two opponents and I ogled each other in bewilderment. There was no such character in this game. I stated the obvious, "Who is Mr. Carbunkle?"

The words hung in the room as I jerked upright in bed. I must have spoken the question aloud. And suddenly I knew the answer, as surely as if the Almighty had texted me.

I'd been praying for weeks about how to use my writing tithe. It wasn't much; just enough to bless someone in their celebration of Christ's birth with affirmation that Papa God cares about their needs.

I actually knew a "Mr. Carbunkle" from church—a quiet, unassuming man who'd been out of work for a year. I hadn't really given him much thought—or prayer—lately. *Hmm.* Although he never complained, his family must be struggling.

So Mr. Carbunkle it was.

You know, there are lots of Mr. Carbunkles who would be blessed by a love-gift from you this Christmas. Doesn't have to be money. . .could be help with yard work, home repairs, a loaf of banana bread, or best of all, a gift of your time. Thirty minutes for a lonely soul who needs to feel a warm hug from Papa God.

Who's your Mr. Carbunkle? Don't have a Clue? I know someone who does. Just ask Him.

*Generous Father,
Whom should I bless
with a love-gift this week?*

Christmas Blessings

"Don't be frightened, Mary," the angel told her,
"for God has decided to wonderfully bless you!"
LUKE 1:30 TLB

My then-three-year-old grandson ripped open the Christmas gift from his little friend. The other boy and his mama stood by in smiling anticipation of Blaine's response.

Blaine's bottom lip slipped into pouty-protrusion mode. "This isn't what I wanted," he said, handing the unappreciated gift back to its giver.

Gratitude. We're supposed to be grateful for the amazing gift of Papa God's Son in the form of a babe in a manger. And we are. For at least ten minutes every day. But what about the other 1,430 minutes?

Oh, c'mon—don't deny that you inwardly cringe when you open those hideous socks. Or that you fight an impulse to flee out back and hide behind the philodendrons when your mother-in-law arrives. Or that you resent hosting Christmas dinner yet again because lazy Cousin Bertha won't take a turn.

Yep, we all feel a bit like three-year-olds at times.

But what if we wake up tomorrow with only the things we thanked Papa for today? Eeek. Things would look a little differently, wouldn't they?

Warm socks would become a treasure on cold nights, a comfort many people lack. The mother of your spouse produced that person you loved enough to marry. And all that food threatening to collapse your table is a privilege not enjoyed by more than half the world.

It's all in the way we look at it, isn't it? Like a selfish three-year-old. Or like the humble recipient of a good and perfect gift from our heavenly Father.

Ever-Loving Lord,
I'm eternally grateful for
the undeserved blessings
You lavish on me today and
forever. Especially for the
marvelous gift of Your Son.

Five Incredible Words

*"You will find a Babe wrapped in
swaddling cloths, lying in a manger."*
LUKE 2:12 NKJV

The young woman holding the guitar looked nervous as an expectant hush fell over the large gathering of women at our church Christmas tea. She fumbled the first few chords then haltingly plucked the familiar introduction. Her soft voice projected poorly, but we knew the lyrics well.

"O holy night. . .the stars are brightly shining. It is the night of our dear Savior's birth."

Oh no—another botched chord and her voice slid off-key. I squirmed in my seat, uncomfortable for her. I could see similar reactions all around me.

"Long lay the world in sin and error pining, till He appeared and the soul felt its worth."

She suddenly stopped singing and just stood there. Her next words shot like an arrow straight from her heart to ours.

"Sorry. I know I'm not a singer," she said apologetically, "but I need to share this today. You see, I have a brain tumor and probably won't be able to speak after my next surgery."

Stunned silence seized the room.

"Five words of this song are especially meaningful to me: *the soul felt its worth*. If you ever doubt your soul's worth like I have for the past few months, remember that Jesus came as a babe and then thirty-three years later died on a cross. . .just for you. Because your soul was worth *that much* to Him. Believe me, there's great joy, regardless of external circumstances, in knowing the true worth of your soul. It was proven that holy night in Bethlehem. So please, this Christmas . . .allow your soul to feel its worth."

Sweet Savior,
Make me acutely aware
today of my soul's incredible
worth. All because of You.

Bending the Rules

"For nothing will be impossible with God."
LUKE 1:37 NASB

Every time I hear someone quote this verse, usually applying it to some hopeless mess they find themselves in, I think about the hopeless mess going down when it first appeared in the Bible. Do you recall?

These incredibly powerful words were uttered by the mighty angel Gabriel as he presented a flabbergasted, quivering virgin with a positive pregnancy test. The plus sign was horrifyingly clear.

No! Impossible!

"But how? I've never slept with a man," Mary gasped (Luke 1:34 MSG). Bible scholars believe Mary was less than fifteen years old. She wasn't being snarky; she was simply pointing out, from her teenage *her*spective, the zit in the face of the plan. Not gonna happen. Nope. A humongous piece of this puzzle's missing, man.

And then the shiny dude dropped yet another crazy impossibility in her lap—middle-aged Cousin Elizabeth, way past menopause, was preggers too!

I picture Mary's already pale face going bone white and her mouth dropping open. *Whaaa . . . ? No way!*

It was then that Gabriel gave her the only explanation she would ever need. "Nothing is impossible with God."

Mary didn't get it at first. For, like us, she never considered that a bona fide miracle could possibly happen in her life. But then it sank in: She was loved. She was special. She was chosen. God was going to bend the rules of possible for her.

Did you know He wants to bend the rules for you too? No, not because you're pregnant with His Son. . .

Because you're loved.

You're special.

You're chosen.

Mighty One,
Like Mary, I thank You for
doing great things for me.
For making the impossible
possible. Holy, holy, holy
is Your name.

A Place for Jesus

Then I remember something that fills me with hope.
The LORD's kindness never fails!
LAMENTATIONS 3:21–22 CEV

It all started last year when I took my outdoor nativity set to children's church as a visual aid in telling the Christmas story on stage to a hundred kids. Everything went great until the chubby eight-year-old playing Mary was startled by the heavenly host and fell on the plastic manger, smashing it to smithereens and sending doll-baby Jesus logrolling across the stage.

No silent night, that.

So this Christmas we had no manger for the wee Savior in our yard. It just didn't seem right to lay the Prince of Peace on the bare ground, so we left Him in the garage until we could find a replacement manger.

There they were Mary, Joseph, sheep, and an angel looking lovingly down at. . .nothing.

The afternoon of Christmas Eve, I was sprawled on a hammock in my backyard praying about our manger-less manger scene. "Lord, we want to honor Your Son's birth, but we've exhausted all manger ideas. Can You help us find a place for Jesus?"

Within minutes, a sunbeam pierced the canopy of leaves and spotlighted something metallic in our debris pile. The bright reflection made me squint—it was an old fireplace grate we'd discarded years ago. . .what d'ya know, the perfect manger.

That grate had been there all along, but I never noticed it until I asked for heavenly guidance.

How about you? Have you found a place for Jesus in your celebration? What crucial element might you be missing this Christmas season because you haven't yet asked for Papa God's help?

Light of the World,
Shine upon the dark corners
of my life in which I've
neglected to include You.

Candy Man

The shepherds returned, glorifying and praising God.
LUKE 2:20 NIV

To get into the spirit of celebrating the birth of the Christ child, I bought a dozen candy canes to hang on one of my favorite decorations—a snowman standing with his little wooden arms extended like a clothesline.

Why candy canes?

Did you know that the candy cane was invented in 1670 by a German choirmaster who melted and bent white stick candies into the shape of a shepherd's staff to amuse the antsy children in his Christmas choir during the long service?

The custom spread throughout Europe and eventually came to America with a German immigrant in 1847, who decorated his Christmas tree with the all-white candies.

Sometime around 1900, a candymaker in Indiana wanted to create a Christmas confection that bore witness to the true significance of the occasion, so he added red stripes and advertised the associated symbolism:

- White: represents the virgin birth and sinless nature of Jesus.
- Red: represents the blood shed by Jesus on the cross so we could have eternal life.
- J shape: represents the name of Jesus, as well as the staff of the Good Shepherd.

No one knows if this same Indianan candy man added peppermint flavor, but someone did at the turn of the twentieth century, and the rest, as they say, is history.

So who can really get you in the Christmas spirit this year? The Candy Man can!

*Reason for the Season,
Every time I nibble on a candy
cane, make me cognizant
of Your most precious gift
this Christmas.*

Christmas Glow

Let the godly rejoice. Let them be glad in
God's presence. Let them be filled with joy.
PSALM 68:3 NLT

Last December, Dr. Katie, my veterinarian friend, was puzzled about the mysteriously ill dog just brought into her clinic. Dr. Katie hung the pooch's X-rays up to study the contents of his stomach. Something peculiar caught her eye.

"Does that look like a camel to you?" Dr. Katie asked her assistant.

"As a matter of fact, it does," the gal replied. "And there's an angel, a shepherd, and baby Jesus Himself."

At that moment, the phone rang. It was the dog's owner. "I just noticed my manger scene on the coffee table—it's empty!"

This interesting technique for internalizing the true meaning of Christmas (ha!) got me thinking. Can people see the core-deep joy that radiates from my innards when I think of the incredible gift Papa God sent the world in His Son, Jesus?

Is my immeasurable gratitude evident as I dash through the hectic season, scurrying to get everything done and reserve enough energy to hold my head up at the end of the day?

I'm afraid I'm often too busy to allow my outside to reflect my inside sufficiently for nonbelievers to recognize that I may view the celebration of Christmas differently than they do. . .all because of the hope that is within me. My joy is obscured by mounds of clutter; gratefulness is sucked out of my soul by the vacuum called urgency.

Today's verse is my Christmas season prayer—that I would *make* the time to rejoice, be glad in God's presence, and let my inner joy shine.

Will you make this prayer your own?

Precious Jesus,
Shine through me to those who
may be quietly desperate to
know the Giver of true joy.

Christmas Surprise

If anyone is in Christ, the new creation has come:
The old has gone, the new is here!
2 CORINTHIANS 5:17 NIV

Not a creature was stirring, not even a mouse. . .which is why the muffled boom awakened us just before midnight on Christmas Eve.

I sat straight up in bed. What was that? Did Santa land on the roof? The sound seemed to have come from our closet.

Chuck and I cautiously crept across the room and peeked in. A thick, dark substance like rancid chocolate pudding splattered the walls, clothes, and shoes. It even dripped off the ceiling light.

"Smells like somebody blew up a truckload of rotten eggs in here," Chuck said, looking around in disgust.

"I think somebody did blow up." I stared, horrified, at the ball of purring fur at my feet. Our snowy white cat, now covered in black sludge, sported a gaping hole in her side.

Turns out Kitty was secretly battling an internal abscess that built up pressure until it burst forth like a cannon shot. Ewww.

As I scrubbed the closet on all fours, I thought about today's verse. When we become new creatures in Christ, we expel the old, festering sin in our lives and start over fresh. . .like Kitty, who practically danced on tippy-paw after her physical nastiness was expelled. The way to experience that kind of new life spiritually is through faith in Christ.

So this Christmas, if you haven't yet received the gift of salvation, you may be harboring a putrid, infected heart.

The Great Healer can expel that and replace it with a clean, fresh heart.

And you won't even have to scrape alien pudding off your boots!

Precious Savior,
Make me aware today
of the state of my heart.

Christmas Wonder

*They [shepherds] hurried off and found Mary and Joseph,
and the baby, who was lying in the manger. When they had seen him,
they spread the word concerning what had been told them about this child,
and all who heard it were amazed.... But Mary treasured up all
these things and pondered them in her heart.*
LUKE 2:16–19 NIV

Ah, Christmas Day. Do you recall the beauty, excitement, and pure wonder of it all when you were a little girl? Truly a day to look forward to all year long.

But then something happened. You grew up. And once it fell to you to "make Christmas happen" for others, endless tasks, responsibility, and stress stripped much of the amazement from the day.

So take a moment now, like Mary, to treasure up images of Christmas and ponder them in your heart.

- The Son of God—the holy Christ child—lying peacefully in a cow trough.
- A sky filled with angels singing, "Glory to God in the highest."
- Astounded shepherds kneeling before the newborn King.
- Smiles lighting the faces of children—you as a child and now your kids.
- Waves of love, awe, and gratitude overflowing your heart for Jesus, your Savior.

Yes, sweet friend, the wonder is still there. Some years it may be buried deeper than others, but it's treasured up and always available if you take the time to ponder each precious memory.

From my heart to yours, I wish you an extraordinarily *blessed* celebration of the birth of our Savior. And remember, to avoid the post-Christmas blues, don't put away Christ with Christmas!

*God in the Highest,
All glory to You on this
marvelous day. Renew my
wonder. Restore my awe.*

Refreshed

*"Come with me by yourselves to
a quiet place and get some rest."*
MARK 6:31 NIV

Christmas is over. Whew. Time to regroup.

We all reach a point when fifteen minutes of quiet time just isn't cutting it. We're exhausted physically, frazzled emotionally, and parched spiritually. We need renewal in every sense.

If you're there, here's what I recommend (it's worked wonders for me): a He & Me Retreat. No whining kids, inquisitive husbands, nagging bosses. . .just time alone for you and your Creator.

How is that possible with your insane schedule?

He & Me Retreats can be three hours or three days; it's committed time set aside to listen for that still, small voice that often gets drowned out in the cacophony of life. To rest. . .revitalize. . . refuel your tank.

The best location is Papa's Cathedral of Creation—a lake, mountain, woods, park, seashore, even your own backyard when no one's home. Somewhere you can unplug from all electronic devices and eliminate distractions. Just you, your Bible, journal, fave praise music, and Papa.

There are many scriptural examples of Jesus stealing away to rest and regenerate. If it was that important to Him, it should be that important to us, right?

I strongly encourage you to schedule uninterrupted time to get to know yourself again, revive your enthusiasm for God's Word, and embrace the opportunity to relax and enjoy His rejuvenating presence. Start with a half day in a secluded place; I guarantee next time you'll want more.

Falling in love with Papa all over again. . .it's something you really can't afford NOT to do. "Get away with me and you'll recover your life" (Matthew 11:28 MSG).

*Prince of Peace,
Give me the backbone
to schedule a He & Me
Retreat for next month.*

Distractions

"Our Father is kind; you be kind."
LUKE 6:36 MSG

I try to pay attention in church. I really do. But it's tough for a gal who's the step beyond ADD. Wouldn't you be distracted too, if you had to deal with these wayward sheep in your flock? Come to think of it, you probably do.

- **Jolly Green Giant**: the six-foot-eight string bean who inevitably sits in front of *you*. The only way to see the pulpit is to peek through Jolly's armpits.
- **Madame Butterfly**: the operatic-voiced woman who adds an unwritten ultra-soaring soprano to every song.
- **Amener**: this overly agreeable person is compelled to agree with the pastor every five seconds with a resounding AMEN!
- **Wheezer/Sneezer**: you're already seated and settled when the first juicy blast of droplet-laden air from behind blows your hair over your eyes. You can just feel the infectious bacteria swimming around your drenched neck.
- **Au Natural Man**: the elderly fellow who somehow forgot to bathe this week. He enters late, sits as closely to you as possible, and smells like he stopped to roll in a dead possum on the way to church.
- **Peanut Gallery**: kids old enough to know better who spend the entire service chattering. Fight the impulse to remove your sock and plug their little mouths.
- **Pyrotechnic Man**: this businessman is so important, he can't remove his cell phone for a one-hour church service, so he leaves it clipped to his belt where it distracts the entire row of people behind him by flashing fireworks with each incoming call.

Are you with me here, sister? Can't you picture these same people in your church? Stay tuned for more tomorrow.

*Lover of the Flawed
(especially me!),
Please help me love them too.*

One Judge

"Don't pick on people, jump on their failures, criticize their faults—unless, of course, you want the same treatment."
LUKE 6:37 MSG

Yesterday we identified some wandering sheep in our church flocks. Here are a few more:

- **The Uzi Laugher**: the lady who responds to every pastoral joke with a staccato machine-gun laugh: *HA-A-A-A-A!*
- **The Hoarse Whisperer**: a covert converser using highly audible stage whispers, often during praise songs as if they're merely the opening act and deserve no respect.
- **Goat-Lady Singer**: this woman warbles with a choppy vibrato that sounds alarmingly like a goat bleating. Just *try* to keep a straight face if you're sitting directly in front of her. Resist the temptation to cluck or moo.
- **Crinkle Chorus**: loud candy wrappers usually heard in the silence immediately preceding the sermon. Why doesn't somebody invent cloth wrappers for church?
- **Bird Nest Lady**: still wearing her teased '70s hairdo, this short, stocky lady thinks big hair makes her look tall and thin. The only way to see around her is to rock side to side like a pendulum.

Okay, having confessed all these wicked thoughts, I shall now beg forgiveness. In truth, Papa God never said His ewes, rams, and lambs should be clones. It would be a pretty boring flock if they were.

It's up to me to chill and learn to take today's verse seriously. I certainly don't want anyone discussing my nanosecond attention span on their way home from church. My mind's tendency to flit like a moth on a lightbulb should be between Papa and me.

Dearest Papa God,
Teach me not to knock Your
flock. I promise to try harder
to remember that there's
only one appointed judge,
and I'm not Him.

Rendezvous

*The Lord would speak to Moses face to face,
as one speaks to a friend.*
EXODUS 33:11 NIV

Wanna study a cool passage? Read Exodus 33:1–11. What stood out to you? Here's what grabbed me:

- Moses had just returned from receiving the Ten Commandments on Mt. Sinai (chapter 32) and found the people worshipping a golden calf. *Seriously?* A cow? God was ticked (33:3).
- People need a rendezvous place *away* from their regular "camp" (home/work) and everyday stressors (verse 7) to meet Papa God unhurried, uninterrupted, and unencumbered.
- The people wouldn't meet with Jehovah themselves; instead, they expected their leader (verse 8) to share what he'd learned. Each of us needs a *personal* word from God. It's no good swallowing food someone else chews for us (pastors and teachers); we need to chew and digest it ourselves.
- God appeared as a cloud (verse 9). He appears in different forms all over the Bible—a burning bush (Exodus 3:4), dove (Matthew 3:16), column of fire (Exodus 13:21), stranger on a road (Genesis 18:1–3), tongues of flame (Acts 2:1–3). . .makes you wonder if you've ever been in His presence without realizing it. Whoa. Sobering thought.
- Jehovah valued private time with His friend Moses (verse 11). His *friend*. Just as He values private time with you. Friendship develops through spending time together; how much time do you spend with Papa God?
- Joshua, Moses' intern, cherished being with God so much, he couldn't leave (verse 11). Even after Moses left, he stayed, soaking up Papa's presence. Do you cherish Him that much?

Girlfriend, isn't it time you and I focus on growing our relationship with our Godfriend?

*Living Lord,
I yearn to call myself Your
friend. Teach me how.*

Trembling Hand

*You will trample our sins under your feet and
throw them into the depths of the ocean!*
MICAH 7:19 NLT

Corrie ten Boom often told about the time she was asked to travel to Munich to share God's message of love and forgiveness with a roomful of Germans. This took place only a few years after Corrie's release from Ravensbruck, the Nazi concentration camp where her family was killed for harboring Jews.

Following her talk, Corrie was approached by a man whom she recognized as one of the cruelest guards at Ravensbruck. The very man who was instrumental in the slow, excruciating death of Corrie's beloved sister, Betsie.

The man extended his hand and said, "How good it is to know that, as you say, all our sins are at the bottom of the sea."

Corrie's first impulse was revulsion.

The man claimed he'd become a Christian and knew God had forgiven his unspeakable deeds. Then he asked Corrie, "Will you forgive me?"

A war waged within Corrie—hatred and bitterness versus forgiveness and obedience. Corrie recognized that forgiveness is an act of the will, not based on emotion.

"Jesus, help me!" she prayed. And He did.

In sheer obedience to Jesus' command to forgive your enemies, Corrie extended her trembling hand to the man she once despised. Jesus' supernatural love immediately filled her heart as literal warmth flooded her body.

Sister, is there someone you need to extend your trembling hand to today?

*Jehovah Shalom (Our Peace),
Please keep reminding me that
if I wait until I feel like
forgiving, it'll never happen.
Forgiveness is an act of the will,
born of sheer obedience because
of my love for You.*

Happy New Year

Rescue me from my enemies, LORD.
PSALM 143:9 NIV

This terrific poem has been around for years in various forms, but sadly, the author is unknown. Kudos to you, audacious anonymous girlfriend!

T'was the week after Christmas,
And all through the house,
Nothing would fit me,
Not even a blouse.

The cookies I'd nibbled,
The chocolate I'd taste
At the holiday parties
Had gone to my waist.

When I got on the scales
There arose such a number!
When I walked through the room
Less a walk than a lumber,

I'd remember the marvelous meals I'd
    prepared:
The gravies and sauces and beef nicely rared,
The dips and the meatballs, the bread and
    the cheese
And the way I'd never said, "No thank you,
    please."

As I dressed myself and struggled to zip
The skirt that was gaping askew on my hip,
I said to myself, as only I can,
"You can't spend a winter as wide as a van!"

So away with the last of the sour cream dip.
Get rid of the fruitcakes, each cracker and
    chip.
Every last food that I like must be banished
Till all the additional ounces have vanished.

I won't have a cookie, not even a lick.
I'll chew only on this here green celery stick.
I won't have hot biscuits or cornbread or pie.
I'll munch on an apple and quietly cry.

I'm hungry, I'm lonesome, and life is a bore...
But isn't that what January is for?
Unable to giggle, no longer a riot,
Happy New Year to all, and to all a good diet.

Father of Fresh Beginnings,
Give me hope, Lord. I'm starting
anew. Teach me what a smidge
of restraint can do. Amen. And
pass the baby carrots.

Deb would love to hear your thoughts about this book
and chat with you via her website, www.DeboraCoty.com.

She'd be more than happy to share some biblical truth
gift wrapped in humor with your civic or church group.
See the speaker page on her website for details.

Enjoy these other fun books by Debora M. Coty:

Too Blessed to be Stressed
Too Blessed to be Stressed Cookbook
Too Blessed to be Stressed Coloring Book for Women
Too Blessed to be Stressed: 3-Minute Devotions for Women
Too Blessed to be Stressed 5-Year Keepsake Journal
The Bible Promise Book: Too Blessed to be Stressed Edition
Too Blessed to be Stressed Planner
Fear, Faith, and a Fistful of Chocolate
Too Loved to be Lost
More Beauty, Less Beast
Mom NEEDS Chocolate

Be sure to subscribe to Deb's "Too Blessed to be Stressed"
blog at www.DeboraCoty.com
and connect with her on Facebook, Twitter,
Goodreads, and Pinterest.

SCRIPTURE INDEX